The Last Eyewitnesses

THE LAST EYEWITNESSES

Children of the Holocaust Speak

VOLUME 2

EDITED BY JAKUB GUTENBAUM AND AGNIESZKA LATAŁA

Translated from the Polish by Julian and Fay Bussgang and Simon Cygielski

NORTHWESTERN UNIVERSITY PRESS

Evanston, Illinois

Northwestern University Press
Evanston, Illinois 60208-4170

Printed in the United States of America

10 9 8 7 6 5 4 3 2 1

ISBN 0-8101-2238-3 (cloth)
ISBN 0-8101-2239-1 (paper)

Library of Congress Cataloging-in-Publication data are available from the Library of Congress.

∞ The paper used in this publication meets the minimum requirements of the American National Standard for Information Sciences—Permanence of Paper for Printed Library Materials, ANSI Z39.48-1992.

Dedicated to all those who, at the risk of their lives,
helped save Jewish children during the Holocaust

Contents

Translators' Note

The members of the Association of "Children of the Holocaust" in Poland are men and women of Jewish origin who survived the war as young children and, for the most part, remained in Poland after the war. They all have fascinating and heartrending stories to tell, stories that convey a great immediacy, since the authors are not removed from the environment in which these experiences took place.

Collectively, the thirty-three personal accounts assembled here constitute an important historical document, which portrays the wartime experiences and emotions of Jewish children in Poland, children who were faced with incredible and often insurmountable difficulties. Their stories depict both the noble behavior of those who helped save them and the devastating betrayal and brutality of others with whom they came in contact.

Unfortunately, difficulties for these survivors did not cease when the war ended. Suffering from wounds not yet healed and haunted by painful memories, they had to resume life without the devoted support of their loved ones. Sadly, in some cases, although relatives were located after the war, political and economic circumstances isolated those in Poland from those who had managed to escape.

The postwar period presented other problems as well. Communist Poland did not look kindly upon Jewish survivors, due both to the lingering effects of anti-Semitic Nazi propaganda and because of Soviet-inspired policies claiming that Jews had divided loyalty. At the height of the anti-Zionist campaign in 1968, Jews were systematically demoted or removed from their jobs.

Because the Holocaust was such a dramatic and unique event in modern history, it is essential that new generations understand its scope and impact. The stories presented in volumes 1 and 2 of *The Last Eyewitnesses: Children of the Holocaust Speak* can provide a helpful resource for understanding the disastrous consequences of hatred and prejudice. Educational programs can benefit greatly from examining and discussing these concrete and varied experiences.

We believe that this collection of wartime and postwar experiences of Jewish children can provide a more comprehensive view of the tragic era of the Holocaust than individual memoirs, and a more vivid tool for teaching and understanding the facts than dry history textbooks. By adding the footnotes, a glossary, and historical notes, we hope to facilitate the reader's comprehension and give a context for the events described.

Because of our roots in Poland (Julian was born in Lwów, Fay's father, in Brzeziny), we have felt a sense of mission in helping translate and prepare these two volumes for publication for English-speaking readers.

JULIAN AND FAY BUSSGANG

NOVEMBER 2004

Introduction

We are pleased to present the second volume of memoirs by child survivors of the Holocaust. Its character is somewhat different from our first book, published by the Association of "Children of the Holocaust" in Poland in 1993 and issued in English by Northwestern University Press in 1998. The first volume consisted mostly of accounts that were not originally meant for publication but had been submitted to the association along with membership applications in response to the item: "Personal history, with special emphasis on the period of the occupation." Thus those memoirs were often quite brief, with little attention paid to literary form.

The present volume has a more diverse format. Some authors describe their lives before the war, others, only individual events—those that have been particularly imprinted in their memories—or the most important ones, the ones that determined their subsequent fate. Why did they write, despite the fact that it was difficult for them? Several authors expressed it thus: "because I want to leave a memorial to my loved ones who do not even have a grave," "because I want to leave a tribute to those who endangered their own and the lives of their loved ones to save me," or "I don't want my experiences to be forgotten; I want them to be a warning for the future!"

Although there have been many publications devoted to the Holocaust, the first book of recollections of Jewish child survivors that we published was received with interest, not only in Poland, where two editions, a total of sixteen hundred copies, were sold, but also in the United States, where it was published by the renowned Northwestern University Press, and in Germany, by the Reclam-Verlag publishing house, recognized for publishing literature on Jewish themes. It should be added that the impetus to produce a subsequent volume was not only the anticipated interest of potential readers but also the fact that, as a result of the printing of the first volume, a few of the authors found long-lost relatives in the United States, Canada, and Australia.

Nearly all the accounts in the second volume are recollections of children who survived by hiding their Jewish identity. Some stories—including the most interesting ones, because they depict little-known situations—describe the fate of children who were in hiding with Jewish groups in camouflaged bunkers, in forests, or among various guerrilla groups that often fought each other (see Ignacy Goldwasser). Only very few relate to children in concentration camps. The account of a thirteen-year-old boy, Henryk Arnold, who joined the Home Army[1] immediately after the outbreak of the Warsaw Uprising[2]—"to get revenge for the years of suffering, for the death of my loved ones"—deserves particular attention.

A large part of many of the memoirs deals with the postwar period. The authors' Jewish identity and their experiences during the war determined their subsequent fate, their physical and mental health, the path they chose in their lives, their choice of partners, and their relationships with their own children. There is dramatic intensity in hiding one's identity for many years, even from one's closest family, for fear of being "unmasked."

The accounts show that during these many years, serious psychological problems, not infrequently actual illnesses, have hounded many of the authors. It is not by chance that many members of the Association of "Children of the Holocaust" must be under constant psychiatric care. Here we must note the role, frequently mentioned in the accounts, played by our organization. For many individuals it has become the first group since the war in which they felt surrounded by their own kind, by people who shared their experiences. It is noteworthy that the present membership of the association reflects wartime conditions. For instance, about two-thirds of the members (as well as the authors of the accounts in this book) are women, which results from the obvious fact that it was much more dangerous to hide a boy than a girl!

These memoirs serve to confirm the well-known attitude of the Polish people toward Jews—who were their compatriots for many centuries—in the face of the Holocaust that was ordered and carried out by the invaders. Nonetheless, noble people, who did not hesitate to endanger their own lives and those of their families in order to save a Jewish child, are nearly always mentioned. We should particularly note the role of the warmly remembered "Polish nanny" in a Jewish home, who hid and fed her truly beloved Jewish wards. Unfortunately, these attitudes were not too common, which really does not come as a surprise. There is no overabundance of heroes anywhere, and giving aid to Jews in occupied Poland was sheer heroism.

The dominant attitude was aversion or even hostility toward those who were being annihilated. It should also be remembered that these are the memoirs of those who survived and who must have encountered people—often, on repeated occasions—who held out a helping hand. We do not know, and will never know, anything about the approximately one million Jewish children who were gassed, burned alive, shot, or tortured to death.

The attitude toward the Holocaust divided Polish society, but not along any conventional lines such as social class, education, profession, or attitude based on religious beliefs. The division was mainly a moral one! It should come as no surprise that these attitudes were such as they were. It is enough to read what was written on this subject in the 1930s in the nationalistic press.

The surviving children writing their memoirs are not a representative cross-sampling of average prewar Jewish children in Poland. To even make a decision to hide, one had to meet certain criteria, namely, to have "good looks,"[3] a good accent, contacts on the "Aryan side,"[4] and financial resources. Only a small percentage of Jewish children met all these requirements.

Each memoir deepens our knowledge of the Holocaust and has a powerful emotional impact. Each portrays the game of survival played with uneven odds and shows how much ingenuity, an understanding of people, the ability to assess situations, and acting skills were necessary to survive each day. How can we comprehend today that in order to survive, a small child knew that she had to talk about Jews in the worst possible terms?

This book is filled with stories of children who found themselves in difficult-to-imagine, extreme situations. Thus these stories constitute an inexhaustible source of inspiration for literary works or films—for centuries.

During our work on this publication, we had to choose the order in which to present the accounts. Since it would be difficult to group them along any unified criteria, we decided to publish them alphabetically, meaning that in terms of content, the order is a product of chance. The only exception is the opening contribution by Dasha Rittenberg, which is not so much a memoir as a depiction of the observance of the Sabbath. . . .

It has been our goal to preserve the style and language of the manuscripts, which were quite varied. Only evident grammatical errors were corrected.

On behalf of the Association of "Children of the Holocaust," I would like to express sincere thanks to everyone who made this book possible, especially the authors and Kasia Meloch, who was tireless in obtaining and preparing the texts.

We wish to express our appreciation to the Claims Conference for sponsoring the English translation of this book and to Stephanie Seltzer for her financial support.

Special thanks are due to Julian and Fay Bussgang, our American friends and honorary members of our association, who, on a voluntary basis, have put so much effort into getting this volume of recollections published. They extensively revised and edited the original translation by Simon Cygielski and have annotated the text to make it more accessible to American readers.

JAKUB GUTENBAUM

PRESIDENT OF THE ASSOCIATION OF "CHILDREN OF THE HOLOCAUST"

IN POLAND, 1991–2000

The story of Father Romuald Jakub Weksler-Waszkinel, which appears on page 232 in the Polish edition of volume 2, is not included here, as it was already published in volume 1 of the English edition.

1. The Home Army was the English name for the AK *(Armia Krajowa),* the organized underground army in Poland that reported to the Polish government-in-exile in London.

2. The Warsaw Uprising, not to be confused with the Warsaw Ghetto Uprising, was an uprising by the general population of Warsaw against the Germans, beginning August 1, 1944, just as the Red Army was approaching Warsaw. See glossary.

3. A person was said to have "good looks" if he or she did not have Semitic features.

4. The Aryan side refers to the area outside the ghetto, where only non-Jews were permitted to live.

The Last Eyewitnesses

DASHA RITTENBERG, NÉE WERDYGIER

Born in 1929

Celebrating Shabbat: How I Remember It

Friday — Preparations for the Sabbath

Our sages teach us that the greatest gift that the Jewish people received from God is Shabbat.[1] I was a child from a Hasidic family, the daughter of a great teacher from Góra Kalwaria.[2] At home, where Shabbat was a great event, we treated this gift with great solemnity, fulfilling all the laws, even the most minute ones, with the greatest precision, even meticulously.

In my family home, where I was brought up, preparations for Shabbat began the moment the previous Shabbat ended—that is, after Havdalah.[3]

Friday was for us like Erev Yom Kippur.[4] The day was filled with joy and anxiety about whether there would be enough time to complete the preparations before it arrived.

I had three brothers who came home from school a little earlier on Fridays to prepare for Shabbat, so as not to be late for anything. One of my many chores was to clean my brothers' shoes. According to them, I was the best shoeshine girl, because I polished their shoes according to their instructions—until they sparkled and I could see myself in their shiny tips as if in a mirror.

The kitchen was, of course, the center of preparations for Shabbat. The cooking and baking was done there, the floor was scrubbed, we washed our hair there, and the hot water was gotten ready. It was an incredible commotion—ironing and cleaning. Grandma soaked her feet so she could put on her Saturday shoes more easily. The atmosphere resembled a festive reception for a bride.

As I remember it, we could eat some of the cakes already on Friday, but I would not dare touch the others, because they were meant for Shabbat.

The difference between Shabbat and a regular day was so huge, that from Friday noon on, my entire mentality, my whole way of thinking, would undergo a change.

The table was covered with a snow-white damask tablecloth, and upon it was set a silver platter with silver candlesticks, which must have already served my grandparents for lighting candles.

And slowly, the holiday spirit would settle in. As in most Jewish homes, Shabbat began the moment the candles were lit. Then my beloved father and brothers, dressed in their holiday best, would set out together for the evening prayers. Mama could finally rest after a full week of work and dashing about. And we—the youngest girls in the family—set the table, said our evening prayers, and waited for the king and the princes to come back home.

Thus would begin the day that is the greatest blessing of the Jewish people. The rest—that's our common tragic history, which, together with its greatness, is gone forever. I am glad that I have this memory. I remember much more, however, not just this—and I hope that I will never, ever forget.

---

1. *Shabbat* is the Hebrew word for the Sabbath.

2. Góra Kalwaria, known in Yiddish as Ger, was a well-known Hasidic center in Poland.

3. *Havdalah* is the ceremony signifying the end of the Sabbath.

4. *Erev* [evening] marks the beginning of a Jewish holiday; Yom Kippur [Day of Atonement] is one of the Jewish "High Holidays," which occur in autumn.

HENRYK ARNOLD

Born in 1930

With Weapon in Hand

I was born on July 18, 1930, at 3 Szkarpowa Street in Lwów. My mother was Fryderyka, née Beigel (b. 1910), and my father was Leon Arnold (b. 1910). My maternal grandparents were owners of a restaurant in Lwów. They died relatively young, leaving orphaned, in addition to my mother, her two brothers, Jakub and Jan. My father's parents, Wilhelm and Anna Arnold, owned a large restaurant in Lwów that faced the courthouse building on Batory Street. It was a well-known restaurant; its clients were mostly lawyers and judges. Grandpa Wilhelm was a very strong man. He was known for having once won a fight with a professional wrestler, for which he received a prize of ten Austrian crowns. His wife, Anna, was a modest and pious person.

My parents owned an auto parts store. My father was an avid sportsman. He participated in wrestling, track-and-field sports, and soccer. He played on the Jewish soccer team *Hasmonea.*

His siblings, two brothers and four sisters, were:

Dawid—an attorney who fought in the ranks of the Austro-Hungarian army and was killed near Lwów in 1914.

Ksawery Albert—who worked at the post office in Puławy. During the German occupation he took part in the underground resistance. He was arrested and murdered by the Gestapo[1] in August 1942.

Cecylia—a physician in Brzuchowice near Lwów.

Lidia—owner of a pharmacy in Magierów near Lwów.

Fryderyka—a dressmaker in Lwów.

These three sisters died in 1943 during the liquidation of the Lwów ghetto.

The fourth sister, Stefania, worked in an oil company in Lwów; she was taken in 1942 to the death camp in Bełżec.[2]

My childhood was very happy. A governess took care of me. I often traveled with my father. We went to Warsaw, Kraków, Łódź, and Gdynia. Our whole family spent our vacations together by the seaside, or in Krynica or Rabka. We were emotionally very close. I remember a prophetic dream that my mother told me about in 1938. She dreamed that someone had shot her in the head and that she fell into a dark cellar. This may well be what happened to her when the Germans executed her in Warsaw in 1942.

I began my education in 1937 at the Rutkowski Grammar School, taking an additional language course in Ukrainian. After Lwów was occupied by the Russians, I studied in a Ukrainian school, taking an additional course in Russian—until the Germans entered in 1941.

During the Soviet occupation,[3] the Jews were not singled out for persecution. Soldiers often came to my father's store to buy auto parts. They warned him that his store would be confiscated. Because of this [warning], he was able to carry away many items and hide them in a safe place. After the store was liquidated, he was employed at the Krasnyi Transportnik shipping company. At the same time, he was secretly selling the auto parts he had hidden, thus earning additional money to support the family.

At that time, many Polish Jews were escaping from the German occupation zone to the Soviet zone. In the summer of 1940, the Soviet occupation authorities shipped many of them deep into the USSR. The militia would surround houses and search for refugees. As fate would have it, nearly all of these people survived the war and returned afterward to Poland. Later most of them emigrated to Israel.

When the Germans attacked the Soviet Union on June 22, 1941, the wives of the officers who lived nearby, hearing the artillery fire, thought it was the British bombing Lwów.

The Germans entered Lwów eight days later on June 30, 1941. The next day everyone had to hand over their radio sets. By chance, the Germans stopped Father while he was carrying a radio. He was put in prison on Kazimierzowska Street. Corpses of Ukrainian nationalists killed by the NKVD [Soviet secret police] were strewn about in the cells. In the prison courtyard were lying many bodies of Jews killed by Ukrainians. Jews were also being killed in the city; a pogrom was raging. Father managed to get out of jail by giving a bribe.

Later, Father got a job (and most important, papers) as a worker at a German military garage (*Heereskraftpark*—HKP for short), which protected him from arrest and being sent to a camp.

In November 1941 we had to leave our apartment and move to 18 Tkacka Street. This house was located in a section of the Jewish quarter that the Germans had not closed off. In addition to Jews, many Poles and Ukrainians lived there, and even a few Germans.

The Jewish quarter was located north of the railroad line. Near it was the only crossing point for Jews. Two others were for use only by Poles, Ukrainians, and Germans. German police patrolling these crossings often stopped older Jews. They were then sent in an unknown direction—as it turned out later, to the death camp in Bełżec. It was rumored that in Warsaw and in Lublin, special groups were active, murdering Jews. There was talk of mass murders in Bełżec, but Jews did not want to believe it. They could not comprehend that Germans were killing them only because they were Jews.

Although Jewish children ten years or older were required to wear armbands with the Star of David, I, to spite the Germans, tried to avoid wearing mine.

Various rumors circulated in the city. There was talk that in Warsaw and Lublin special units were active, the so-called *Him-*

melkommando, murdering Jews or shipping them to death camps. Everybody had heard about Bełżec, but not everybody wanted to believe these reports. The occupation authorities introduced precise record keeping for the Jewish population. Father, as a worker at a military garage, obtained a document with the stamp INDISPENSABLE TO THE GERMAN ARMY. Mother also had an appropriate document classifying her as WIFE OF A PERSON INDISPENSABLE TO THE GERMAN ARMY. I, as a child, was not eligible for any documents or stamps, which greatly worried my parents.

At six o'clock in the morning on August 10, 1942, we got word that the entire Jewish quarter was surrounded by the SS[4] and German and Ukrainian police. A mass deportation of Jews from Lwów had begun. Father was able to get out of the surrounded area in a Wehrmacht [regular German army] truck driven by a Pole. I was hidden in the back. We avoided being deported, but we could not stay in the Jewish quarter any longer. My parents decided to hide me with their friends, a Polish family who lived at 8 Kościelna Street, in the same building where we had once lived. From the windows of my hideout, I could see streetcars packed with Jews being taken to the camp on Janowska Street,[5] where the selection[6] took place. Young and healthy men were sent to work, while the rest—women, the elderly, the sick, and children—were taken to the death camp in Bełżec.

There were searches for Jews on the Aryan side[7] as well, where many Jewish families still lived. Apartments of Poles began to be checked for hidden Jews. Sheltering them was punishable by death. One day two SS men burst into the apartment where I was hiding. They started searching in the attic, where my host, Mrs. Adamczewska, raised chickens. Satisfied with the fresh eggs they found there, they gave up searching further. The frightened landlady demanded that I leave the apartment immediately. I had to return to my parents, to the ghetto. Meanwhile, the document that protected my mother expired. She managed to avoid deportation by hiding in the attic during moments of danger. My hideout was the cellar of the HKP garage.

I used to hide on a shelf with old tires and other junk. Father, who was still working, brought food to me.

All the Jews who were still hiding in Lwów disappeared into their hideouts during the day. At night they came out in search of water and food. The Germans organized searches and tried to uncover their hiding places. The deportation action ended in August 1942.

In anticipation of further deportations, we decided to move to Warsaw, where we had some friends and where nobody knew us. We left Lwów on September 8, 1942, on a truck carrying furniture that belonged to a Polish acquaintance. When we passed by Bełżec, we smelled the stench of decaying bodies. That smell has tormented me to this day.

As it turned out later, this was indeed the last chance to leave Lwów, because on October 17, 1942, the Jewish quarter was surrounded by barbed wire and closed off. The Lwów ghetto existed until June 1943.

In Warsaw we found shelter at 18 Wspólna Street, in an apartment owned by a Polish woman who was hiding more than a dozen Jews. An acquaintance, Mr. Drut, secured false documents for us under the name Rudziński. I was changed into Ryszard, born in Kołomyja on December 18, 1930, son of Józef. My mother's maiden name was turned into Ziółkowska.

For security reasons, we were forced to split up. Father moved in with Mr. Alfons Karny, a well-known sculptor, at 67 Wspólna Street. Mother and I went to live on Śliska Street at the home of Mrs. Wanda Melfior-Rutkowska, a writer. Her husband was an officer in the Polish Armed Forces and was stationed in England. We lived peacefully for several weeks, but it was an illusory peace that ended in tragedy.

In order to support ourselves, we sold things we had brought with us from Lwów. In October 1942 Mother went to 18 Wspólna Street, where she was supposed to meet Father and talk over the sale of a fur coat that she had put in storage. Several other Jews were there at the time. Suddenly, the Gestapo appeared. My father managed to escape. All the other Jews, including my mother, were arrested, taken to the prison on Szucha Avenue, and later shot.

In order to remain in hiding, we had to immediately move to another place. For several days after Mother's arrest, we hid in Podkowa Leśna, and later in Milanówek, at the home of Mrs. Dręgiewicz. There our ways parted. I returned again to Mrs. Rutkowska's place on Śliska Street, and Father returned to Wspólna to stay with Mr. Karny. However, these were not safe hiding places. I finally found relative peace at the apartment of Olga Dudziec on Krakowskie Przedmieście Street, where I stayed for a month.

Later, Father and I moved to the Wola district, where we stayed with a man named Feliks (I do not remember his last name). It was a miserable hovel, without light or running water. It was an unlucky place. After several weeks, we were discovered by *szmalcownicy* [blackmailers], who demanded a ransom. Father gave them thirteen hundred złotys,[8] but they searched us and found dollars that were sewn in my jacket. During a scuffle, my father grabbed a knife, and screaming, "Mr. Feliks, help us!" he threw himself at them. I managed to put out the oil lamp. The blackmailers ran away. Because of the police curfew, we had to spend the night in the "burned"[9] apartment.

In the morning, my father ripped the dollars out of my jacket. At six in the morning we went out on the street, but they were already waiting for us. While Father engaged them in conversation, I tried to escape. They caught me, and after checking that I did not have the money, they called a blue-uniformed [Polish] policeman. He declared that the matter should be taken to the Gestapo and walked away. My tormentors also gave up and left. Sneaking around and checking whether anyone was following me, I went back to the home of Mrs. Olga Dudziec. Father found shelter with Mr. Karny.

Mrs. Dudziec lived with her ten-year-old nephew, whose father was a *Volksdeutcher.*[10] He attended a German school, and there was danger that he might tell someone there about the boy who lived with them who did not attend school. In this situation, we decided that I should move in with Father. Our fears soon proved to be justified. One day the Gestapo came to the apartment of Mrs. Dudziec. By chance, Father just happened to be there, but he managed to hide in a cubby.

Mr. Karny rented a room for us from a friend of his, a painter. When our host was not there, we had to remain inside, locked up.

We constantly had to change our place of stay. We moved to Kolejowa Street, but we had to escape from there in January 1943. Later we found shelter at the home of a sister of Mr. Feliks, who himself had meanwhile died of tuberculosis. In the same apartment lived a certain Mietek who sent a blackmailer after us. Father had six hundred złotys. The blackmailer showed mercy—he took only four hundred złotys from him, leaving the rest.

We had to be on the run again. For two days we slept on chairs in the home of a Mrs. Filipska, from whom father used to buy auto parts before the war. Father returned to Mr. Karny, and I moved in with Mrs. Kwiatkowska, who was a neighbor of Mrs. Dudziec's on Krakowskie Przedmieście Street.

April 1943 came. The uprising broke out in the ghetto. German patrols roamed through the city searching for hidden Jews.

In the building where Mrs. Dudziec lived was the office of her sister Zosia's lover. Zosia's husband was in the Polish army in England. Zosia told my father that she knew someone who would hide me for two weeks for fifteen hundred złotys. He gave her the money she requested. She told me to meet her at 7:45 P.M. near Trzech Krzyży Square. I suspected something, because it was too close to the police curfew of 8 P.M. I arrived at the agreed spot at 7 P.M. and waited until 7:55. Luckily, Mr. Karny lived nearby at 67 Wspólna Street. I managed to get there just before the gate was locked and spent the night in the trash bin. It turned out later that Zosia had told me to meet her so late on purpose, counting on my getting caught for breaking curfew, so she could keep the money for herself.

I was already so desperate from continuously having to seek shelter that I considered jumping out of the fourth-floor window. However, Father persuaded me to try to find shelter with Mr. Stanisław Fajkus in Podkowa Leśna.

Mr. Fajkus agreed to hide us in his attic, which was accessible only by ladder. We could only spend nights there, because there were too many searches during the day. Thus we spent our nights in the attic and our days roaming the streets of Podkowa or Warsaw. Once, around 3 A.M., we heard, "*Aufmachen! Licht!*" [Open up! Turn on the light!] I told Father, "Grab a crowbar and strike whoever comes in." "No, they'll beat and torture us," he responded. We heard someone placing the ladder against the attic's trapdoor. Mr. Fajkus's face appeared, gray with fright. "Run away, the police are at the landlady's!" We jumped into the garden from Fajkus's kitchen and got through the barbed-wire fence and into the field. Father no longer had his shoes on, and I cut myself going through the barbed-wire fence. After some time, we returned. It turned out that the Germans had not come for us but to the landlady's. She was hiding a Jewish family—who managed to bribe their way out.

The mounting terror made it necessary to continuously change our place of stay. For a time I lived in Żoliborz with Mr. Wajsman and his family, who were also Jews in hiding. Their landlady did not know about their origins and had no idea at all that I was living there for over four months. I could go to the toilet only at night. The landlady saw me in September 1943, and I had to leave. I moved in with Father, who was staying with Mrs. Tosia on Królewska Street. She suspected that we were Jewish but was not sure. She told us one time, "If it turns out that you are Jews, I'll chop off your heads with an ax at night and take them to the Gestapo." We had to flee.

Father rented a room from Mr. Sankowski at 14 Krzywe Koło Street, and I returned again to Mr. Karny. My stay at his place was limited to nighttime only, and I spent my days wandering aimlessly around Warsaw. This was very dangerous because of the inspections, roundups, and blackmailers. One day, two streetcars came up, one right behind the other. I got into the first one. It turned out to be sheer luck, because the second one got stopped by an SS unit, and all the passengers were arrested.

Finally, as a result of Father's insistence, Mr. Fajkus agreed to have me spend nights at his place in Podkowa Leśna. However, I had to take the train to Warsaw every day at 6:30 A.M. I used to get out at Nowogrodzka Street. There was a clinic nearby where I had once been treated for an eye infection. I would let everyone in line get ahead of me, which allowed me to sit in the warm waiting room for a few hours. I spent most of my time on streetcars, riding them from dawn to dusk.

In December 1943 Father found me a hideout on Nowy Świat Street with Mr. Brudziński, a photographer and a very decent human being. Father paid him fifty złotys a day, which was about half the going rate. Once I got caught by his landlady, who had a key to his single room. I told Mr. Brudziński about it, and he got very worried. "She is dangerous, because she has a loose tongue," he said. But the next day the woman had a stroke and was taken to the hospital, where she died.

From January 1944 until the start of the Warsaw Uprising, Father and I lived together at Mr. Sankowski's on Krzywe Koło Street. He and his wife did not know that we were Jews. In the morning, we would leave the house—I, supposedly to school, Father, supposedly to work.

At the end of July it became clear that the Germans were retreating under pressure from the Russians. This gave us great joy. My father's acquaintance, Mr. Hilczyński, gave him a key to the apartment at 18 Wspólna Street, where my mother had been arrested. "Your son can sleep there." This is where I was when the uprising[11] began. To complete the picture, I must add that father was blackmailed several times by the *szmalcownicy.* In the summer of 1943, when I was staying with Mr. Wajsman, Mietek from Kolejowa Street brought with him some blackmailers and an SS man who wanted to shoot Father, but Father promised him a fur coat in exchange for his life. Father led him to a house on Krakowskie Przedmieście Street that he knew had a rear exit from the stairwell. Father, who used to wrestle in his youth, gave the SS man a heavy blow. When he fell, Father escaped through the rear exit. Another time two blue-uniformed Polish policemen stopped Father in the Old Town. They were easily bribed, though.

Starting in January 1944 we received fifteen hundred złotys a month from the Żegota organization.[12] This assistance, without a doubt, made it possible for us to survive in hiding.

On August 1, 1944, shooting began in the streets. The uprising had begun. At first I did not know whether it was the Russians who had entered the city and were fighting in the streets or whether the Germans were shooting at civilians. I went outside. Barricades were being erected in the streets. German tanks were rolling down Jerozolimskie Avenue. The police surrounded houses on Wspólna and St. Barbara Streets. The inhabitants were being evicted and murdered.

I immediately decided to report to the AK [*Armia Krajowa*][13] as a volunteer and take part in the fight against the Germans, to take revenge for the years of suffering, for the deaths of my loved ones. However, it was not at all easy for a fourteen-year-old boy to become a soldier. Mr. Kazimierz Mojsiejuk, an underground activist, helped me in this. I was accepted by the Home Army, in the Fifty-ninth Communications Platoon, where I got my alias—Ryś. Our commander was Second Lieutenant Roman Grodzki (alias Roman), and his deputy was Second Lieutenant Alfred Kazanowski (alias Teodor). At first, the platoon was stationed at the dairy plant on Hoża Street. We were then moved to Widok Street and assigned to maintain communications between the AK headquarters and the various insurgent units. Around September 10, at Colonel Monter's orders, Teodor's squad, to which I belonged, was assigned to guard General Bór's headquarters at the so-called little PAST[14] [Polish Telephone Corporation] building on Piękna Street.

To this day I remember the first shot fired in my direction. The bullet passed just by my leg. It came from one of the "pigeon keepers," German snipers, hidden on the rooftops of houses in the districts controlled by the insurgents.

My squad protected the AK headquarters and those fighting near Bracka Street and on Jerozolimskie Avenue. At that time the Germans controlled the main railroad station on Towarowa Street and the Bank Gospodarstwa Krajowego [BGK—National Economy Bank] at the intersection of Jerozolimskie and Nowy Świat. As a liaison, I was often at combat outposts.

At that time Father was staying at 7 Poznańska Street. I often got a pass and could visit him there at night. I always carried a grenade with me. I felt safer that way. One night I got stopped by a patrol of the insurgent military police and had to spend a long time explaining what I was doing on the street at night with a grenade in my pocket.

After the fall of the Old Town, the Germans attacked the riverbank, which soon also fell, and its defenders had to retreat to the center of the city. It was then that the SS Dirlewanger units, commanded by SS Oberführer Oskar Dirlewanger, moved in from the riverbank toward Nowy Świat Street. These units were composed of criminals. The attack was conducted with heavy air support. I found myself in a group of twenty-three insurgents assigned to fend off the attack. Because I was the youngest in the unit, I served as a paramedic, together with two nurses. Passing around through the back of Nowy Świat, near Górski Street, we chanced onto a courtyard full of dead bodies. They were mostly women whose faces were covered with newspapers. One of the nurses accompanying me couldn't bear the sight and broke down, sobbing terribly.

When we calmed her down a little, we heard screams from the adjoining building. We walked in and found ourselves inside the hall of a movie theater that was on fire. A civilian who had been wounded in the stomach was lying on the floor. He must have been suffering terribly, because when we were carrying him out, he was still screaming and cursing everyone, even blaming us and the uprising for his wounds. We carried the wounded man to the nearby Górski Gymnasium. In its hallway lay bodies of girls killed by the Germans.

From September 7 on, I was stationed at Górski Street. We didn't know exactly where the German positions were. One day we noticed two insurgents escaping through a garden that bordered on Warecka Street. The Germans managed to set up a machine gun and opened fire at them. They killed one of them. The other one was wounded, and they took him prisoner. This is when Lieutenant Giewont (Jerzy Stawski), the platoon's second-in-command, gave the order to capture the machine gun. During our attempted attack, we encountered heavy fire. At a certain point, Lieutenant Giewont was wounded in the head. Realizing the Germans had a big advantage, he ordered us to retreat and to leave him where he was. We did not obey the order, however, and managed to carry our commander through a hole in the wall and out of the range of the German weapon. We later got through to the Górski Gymnasium building.

I often stood watch with twenty-two-year-old Private Gałganek (Stefan Jędrzejczak). He had an uneasy premonition and constantly repeated that he was going to die. Indeed, one day while on watch in a garret, he was hit by a sniper from the Dirlewanger brigade.

There were also humorous incidents. One time each of us got a can of sardines. We prepared sandwiches and were about to eat them when a Stuka bomber dove over our positions and dropped a bomb. Because the explosion was delayed several seconds, I thought we were done for and felt regret that the sardines were going to go to waste. I swallowed them quickly. Luckily, nobody got hurt, but the blast of air was so powerful that everybody's sardines fell to the ground, and we had to be satisfied with dry bread. The bomb made a sizable crater a few meters from our position.

Delivering reports to the main post office was one of our most dangerous missions. We had to make our way through places barely ten to twenty meters from the German positions.

One of my fellow soldiers, Zbyszek—despite being lightly wounded himself—shot an approaching German, wounded him in the knee, and took him prisoner. While interrogating him, we found out about the "Goliaths,"[15] newly introduced into battle. From our insurgent newsletters we learned that the Allies had recognized us as soldiers, and we were thus subject to the Geneva convention, which forbade killing prisoners. We were very skeptical whether the Germans would abide by these principles.

The Germans began to bomb our positions from the air. As a result, a group of insurgents in the shelters inside the railroad tunnel running along Jerozolimskie Avenue got buried. Some of them perished. We were given an order to get through to the men who were buried. In order to accomplish this, we had to make our way through an area exposed to German fire from the BGK building. Paying no heed, we tried to get to the buried men to give them help. Several attempts, including one by a team led by Second Lieutenant Antoni Bieniaszewski (Antek), failed. The Germans shot at the insurgents who were trying to break through. I volunteered. I knew the area well and knew where the Germans were shooting from. I got through without drawing their attention. Approaching the ruins, I heard cries of "Help, we're buried!" I was able to establish voice contact with the buried insurgents and inform them that we knew about their situation but that it would be impossible to help them during the day. I tried to reassure them, telling them that help would surely come at nightfall. This is exactly what happened, and those who had survived were rescued.

After we returned, I set out toward Jerozolimskie Avenue with another soldier, both of us equipped with bottles filled with gasoline. A tank was rolling along the street. My dream of getting revenge against the assassins, while winning a medal for valor at the same time, seemed within reach. After firing several shots in a row, the tank turned back toward the German positions. We had to give up further action. The same day I was given another assignment, to deliver a bucket of tomato soup to insurgents cut off from supplies. Going over a pile of bricks, I suddenly found myself under fire from the BGK building. I scooted down on my rear end, with half of the soup landing on my uniform. I then sat in a bomb crater with a firefighter's helmet on my head, yelling to our guys after every shot, "I'm still alive!"

On the evening of September 9, I was standing watch about a hundred meters from the Germans in the BGK building. I saw a searchlight about one hundred fifty to two hundred meters away from me that was trying to pick out the positions of the insurgents. I tried to take a location directly opposite it. I shot in the direction of the searchlight, and it went out.

There remains in my memory of this period the horrifying vision of Warsaw streets full of human remains and wounded and crying people. I remember an artillery barrage during which I hid on the second floor of the nearest building. A shell partially destroyed the staircase. Walking out, I nearly slipped on a corpse lying on the stairs. On another occasion, going to meet my father, I came across a courtyard full of dead bodies of men and women. Some kind hand had covered their heads with newspapers. I was terribly worried that Father might be among them, but fortunately my fears were unfounded. He had hidden in a cellar and, thanks to that, survived.

Two days later I fell ill and went to a pharmacy on Hoża Street that was still operating. As I waited in a long line, we heard the howling of a diving Stuka. People began to crowd into the entryway, screaming. A moment later, there was a strong tremor; beams began falling down from the ceiling, wounding many people. One of the falling beams hit my spine. To this day I feel pain, most likely because of this. It turned out that the bomb had fallen on the neighboring house, killing about fifty people.

The last mission in which I took part was to conceal the documents of the AK headquarters. They were buried in the cellar of the PAST building on Pius XI Street.[16] The documents of my platoon, the Fifty-ninth Communications, were buried in a separate container. These documents are probably still there. A parking lot is at that location now.

On October 5, 1944, the day of surrender,[17] I was with my platoon near Marszałkowska Street. My father, who had joined me by then, and I were both terrified at the prospect of falling into the grasp of the Germans. I could have left Warsaw with the civilian population,[18] but I did not want to leave my comrades in arms. My decision was also influenced by the fact that the insurgents were under the control of the Wehrmacht, while the civilians were under that of the Gestapo.

I thus became a prisoner of war as a soldier of the Fifty-ninth Communications Platoon, commanded at that time by Lieutenant Stanisław Jankowski (Agaton). Father was with me, to which he had the right, in accordance with an order allowing certain family members to join prisoners of war. This served to save those closest to us from the hands of the Gestapo. Our farewell to Warsaw took place on Koszykowa Street, where we sang the national anthem. Many wept. Then the Eighth Company, commanded by General Bór, marched in style along Koszykowa to the Warsaw Polytechnic, where it laid down its arms. The officers were allowed to keep their swords, which was a sign of respect by the Germans for the bravery of the insurgents. Because we were not allowed to wear the captured German uniforms, most of the prisoners were dressed in civilian clothing.

My unit, guarded by soldiers of the Wehrmacht, was taken to Ożarów. Along the route of our march through Warsaw and beyond the city limits, people gathered and applauded us. The German escorts did not react. We spent the first night of our imprisonment in the hall of a cable factory. During the march, Father and I had an opportunity to escape, but we didn't really have a place to which we could run. We thought about hiding in Podkowa Leśna with Mr. Fajkus, but that was too far. After the war we learned that German officers were stationed at his home at that time, so we could have fallen into a trap.

The next day a freight train rolled up, and we were herded into the wagons, more than fifty people in each. It was horribly crowded and stuffy. We took care of our bodily needs through a hole in the floor. We suffered from thirst. Despite our pleas, we were not given any water.

After dozens of hours of travel, we came to the town of Lamsdorf (presently Łambinowice) near Opole. After being forced by the Germans to run eight kilometers, we found ourselves at a prisoner-of-war camp, Stalag 344. During this run, we witnessed a midair collision of two German airplanes, which raised our spirits tremendously. In the camp, those under eighteen years old were segregated. I was once again separated from my father, although we could still see each other.

In Lamsdorf, at age fourteen, I was registered as prisoner number 103226, as a Warsaw Uprising soldier named Ryszard Rudziński, born on December 18, 1930, in Kołomyja, a Pole, the son of Józef and Ziółkowska, all in accordance with my false documents. From the surviving documents from Lamsdorf, it is apparent that I was one of the youngest prisoners there. Camp life was incredibly harsh. Hunger, inhuman sanitary conditions, freezing cold (it was already fall), and roll calls that lasted for hours dominated our lives. My companions treated me well. I was liked, because due to my sharp memory, I remembered and recited verses, not always decent, to everyone's amusement.

On November 19 Father was transferred to a camp in Żagań. Before leaving, he managed to pass on to me a can of sardines, which I don't know how he obtained. The next day I was taken to Stalag IV B in Mühlberg, Saxony. We traveled several days, in better conditions than before. There were fewer people in the wagons, the train stopped several times, and we were given water.

After several days, I was sent with a group of fifty prisoners to a glass factory in Brockwitz near Meissen, eighteen kilometers from Dresden. There I worked in a plant that manufactured land mines made out of glass, which could not be spotted by metal detectors. The same factory also assembled Messerschmitt Bf 109 F fighter airplanes, tractors, and artillery guns.

In Brockwitz our status was changed from prisoners of war to that of civilian laborers, and we were handed over to civilian authorities. Our food rations were very meager. In the morning we were given three slices of bread, twenty grams of sausage or processed meat, a spoonful of marmalade, and a mug of ersatz coffee. For our main meal we were given a bowl of soup. These were starvation rations. Twice we received Red Cross food packages. We also received American military overcoats from the Red Cross.

Despite our hunger and exhaustion, we were forced to work hard. We sorted broken glass and loaded and unloaded freight cars. In preparation for the approaching Soviet offensive, we dug trenches and antitank barricades. We suffered greatly from the cold. We worked about ten kilometers from the camp. If, after our return to camp, it turned out that any shovels or other tools were missing, the whole unit was forced to go back and find the forgotten equipment. Once while we were digging a trench, its wall collapsed on me, and I was buried with sand up to my neck. The German officer who oversaw the work did not exactly rush to the rescue but yelled and threatened. Fortunately it ended with the yelling.

I clearly remember the day when, at the beginning of March 1945, the Allies bombed Dresden.[19] We saw the glow of fires extending over the city.

One time we were sent to work in the field for a local peasant. The work was hard, and food was handed out very sparingly. Instead of soup, the farmer gave us water in which he had boiled his sausage. We complained to the noncommissioned officer who supervised us, and he scolded us for lying, because we "had it too good, while Germans were suffering."

Not all Germans were hostile toward us. One example was a German woman, who, seeing how greedily we were devouring a pumpkin we had acquired somewhere, began yelling that starving prisoners was a scandal. She even wanted to go to the town hall to lodge a complaint, but I managed to persuade her not to, knowing from experience that this could have ended badly both for her and for us.

We tried to somehow supplement our starvation rations. Red

Cross packages were a big help. For a packet of coffee, we could either get ration cards for bread or lots of jars of pickled pumpkins, which was one of the few food items available for sale in unlimited quantities. Unfortunately, my stomach couldn't handle such food in very large portions. One time a friend and I decided to go at night after a pile of rutabagas in a field, despite being warned of the threat of a death sentence for such escapades. We took six rutabagas each. Each of us ate one on the spot, and the others we tossed over the factory wall. We benefited only from the ones we ate, because someone stole the others, which we had hidden in the latrine.

In mid-April 1945 the Soviet offensive got under way. On the twenty-sixth of April, the first evacuation march of prisoners began. The first day we walked about fifty kilometers due south, escorted by a couple of teenagers from the *Volkssturm.*[20] In the evening they announced that the war was lost, *Hitler kaputt,* and that they had had enough of it all and were going back home. We were left alone. At night we heard explosions; it was the Germans blowing up the bridge on the Elbe River.

For two days we camped out in the vicinity of a town called Glashütte. Our nourishment was potatoes we had bought with marks.[21] On the first of May, coming back from a field with a friend, loaded down with potatoes, we ran into a peasant who told us that Hitler was dead. We headed toward the town in high spirits, but a member of the *Volkssturm* stopped us and led us at gunpoint to a military police post. There we got charged with stealing potatoes. As if all those years of terror had not happened, a report was drawn up, and a fine was levied. Since we had no money, our potatoes were taken from us, and we were set free.

We soon found out that the British were already in Hamburg. It was clear that despite the fighting still going on, the war was over. On May 8 we went through heavy bombardment. While a German armored division was going through town, Soviet airplanes flew in and decimated the Germans. At the same time, they also bombed our column. Three among us were killed, and many were wounded. A horrifying image of starving former prisoners cutting a dead horse into pieces has stuck in my memory.

On May 9 a Russian officer rode through the railroad tunnel into town on a motorcycle. He rode through the streets and then turned back. Soon a lot of soldiers appeared, riding on horse-drawn carts. We ran up to them, embracing and kissing them. This was what my liberation looked like.

My happiness was marred because I didn't know what had happened to my father. To make matters worse, I had cut my foot on a broken glass, and I had to remain in Glashütte, despite the fact that my colleagues set out to return to their homes. Fortunately, one of them came back with a confiscated horse-drawn cart on which he loaded me and another insurgent, who was seriously wounded. We reached bombed-out Dresden. We left the wounded fellow in a military hospital there, and I rejoined the column.

A few words about Jews in Brockwitz. Among the fifty prisoners, there were four Jews besides me:

1. Paweł Borkowski (alias Cwaniak).

2. His brother Zenon Borkowski (alias Miki), decorated with the Cross of Valor. Their real last name was Hochman. During the occupation they sold newspapers; after the war they left for Israel.

3. "Pistolet" [Pistol], whose real name I don't know. After the war he remained in the American zone and encountered my father, who learned from him that I was alive.

4. Eugeniusz Krawczyk (alias Żbik) was a mute. I don't know what happened to him.

In our fifty-man group no one was older than sixteen. They all knew we were Jews. Most of them behaved very decently, but some are inscribed in my memory as having behaved very poorly. They threatened that they would go to the Gestapo and expose us. They beat me. I couldn't defend myself; I was very depressed about being separated from my father. As luck would have it, the two worst ones got killed in the bombing. Some of the Germans in the factory knew about our origins. A Polish corporal, who had passed himself off as a cadet officer, was in charge of our group. He did not defend us. We were supervised by a German civilian named Franz Vycisk, who spoke Polish. He was a very decent person; I think he was a Communist. Several of the Russian prisoners also came to our defense.

The return to Poland took a long time. We walked toward the border for ten days. In Poland I managed to reach Kalisz, by hitching a ride on a passing truck, and from there got to Warsaw by train. I found out that my father was alive, freed by the Americans.

At the Jewish Committee in Warsaw, I was told that in Helenówek, near Łódź, there was a home in which surviving Jewish children could find care. I was admitted there without difficulty. After so many years, I could return to my hidden Jewish identity and my real last name, Arnold. Because I was so used to it, I introduced myself with my alias from the uprising, so everyone in Helenówek called me Rysiek. And that's how it has remained to this day.

In Helenówek, I was able to continue my interrupted education. I was accepted to the first grade of the Stanisław Staszic Gymnasium[22] in Zgierz. In spite of the interruption of several years, I quickly made up the lost time. I never stopped searching for contact with my father. I finally received a message through family in Switzerland that he was in Baden-Baden, the capital of the French occupation zone. I went from Helenówek to Wałbrzych. Later, thanks to contacts with various Jewish organizations that organized emigration to Palestine, I managed to leave Poland. Through Kłodzko, Nachod, Bratislava, Vienna, Linz, Salzburg, and Munich, I finally reached my father.

Father continued to live in Baden-Baden, while I at first stayed in Brussels in a dormitory for Jewish children and later in Chelles near Paris. In the fall of 1947 I came to Baden-Baden, where I attended the French Gymnasium named for General de Gaulle. In 1950 I began medical studies in Strasbourg and completed them in 1956. I settled in Troyes, France. I worked in a hospital and had my own private medical practice. In 1984 I was awarded the Warsaw Uprising Cross by the Council of State.[23] I have been retired since 1995 and am engaged in charitable work. Father died in November 1996.

The original Polish version of this chapter was prepared by Anna Cybulska-Piotrowska, based on the account of Henryk Arnold.

1. The Gestapo, short for *Geheime Staatspolizei,* was the German secret police, known for its brutality.

2. Bełżec was a death camp in southeastern Poland where 600,000 Jews were killed.

3. The Soviets occupied eastern Poland from September 17, 1939, until June 30, 1941.

4. The SS, short for *Schutzstaffel,* was an elite military unit of the Nazi party that served as a special police force; also called "Black Shirts."

5. Janowska/Janowski was a labor and extermination camp on the outskirts of Lwów (now Lviv, Ukraine) where 40,000 Jews were killed.

6. A "selection" was the separation of those fit to work from those to be killed.

7. The Aryan side refers to the area outside the ghetto, where only non-Jews were permitted to live.

8. The złoty is the unit of Polish currency.

9. A "burned" apartment was one that was no longer safe.

10. A *Volksdeutscher/Volksdeutsche* was a Polish man/woman of German origin who received extra privileges by declaring loyalty to Germany.

11. This is the Warsaw Uprising, which began in August 1944, not the Warsaw Ghetto Uprising. See glossary.

12. Żegota was a branch of the Polish underground organized to give assistance to Jews.

13. AK, *Armia Krajowa,* known in English as the Home Army, was the organized underground army in Poland that reported to the Polish government-in-exile in London. Its commander was General Tadeusz Bór-Komorowski.

14. PAST, *Polska Akcyjna Spółka Telefoniczna.*

15. The "Goliaths" were powerful German mines that could be automatically detonated from a distance.

16. Pius XI Street is now called Piękna Street.

17. Refers to the surrender of the insurgents of the Warsaw Uprising.

18. Much of the civilian population of Warsaw, as punishment for having participated in the uprising, was forcibly moved out of the city to internment camps.

19. The bombing of Dresden actually took place on February 13–14, 1945.

20. *Volkssturm* [people's militia] was a civilian corps of males age sixteen through sixty, recruited to defend Germany's home soil.

21. German currency.

22. Gymnasium/*gimnazjum* corresponded at that time to U.S. grades seven through ten.

23. The Council of State was the name of the governing body of Poland after World War II.

IRENA (AGATA) BOŁDOK, NÉE LIKIERMAN

Born in 1932

Back to Being Myself!

I constantly feel as if I am about to see my father, sister, family. . . . All the time I am waiting for someone familiar to suddenly appear. My father's name was Henryk Likierman. He married Anna, née Hampel. I am Irena, née Likierman. I had a sister, Helena, who perished. She was eight years older than I. Before the war we lived on Marszałkowska Street, house number 49, apartment 34—this I still remember.

I remember the apartment, the color of the wallpapers, and our normal family. I remember that Mama used to take me to the Botanical Garden, which she should not have done, because I was allergic to roses. Besides, children were not allowed there. I spent my childhood in the Ujazdowski Garden. I used to go to the playground on Bagatela Street to the little Jordan Garden for several hours a day. Mama used to take me there. I remember taking strolls with my mother and trips to the seaside. Mama fed us vegetables, because she thought they were healthy. I remember that my sister hated spinach, but I liked it very much. I remember that we walked around in our stocking feet until the first snow. I remember how my mother used to scrub me and say, "You have to be so clean that your knees shine!" She took good care of me. I think my sister was a bit jealous of me—she had been an only child for a long time.

Father was a bookkeeper. He worked for the firm Plutos. Of course, mother did not work. We had a maid before the war. I assume that my parents were rather well off. Mama was very talented artistically; she devoted time to the arts. She sketched, sang, and danced. She may have even danced professionally before we were born. She told me to step on my toes, not my heels, and taught us movement to music at home.

My sister told me wonderful fairy tales; I could be talked into doing anything she wanted in exchange for her stories. We devised our own language, which we used with each other. It wasn't for everyday use. She drew very well, took drawing lessons even in the Warsaw Ghetto.

The Germans, while looking for radios that were supposed to have been turned in, came to our home, in 1939 or 1940, and killed my dog in front of my eyes. After that I got meningitis. When we moved to the ghetto, I wasn't able to speak or walk; my parents wheeled me in a cart. I don't remember this very well, but I do remember it. In the ghetto we lived at number 30 or 60 Sienna Street—I get the numbers mixed up. It was somewhere near where the Palace of Culture is today. The four of us lived in a little room, somewhere very high up, on the sixth or seventh floor. How we supported ourselves—I don't know. Our neighbor from Marszałkowska helped us for a while. Her name was Wiernicka. Earlier, at that woman's suggestion, my mother had me and my sister baptized at the Church of the Holy Cross.

Later . . . I remember only that my mother left the ghetto with me; we went through some hole in the wall and went to Międzyrzec Podlaski, where my father's sister lived, married to a Doctor Kozes. They had a house there. I remember the trip to Międzyrzec. Mother, who spoke good German, entered with me into a compartment for Germans, which was dictated by necessity (or was it impudence?), because the train was terribly crowded. The officers in this German car were very gallant and let my mother ride with me. However, a conductor came and threw us out of there, stuffing us into some other car.

We thus lived for a time with our family in Międzyrzec, but then my mother decided to go back for my father and sister, who had stayed in the Warsaw Ghetto. With a Polish last name (on Aryan papers[1]), as Anna Szonert, she went back to Warsaw. She took a certain amount of money, or gold, to bribe the blue-uniformed [Polish] police. Unfortunately, during a street roundup, she was taken for forced labor in Germany. She worked in a marmalade factory there. Later, for participating in sabotage, she was sent to the camp at Ravensbrück.[2]

I don't remember the order of events clearly . . . but I think it must have been that Mother was still alive, Father's family, too, and I was staying with peasants in a village. I was placed there (for money) for "safekeeping." But when I got jaundice and scabies, they drove me close to Międzyrzec and dropped me from the cart like a sack of potatoes, saying that I should go back to where I had been before. So I went back to my aunt and uncle and stayed there for some time. But at that time transports to Treblinka[3] were already being organized. A German lived in one of the rooms of that house (a multifamily house on the market square of Międzyrzec). But things get a little mixed up for me here . . .

There was also a time when Mother was still living in Międzyrzec and we were all herded together in the market square for deportation. However, I stayed at home and hid (aware that they were going to their deaths) in that German officer's room, behind his overcoat. Eventually, someone came and dragged me out from behind that coat. Here I must return to 1940 or maybe 1941. Why weren't we shipped off when everyone else was taken? It seems that my mother showed our certificates from the church, and we managed to get out from there. And then I think Mother went to Warsaw.

During the next roundup, my aunt, I, and our whole family from Międzyrzec were packed into a railroad wagon for deportation, most likely to Treblinka. Mother wasn't with us then. And then, my uncle—the doctor—injected himself, his wife, and their child with morphine. He wanted to give me an injection, too, but there was terrible crowding and confusion; someone pushed me away, and I found myself near the door. I did not quite realize that they were no longer alive, even though I knew. . . . My uncle had said that it was a deadly injection, that we were going to our deaths anyway, so to protect everyone . . . Maybe I ran away from that shot myself? I don't remember.

In any case, I found myself near the door. A railroad worker who was there asked, "What's your name, little girl?" I answered, "Irena." He said I had blue eyes, like his daughter. He pulled me out of there, saying, "Come quickly, don't say anything." He hid me in the station, in the toilet. When the transport left, he came for me. Where did he take me? If I could only remember . . . I get the sequence of events mixed up. So when the railroad worker told me to go, I think I went to the house of my mother's friend, a gentile. Her name was Cydzikowa. My mother must have been there with me at some point in time. We had hidden in the barn. A peasant came in there with a pitchfork and looked for us. He poked the pitchfork into the hay and said, "I'll scare those Jews out of here right away." Apparently he had seen us when we sneaked in. He poked the pitchfork in time after time. I remember that I was terribly afraid that I would scream. I don't know whether he threw us out of that barn or whether he didn't find us.

I came from the train station to Mrs. Cydzikowa's. I had jaundice. I remember that I looked completely different from the other kids. My mother's friend let me stay for a while, but then she said, "You know that I have two sons. I can't take such a risk." She turned me over to the nuns. These were the Sisters of Providence—located at 69 Lubelska Street, a place donated by Count Potocki. There was a barracks for orphans there. I was the oldest, but there were thirty other little ones. This might have been the end of 1942 or 1943. The nuns knew very well that I was Jewish. I was emaciated, with little braids, yellow like a lemon because of the jaundice.

I don't know how long I stayed with those nuns. One time, Germans came and told the nuns that if they had any Jewish children, they would have to give them up. They ought to go back to wherever they came from. The nuns decided to send me back to the woman who had brought me there. You should have seen the expression on Mrs. Cydzikowa's face when she saw me. She said that she was very sorry, but that unfortunately, she could not take me in and that I should return to the nuns. I didn't really know what to do; I went back and forth maybe twice. During those trips, somewhere midway, I was caught by nightfall. It could have been late fall, because I was already wearing a winter coat (I remember that coat; it was dark green and had a leopard-skin collar). I spent the night on the doorstep of a church mortuary. I was very cold and got a bladder infection, so I had to go pee very often. Gendarmes came in the morning. They asked, "What are you doing here, little girl?" I answered astutely that I was waiting for my mother, even though she wasn't there, of course. "Where's your mother?" "She went to the store."

They came back once—I was still sitting there. A second time—I was still sitting. They said, "Come with us, your mother probably won't come back." They took me to the town hall, to the mayor. The mayor was a *Volksdeutscher;* I think his name was Majewski. I believe this happened after all the Jewish transports had gone. I don't know what year it was then. The mayor got the idea to send me to a home for the elderly, so that I could wait out the worst period there. He figured out that I was Jewish. When someone asked me what my name was, I answered "Irena Likierman." What more did he need?

At the home for the elderly, I sat under someone's bed. I would only come out to eat and wash myself. I was already there for some time (months or weeks), when I once went outdoors. Did I come out because I couldn't stand it under the bed any more, or was it because I was allowed to? In any case, some woman saw me and began screaming, "A Jewish girl has stayed behind here; I'll take care of her right away!" I ran back into the home, and the nuns that were running it, afraid that this woman would come after me, took me back to the sisters where I had stayed before. I spent the following year with them.

One time, before 1944, when I was not supposed to go into

town, I went to see the Kozes' house. I stood in front of the window of their pharmacy. I was thinking about everything that had happened. I could feel a German with a dog come up behind me. I saw his reflection in the window. The dog started sniffing me. I remember my determination. I was scared to turn around. The German grabbed me by the arm and turned me around to face him. *"Jude?"* [Jew?] *"Jawohl!"* [Yes!], I answered. He pushed me and said, *"Raus!"* [Out!] I didn't run. I walked (this German was supposedly the butcher of Międzyrzec).

In 1944 the Russians entered. Some time before this, when the front was approaching and there was nothing to eat, the nuns handed me over, as the oldest of the girls, as a servant to a woman teacher. I was twelve years old already. The story about the teacher is a separate matter. It is sad, colorful, and long. This teacher did not let me read books, because she thought I was too smart. So why? . . . Around that time the uprising broke out in Warsaw, and she held it against me that I, a Jewish girl, was tucked away safely, while her nephew was in Warsaw, and it was not certain if he would survive. The last day of the war for me conjures up only the sight of a peasant with an ax, and his words, "They didn't finish you off, but I will."

When the front passed, I went back to the nuns (those at the orphanage, not with the elderly), and in 1945 I went to school. I had never gone to school before; when I was supposed to go to first grade, the war broke out, then the ghetto, the nuns. . . . Evidently, I learned to read and write when I was still at home, when I was six years old.

Some nuns were good to me, others were not. Sister Bolesława was always very good to me, and I liked her a lot. When after the war she became mother superior in Wodzisław Śląski, she invited me for vacation and sent me to a scout camp near Kłodzko. Professor Jerzy Soplica took care of our team. He immediately realized that I was a Jewish girl. He told me, "You are a child of the nuns, but remember, if you ever have any problems, you can count on me; I'll help you."

I didn't want to be the "good girl" who has to be nicer than the others just because she's a Jew. I didn't get along with the nuns any more. I was difficult—it was my adolescence. Some of the nuns from Zamość (I moved there from Międzyrzec) had probably been raised in small towns and had known Jews. They would wake me at night to try and force me to speak Yiddish, but I didn't know a word of Yiddish. But they still didn't believe me and wanted me to "confess." I told them all kinds of stories—that I had a Jewish father and a non-Jewish mother or vice versa. I used various ploys. That remains with you the rest of your life. . . .

After completing the first or second year of lyceum,[4] I got on a train, and, supposedly traveling to "my nun," I went to see the professor. What was I counting on? I simply knew that I could not stand being with the nuns any more. In addition, there were problems with a priest; he was very amorous and pressed me against the wall. After all, at that time I was a believer, zealous as a neophyte, who relies only on her faith.

When I appeared at the crack of dawn at Professor Soplica's, he looked at me as if he had seen a ghost. He gave me something to eat and drink and told me we would go to Długopole Zdrój, where I would work in the library, and after vacation he would place me in a boarding school where I could continue my education. We went to Długopole. One time I heard the professor speaking to an acquaintance who had come to visit him. She asked about me, "Who is this young girl?" He answered, "She is my cousin." To that she said, "Since when do you have Jews in your family?" This made me uncomfortable, and I began thinking that after all, I really was a Jew and should find another place for myself. But at that time I didn't know any other Jews besides myself.

Some woman came to the library in Długopole and told me she was working at the Israeli Embassy. "Are you Jewish?" she asked. "Jewish," I answered. "What are you doing here? You're young, you should go to Israel. Go quickly to Warsaw."

She gave me two addresses—one of the Israeli Embassy and

the other of the Jewish Committee. She told me to write to the Jewish Committee for money for the ticket to Warsaw. She advised me that once I was in Warsaw, I should not go to the committee but to the embassy. I wrote, telling them where I was. I got an immediate response and money for the ticket. They wrote me to report to the committee. To tell the truth, I did not know the difference between these two institutions. I reported to the committee, but the committee was geared toward building communism in Poland. I told them in the committee that I came to Warsaw to go to Israel. The people who were interviewing me said the following, "You want to go to Israel? Do you have anyone there?" "No, I don't." "Do you want to continue studying?" I did. "You will go to Nowy Dwór for vacation," they decided. "At the start of the new school year, you will go to school in Warsaw."

I was confused. I thought, "Why should I go to Israel if I can be in Warsaw?" And that's what happened. They took me—as I was, in my only dress—to Nowy Dwór. There was a camp for Jewish youth there. At the beginning of the new year I went to lyceum. I moved into student housing at Jagiellońska Street. I then passed my matriculation[5] at the pedagogic lyceum.

I skipped over some important elements in my life. My mother survived Ravensbrück and came to Łódź (to Radogoszcz) in 1946. She had stomach cancer and soon died, but I still managed to see her alive. We saw each other for two hours. She asked, "Do you know you are Jewish?" "Why are your hands so swollen?" (I had second-degree frostbite), "Why are your teeth so horribly yellow?" (I didn't brush my teeth at all while staying with the nuns). Mother died, which I learned about by mail, but before she did, she sent some people—Jews—for me to Międzyrzec. But what did I want with Jews? I was deeply involved in the Catholic "holy faith." I considered Jews to be something inferior. The nuns had instilled this conviction in me. "They crucified the Lord Jesus!" And I was supposed to go with Jews? I wouldn't hear of it. They tried to convince me for a long time. I, a young squirt—I must have been thirteen then—made stupid faces behind their backs. I was showing off in front of the nuns, saying, "I am not going to renounce the holy faith. I am not going to any Palestine (there was no Israel yet) with a bunch of strangers." They even went to the police, trying to take me back. Nothing came of it. Those nuns, with their attitude toward Jews, had created within me a barrier, a kind of resistance, during all those years I had spent with them.

I was attracted to my colleagues from the Jewish dorms and at the same time repelled by them. When I heard them speaking Yiddish, I got goose pimples. I was unable to get used to it. I thought that somebody would come soon and put an end to "it." It seemed impossible that they could be so calm, that they should talk and laugh. I could not find a place for myself among them. I looked at them, and the people I liked the most were those who looked the least Jewish. Those who looked the most Jewish scared me. I ran as far away from them as I could.

This also happened later. I would run away from Jews, then I'd come back to them. At times I thought I could be with some Jews, but then I really couldn't. I ran away and pretended I didn't have anything in common with them. Then I'd be drawn to them again, and I would come back. From the time I was a little child, I had to deny being Jewish, and this has left traces that did not allow me to think, see, or live normally. There was a popular book by Chagall's wife called *Burning Lights.* People thought it was a wonderful book and admired the Jewish folklore. When I picked it up, I suddenly realized that it encompassed a Jewish world that people had tried to eradicate from within me, which I was trying to forget. I couldn't even say what all that attraction and repulsion was all about.

I constantly come back to our (Jewish) milieu, but somewhere at the bottom of my soul, there is still some resistance. To survive, I could not "admit" to being Jewish; it was something that couldn't be mentioned. I was supposed to go to Israel, to see a friend from the Jewish dormitory on Jagiellońska. An old hag—an awful, nosy one—in the neighborhood pharmacy asked whether I was going with a pilgrimage. I said, "Yes, with a pilgrimage." I later tortured myself, blaming myself and my soul for my cowardice. But I also thought that this could have been the last voice of the past, perhaps some echo, all that was left. After all, there are plenty of moments in life when I feel like a stranger, and I don't know where I belong. What can I say about it? It's difficult to talk about it without sounding as if I am making things up. This is the "foreigner" syndrome.[6] Even today, even though I have come to terms (that's the wrong expression) with my origins, I still don't feel entirely "here" or "there."

What's left of those years, what has been depressing me as an older person, is my undeniable egoism. I think that if I had not been self-centered when I was eight or nine years old, I would not have survived. As a ten-year-old child I had to make many decisions that forced me to take only my own good into consideration, only in order to be able to survive. I clearly remember one instance when my mother was still with me, and she (or my aunt) was supposed to give me back to the peasant in the village. Mother asked me whether I was sorry to have to go there, and I, completely aware that I had to go if I wanted to save myself, answered, "I can do anything, just to survive." For sure, my mother must have felt pained by this.

During all my years of staying with the nuns, I didn't have anything of my own, and there wasn't anything lasting within me. When I got used to somebody, they would be taken from me. The nuns around me changed, so did the children. I didn't have my own bed, nothing of my own. This created within me the conviction that nothing was permanent. That has probably weighed on my emotional life in later years—a feeling of instability, the conviction that I shouldn't get used to anything or get too attached to anything, because it would be taken from me anyway. Also, the feeling that change and instability were permanent factors with which people had to learn to cope was not a positive influence on the life of a growing girl and later, on my family life.

My first husband was a Jew. I met him in the dormitory on Jagiellońska Street in Warsaw. He studied at the Wawelberg

School. He was calm and placid, which I considered a positive trait at the time. I was alone. In 1952 it was clear that nothing would come of this marriage. In 1953 my son was born. When I got divorced, I turned away from Jews radically. I started working and entered a whole new social circle.

My escape from my Jewish identity also took on the following form—I suddenly decided to stop being Irena. My middle name is Augusta, and some of my acquaintances knew me by this name. This was a way of hiding—having a different name, a different surname, being a different person. My second husband (we worked together in the same publishing company) knew me only as "Agata." My closest acquaintances know me as Agata. Then, not too long ago, I thought, "How typical that I would even hide under a changed name . . ."

This is the end of Agata. Now I am back to being Irena again!

Excerpts of an interview with Irena Bołdok conducted by Katarzyna Meloch in 1991.

1. Aryan papers were documents attesting that the person named in them was Aryan, not Jewish. Jews who were able to obtain falsified Aryan papers were able to live on the Aryan side, though always in danger of being "unmasked" and denounced.

2. Ravensbrück, a women's concentration camp containing numerous satellite camps, was located fifty-six miles north of Berlin.

3. Treblinka was a death camp fifty miles northeast of Warsaw where most of the Jews of Warsaw were deported. More than 800,000 Jews were killed there.

4. Lyceum/*liceum* corresponded at that time to the last two years of U.S. high school.

5. Matriculation/*matura* was the final examination upon completion of lyceum [high school], a prerequisite for admission to university.

6. Reference to the book *Cudzoziemka* [*The Foreigner*] by Maria Kuncewiczowa. (Author's note)

ILONKA FAJNBERG

Born in 1939

I Found My Roots

I constantly invoke in my memory my family home, the small bed with netting, and above it, in a silver frame, a large portrait of a smiling child with two small teeth showing in front. During the day the house empties, quiets down, and during the evening it fills with people. There are no other children there, and Mama is always with me. She plays with me, holds my little hand, does not let me out of her sight. . . . Suddenly, everything changes, I hear, "Mama is sick, very sick. You must not enter her bedroom." Yet, each morning I quietly sneak in there through the dining room and, unnoticed, run up to her bed, slip in under the covers, and snuggle up to her. Only by her side do I feel calm and safe.

One morning, as usual after waking up, I run into Mama's room and see an empty, made-up bed. I am in despair. I begin to sob loudly. A tall man picks me up, takes me in his arms, embraces me, and comforts me, "Don't cry, Mama went to the countryside. You will go to her. I will go, too. We will all go there." In the evening, at dusk, he stands me up on a stool dressed in a fur jacket and says, "Remember, your name is Marysia Kołakowska. Repeat—Marysia Kołakowska."

Afterward there were other places, other homes, faces unknown to me. In one of them, while falling asleep, I hear a woman's voice, "Poor child. Everyone has perished." Later, whenever these words came back to me, and it was often, I would lose faith in the possibility of finding my dear ones.

In the spring of 1943 I found myself in the Sisters of Charity convent in Kamionek. From that time on, my guardian was the mother superior in this convent, Sister Maria Pietkiewicz, a woman of great heart, which she, however, tried not to show. She was stiff and unapproachable and aroused fear and respect, not only among the girls in her care.

At the convent I was the only fully orphaned child, left without even an extended family. It was very sad for me when families took the other children on Sundays and holidays, and I had to remain alone. When I grew up a bit, I complained about this to Mother Superior, and she became angry, "What do you mean you have no family; we're your family!"

And that's how it was left.

After the war ended, many families wanted to adopt children. I remember well a conversation with a nice couple who were on their way to the United States. They told me that there was a big war in which we all got lost, but that they were very happy that they had finally found me. I believed their every word, but Mother Superior absolutely refused to hand me over, despite having been favorably inclined initially. She said she would not give me up to anyone. This is when I began to feel that I was somebody important to her and maybe even loved. Indeed, she really did care for me, dressed me up in secondhand clothing from UNRRA[1] aid packages and liked to take me to town. Passersby would stop in the street and say, "What a lovely child . . . like a doll." She was very proud of me, but in the convent she instructed the staff not to praise me like that. She worried that I would become conceited. I remember also that she would not allow me to hang around in the kitchen with the laywomen.

Sometimes in the convent they would organize religious plays or Christmas pageants, and I was cast as the Virgin Mary. She used to say that that is how she imagined the Blessed Virgin, who, she instructed me, had also spent time around the temple as a young girl.

Mother Superior always occupied a small room in the basement behind the refectory. The kitchen, pantry, dining rooms, dressing rooms, as well as the servants' quarters were all nearby. When I grew up somewhat, Mother Superior moved me from the dormitory and arranged a corner in the dining room for me to sleep in, separated from the tables by a large Danzig wardrobe. In this way I was now constantly near my guardian. She entrusted me with taking care of the pantry. My duties included cleaning and making sandwiches for the children living in the dormitory. When I began to mature, Mother Superior began to worry whether the girls returning from vacation might initiate me in the matter of sex. This was because one of the girls brought back a photo from the seaside; she was dressed only in a swimsuit, and boys were also visible in the picture. The photograph was considered evidence of depravity, and the girl was expelled from the dormitory. Mother Superior kept questioning me about my conversations with the other girls and was very satisfied when it turned out that we had not talked about "those" subjects.

When I turned eight I was placed in Sister Stefania's class. This sister showed a great dislike toward the girls from the dormitory, and especially toward me. During the three years during which she was my teacher, I experienced a lot of unpleasantness and humiliation. When she entered the classroom, I hunched down into my school bench, trying to become invisible to her, but to no avail. She kept sending me to Mother Superior, complaining, for instance, that I was wearing too short a skirt and was demoralizing the other children, or that I did not bring some school paraphernalia such as an eraser or a crayon, even though the rest of the class might not have them either. She often threw me out of the classroom. I felt so lonely, humiliated, and helpless that I often prayed fervently to God to take me to him, as he had earlier taken my parents. I recall with great bitterness one of her punishments, being left alone in a dark vestibule.

When everyone had forgotten about me, I spent the night sobbing, snuggled up to our friendly dog on its mat.

After finishing elementary school, I was invited by a classmate to spend the vacation with her at her grandmother's house. The grandmother gave us plenty of freedom, so we pranced about in forests and meadows. I had not known such scenery, because I had never gone out of the convent. I remember this vacation as the most beautiful moment of my childhood.

Happy as I was about the convent school being shut down,[2] the closing of the dormitory terrified me. I was afraid of being sent to an orphanage, to total strangers. I was then fourteen and longed very much for my dear ones, even though I had hardly known them. I was sure that if any of them had survived, they would have found me. This is why I viewed with increasing resignation a characteristic birthmark on my left leg, which I imagined could have been readily used to identify me. It was gradually fading and getting smaller and smaller.

When I could finally go outside the confines of the convent, I contacted the Polish Red Cross, but nobody was looking for a Marysia Kołakowska.

After the convent school was taken over by the state and the dormitory closed, Mother Superior lost her position and understood that she would no longer be able to help me. She agreed to have me adopted by a family who had two boys and wanted to also have a girl. They took me to their home for Sundays and holidays, and I was thrilled. I waited impatiently for the weekends. I made friends with the boys and their father, whom I called "uncle." They liked me and showed me much warmth. But my relationship with the mother of the boys did not blossom, as she saw me not as a daughter, but as a rival for the affection of her maturing sons and her husband. It was inevitable that this family and I would part. After that I felt even more lonely.

Shortly afterward I was accepted to study at the Catholic University of Lublin (KUL) and left Warsaw. Like most of the KUL students, I lived in a student dormitory. This was the happiest time of my life, a time of wonderful friendships that have survived to this day. I was flattered by attention from the boys, their compliments and adoration. However, when they confessed their love for me and proposed marriage, I was terrified. The convent upbringing, the isolation from family life, and the lack of support from close relatives made me fear marriage.

The man I chose was, like myself, very lonely. He never imposed on me, but I always felt his presence. I believed that I could help him, that I was indispensable to him. His patience and gentleness gave me courage, and in the end, I decided to start a family, but all this happened many years later.

After finishing my studies, I returned to Warsaw. I went to see my guardian, who was living in the little room, very familiar to me, behind the refectory. She had held up bravely, walked proudly and straight, even though she had to increasingly rely on a man's black umbrella substituting for a cane. Her face showed previously unseen fatigue and a certain gentleness. At that time she showed me more affection than before. One day she began to unburden herself and to recall the former days. She judged herself very severely, finally saying, "God will never forgive me for this." I was so surprised that I did not ask why she thought so.

Many years later, after Mother Superior's death, I visited a nun with whom I had made friends. I was married by then and had an adolescent son. I confessed that I had wanted very much to have been placed in some family and that I did not understand why my guardian had opposed this. Then, after a long pause, the nun told me the story of my life and Mother Superior's dilemma. She knew that I was a child from the ghetto. My father had been an educated man and my mother a strikingly beautiful woman who died young. They had only one child. Mother Superior made the nun swear on the cross that she would never tell the secret to me or to anyone else. "I am telling you about this to ease your resentment toward her," the nun said. "You have no idea how much she loved you. During the war she risked her life for you.

Later she couldn't part with you. She thought the convent would become your home forever. You don't even know how happy you made her by finishing Catholic University. You were the most important person to her after God."

Several years after that conversation, I contacted the Association of "Children of the Holocaust" in Poland. I never suspected that this would lead to improbable things, bordering on miracles. My life was to change.

At one of the first gatherings in Śródborów in 1993, I met a cousin on my father's side, Halina Anita Janowska, who is the author of many excellent books, including *My Guardian Demon* and *Crossword Puzzle.* She and her sister, whom I also met, told me about my family history.

My father, Józef Fajnberg, was a well-known lawyer in Łódź before the war. A year before the war, he married a twenty-one-year-old girl, Henryka Gutstadt, who was known in Łódź for her beauty. Their wedding was a huge social event. A year later I came into the world.

When the Germans entered Łódź, the persecution of Jews began. Father was badly beaten in the street. An awareness of the deadly danger made him decide to escape. I was then a few-weeks-old newborn baby, and for that reason, my mother could not accompany her husband. She left for Warsaw with her parents, where they perished in the ghetto, whereas Father and his younger brother went to Lwów, where he intended to bring his whole family. Father and his brother were arrested by the NKVD (Soviet secret police). They were exiled to Kazakhstan for their refusal to take on Soviet citizenship. There they worked as loggers cutting down trees in the forest. When the Anders Army[3] was being formed, they both wanted to join, but the assembly point was too far, the freezing temperature reached minus thirty degrees centigrade, and they owned only one pair of shoes. So only the younger brother became a soldier; he was evacuated with the army to Iran and then to Palestine. He stayed there and became a well-known architect.

At the first opportunity my father returned to Łódź, but he found that his family was no longer there. He learned that his wife had died and his daughter had been placed in a convent. He tried to find his lost daughter for many years afterward. He placed advertisements in the press and on the radio. He offered a very large reward to anyone with information about the location of Ilonka Fajnberg. In response, he received hundreds of letters. He chose the most likely cases and personally contacted the people indicated. During one of those travels, he met his second wife and started taking care of the girl she was bringing up, who is my age. He died in 1969.

I feel great bitterness and sadness at the thought that my father was living in Poland and, despite such great efforts, never found me. I only have a photograph of him and a portrait of my beautiful mother. I am convinced that if she had survived the war, she would have found me somehow.

I met my relatives from Israel. I became closest with Professor Jakub Goldberg and his wonderful wife. The professor often comes to Poland and a few years ago received an honorary doctorate from the University of Warsaw.

I also recently met a charming person who lives in Paris, who in reading Hanna Krall's book *Evidence of Existence* recognized me as the little girl who had lived in the same apartment building in the ghetto. She wrote, "I remember your mother, as if it were yesterday. A stunningly beautiful young woman with her tiny daughter, Ilonka. She was slender, had dark, beautiful hair and absolutely fantastic eyes. The people in the ghetto were dressed modestly, but your mother had a natural elegance that attracted attention. I remember how she used to push you in a stroller, how she held your hand. You looked like a real doll; you had blond curly hair and your mother's radiant smile. . . ."

After the war my father asked her for help in finding his daughter, because she was the only person living who had known the child in the final period before his wife's death. It was, as she wrote, "the goal of his life." Father, after his return from Kazakhstan, found out that his wife had died but had left a message that she had sent the child to the Aryan side. Whenever someone responded to the advertisements placed by my father and wrote that a Jewish girl had been hidden somewhere, the woman would go with him there. Unfortunately, all the trips ended in failure. The woman herself left in 1947. Our meeting in Paris was very moving and unforgettable.

Since I learned about my family, I have experienced many joyful and emotion-filled moments. I would like to particularly thank my wonderful friend Renata, as well as Inka,[4] and many others, for their initiative and assistance in finding my relatives. I am very happy that I have met so many dear and warm people.

---

1. United Nations Relief and Rehabilitation Administration.

2. In 1948–52 the state authorities closed down nearly all schools and other institutions operated by nuns. (Author's note)

3. The Anders Army, also known as the Polish Second Corps, was an army of Poles under the command of General Wladysław Anders. When Germany attacked the Soviet Union in 1941, Stalin, in order to get the cooperation of the Allies, agreed to release Poles who had been exiled to Siberia during the Soviet occupation of eastern Poland (1939–41) and allowed them to form this army. The Anders Army left the Soviet Union and went to Iran, Iraq, and then to Palestine, where it became part of the British Eighth Army. It took part in the Italian campaign, including the famous Battle of Monte Cassino.

4. Renata Zajdman and Joanna Sobolewska-Pyz.

MARIAN FINKIELMAN

Born in 1928

Wanderings

It is very difficult to write about oneself, especially when one's experiences were so tragic.

When the Germans invaded Poland on September 1, 1939, I was eleven years old. During that memorable September, my father was killed in the siege of Warsaw. Thus from the very beginning of the occupation, Mama and I were left without any means of support. In order to make ends meet, she began to sell off certain items from our home. Time was not on her side, because after the establishment of the ghetto, the number of such sellers kept increasing. Beginning with the spring of 1941, I took upon myself the sale of particular items and the buying of food supplies, making these transactions outside the ghetto walls.

Encouraged by my achievements on the "other side," in June, I began going to the countryside to get provisions. I was helped by my "good looks" and good pronunciation—without a Yiddish accent. Thus, posing as a Polish Catholic boy, I managed to do well in the countryside. I also realized that if I wanted to spend the night there, I would need a permit from the village administrator. When a farmer saw such a note, he would not ask many questions and would serve me supper before going to bed and a hearty breakfast in the morning. In the countryside certain "manners" (specific types of behavior) were important. I quickly adopted them, which is why I had no major difficulties.

Paying no heed to the great danger, I made rounds as a smuggler between the Otwock ghetto and the surrounding villages. I brought things wanted by the peasants and exchanged them for food articles. This acquired experience of moving about outside the ghetto was to help me survive in the later, more difficult period. But for the time being, still in 1941, I was enjoying good food while spending nights with village farmers. Unfortunately, this was only a temporarily idyllic time. A typhus epidemic that decimated the population also affected Mama and me. When I left the hospital in the beginning of December, my mama was no longer among the living. The winter of 1941 to 42 was unusually cold and was particularly harsh on the people confined inside the ghetto. The freezing cold and the still spreading typhus increased the "reaper's toll."

In this atmosphere, I experienced my tragedy all alone, suffering at the same time from hunger. Despite the freezing cold, I again began going to the countryside. Perhaps this was what saved me, because I soon regained my psychological balance. Just the fact of being outside the walls of the ghetto demanded full concentration, which diverted my attention from other thoughts and the despair at having lost my mother. Thus, whenever the weather was favorable, I would get under way, marching along the Lublin highway to various villages. Having no problem obtaining permits from the administrator for staying the night, I would extend my stay in the countryside.

When I finally returned to Otwock, I stayed with my schoolmate, Juda Cytryn. One could say that at that time the Cytryns became my substitute family. I gave them provisions that I brought from the country. Even though I officially lived near the Marpa Sanitarium (while my mama was still alive), at that time, upon returning from the countryside, I stayed with my friend at 1 Dłuskiego Street. But in reality, I lived nowhere. I was simply going back and forth between the villages and the Otwock ghetto. I began to wonder whether these dangerous trips made any sense. I had an uncle who lived in Dubeczno, near Włodawa, on the Bug River, and therefore I decided to go to him.

At the end of March 1942 I said goodbye to my dear friends, the Cytryns, and left Otwock. I traveled to Włodawa by train, with a transfer at Chełm. By the time I left Włodawa and was on the way to Dubeczno, it was already evening. Where could I go at night, into the unknown? I therefore decided to use my old method of getting lodging with a permit from a village administrator. After having spent the night in a country hut, the next morning I marched off to Dubeczno and arrived at my destination in the evening. But, as it soon became apparent, this was only a short stopover in my travels. My unexpected appearance was an unpleasant surprise for my uncle and his family. I therefore decided to leave their inhospitable home.

Already earlier some villagers along the road to Lublin (near Kołbiel), had offered to hire me in the spring to mind their cows at pasture. I decided to do this near Dubeczno. Posing as a Polish Catholic boy from near Warsaw, I looked for such a job. I was hired to mind cows in the village of Kozaki, about eight kilometers from Dubeczno. But it turned out that it was easier for me to pose as someone I was not when I went to the village for provisions and stayed with a villager for just one night. On the other hand, it was totally different when I had a permanent job, and especially with a Ukrainian (this was a Ukrainian village). Because it was the beginning of my new job, I got confused as to how to behave. In addition, I had no documents to prove my identity. As a result, the villager immediately guessed who I was. At first he didn't tell me about it, but somewhat later his wife did, threatening that she would put a noose around my neck and take me to the Germans.

I therefore ran away from this village, but my existence was dependent on my finding a job in the country. I therefore continued to go from village to village, looking for work. Because the local villages were mainly Ukrainian, I had additional troubles. I finally found a job after a few days, and I settled on appropriate wages. I minded cows, and in the evenings I helped to clean them. One day the farmer asked me whether I would like to stay with him through the winter. Of course, I agreed. He then told me that I would have to register, so I should write home to have them send me my birth certificate. The next day, when I drove the cows to pasture, I left them there, with regret. I don't remember the name of this farmer, just as I don't remember the names of the villages and the names of other farmers with whom I stayed briefly and then left when I sensed I could be recognized.

I then found myself once again in a Ukrainian village, called Sokoły, working for a villager by the name of Franiuk. I spoke only Ukrainian with the boys out in the pasture and thanks to that improved my knowledge of that language. When the beginning of October came, the local administrators were ordered to deliver horse-drawn carts for the transport of Jews from a nearby town to an assembly point. Franiuk was the local administrator, and upon getting back from the town offices, he told me that I must leave him, because he had to comply with the registration rules, and, as I had no documents, I could not be registered. He also discouraged me from going to the nearby town. The next morning, kind old Franiuk, dishing out my food, once again admonished me, "Remember, don't go to Persow!" I decided to return to my uncle, and I soon found out why Franiuk had advised me against going to the nearby town. Walking through fields and meadows, I reached the road leading to Dubeczno, and after two days of travel (I slept in a haystack), I reached my destination.

I was once again in my uncle's house, where everyone, including the neighbors, were gathered in the kitchen. When she saw me, my aunt exclaimed, "Look at him! Why did you come back here? Tomorrow morning we are all going to Sobibór."[1] Then a neighbor said, "You know what? Let's stoke up the stove, stick some shoes into it, drink some vodka, and when we fall asleep, we'll all suffocate right here. Why should we go to Sobibór, just to be put in an oven there?" Hearing this, I jumped up from my seat and yelled, "I'm not going to Sobibór! I'd rather die from a bullet. I will hide as long as I can, and when they finally catch me, they'll at least shoot me on the spot."

I lay down on a bench near the stove and immediately fell asleep. In the morning, my aunt woke me up, "Get up! It's six o'clock already; the gendarmes may show up at any moment to take us to Sobibór." I got up and noticed that everyone sat numb in the same place where they had been in the evening. No one had drunk vodka, and no one was able to bring himself to start the fire. Exhaustion and despair were written all over their faces. I got up, picked out some shoes lying on the floor, put them on my feet, and left. It had been easy to say I would hide, but where? Somehow, despite myself, I turned in the direction from which I had come.

When I again arrived in the village of Sokoły, it was already evening. I went there in desperation, because I simply did not know where I could go. Besides, in my youthful naïveté (I was fourteen), I thought Franiuk would help me. When I entered the kitchen, Franiuk's wife looked at me as if she had seen a ghost. She crossed herself and exclaimed, "Oh, God! Why did you come here?" I told her about what happened in Dubeczno and about my intention to build myself a hideout in the forest and that therefore I needed a shovel and an ax. I asked about her husband. "Go behind the barn and wait. I'll tell him you are here when he comes back."

I went behind the barn, and Franiuk appeared after a time. Handing me some bread, he said, "Forgive me, but I cannot help you with hiding in the forest and have you come to my house. I can't risk that, because I have children. Don't come here again. Go! But don't go through the village; someone could notice you. Go back through here behind the barns." I went to the meadow and dug myself a place to sleep in a haystack. Sobbing and eating the bread I had been given, I fell asleep.

A heavy rain was falling the next morning. Nobody brought the cows to pasture, so nobody saw me. There was another village on the other side of the meadow, and thus I headed in that direction. In a house along the way, I was told that by going farther down the road, I would get to the small town of Komarówka, about twenty kilometers away. Toward evening I arrived in this town, in which a deportation was to take place the next morning. A Jewish policeman stopped me and led me to a shed with several people already inside. More arrived throughout the night. The policemen made sure that the German order to deport people for extermination was carried out precisely.

The rain stopped at dawn, and a beautiful and sunny morning followed. The doors of the shed slid open, and on the left-hand side of the shed stood a row of horse-drawn carts, which drove up one by one, and each was loaded with four people. I noticed that on the other side of the street there was a fence with a gate through which townspeople were also coming with their small bundles in hand and boarding the carts. Soon I also found myself on a cart and, like the others, I knew I was heading to my death. The carts set out in the direction of Międzyrzec Podlaski, to the railroad station. The policemen kept order, while the soldiers armed with rifles ensured that no one escaped. Despite this, I constantly thought about escaping.

After several hours of riding, the carts drove into a forest. "Finally there is a chance to escape," I thought. Looking to see to which side I should jump from the cart, I spotted a soldier waiting for potential escapees behind a tree.

The caravan of carts kept moving ahead all day without stopping, and in the evening, the carts arrived in a large village. The Germans allowed the peasants to feed and water their horses, and they let the people get off the carts, also, to drink some water. I jumped off the cart and headed for some farm buildings on the other side of the road. When I got closer, I noticed that there was nobody in the area of the farm. Heading for the well, I passed it by and walked toward a barn from which a path led to a garden gate. Farther, beyond the garden, the path led to a haystack in a meadow. I turned to look around only after I got to the haystack. There was no one around. Quickly and skillfully, I pulled the hay out of the haystack to make myself a hole in which to hide.

Early in the morning, after leaving my hideout, I walked toward a field and some railroad tracks, which I had noticed from a distance. Along the way, I pulled up rutabagas and briskly walked ahead. I was happy to have escaped from the transport. For such an eventuality the Germans had issued a special order ahead of time, that anyone helping, hiding, or providing food to Jews would receive the death penalty. So after having escaped the transport, my chances of surviving—without help from anyone—were minimal.

Walking along the tracks, thinking about how many more villages I would still encounter in which I could stay over the night before I reached the town of Gołąbki, and then farther to Siedlce, I met a railroad worker returning from inspecting a rail switch. After scolding me for walking on the tracks, he started talking to me, questioning me about a multitude of things. In the end, he offered me work on his small farm. Of course he thought I was a Polish boy.

So in the middle of October 1942, after my escape from the transport, I found a roof over my head as a servant, and what was most important, I was treated like a member of the household. During long winter evenings I was able to read books, and above all, I read and memorized entire sections of catechism. I realized that one inappropriate gesture, one word spoken wrong, could mean disaster for me. That's why I tried to make myself think that I really was the person I pretended to be. To underscore this, I would kneel and say my prayers in the morning and evening, cross myself at the table before meals, and go to church on Sundays.

But despite all my efforts, I still had no documents to prove my identity as Czesław Pinkowski. Knowing well my situation, I tried to create an alibi, claiming that I had come from Dubeczno. This place was not known to many people. As a base, I used my uncle's house, which I described in detail, but I would say that my mother lived there. I often talked about Dubeczno and its surroundings, saying, consistent with the truth, that Ukrainians lived in some of the villages. The local Poles, in addition to their own language, also spoke Ukrainian, and that is why I knew the language. Evenings, while weaving baskets, I deliberately sang Ukrainian songs.

In the early spring, walking through the village, I made an agreement to mind another villager's cows during the summer. After six months of my stay with the railroad worker, for whom I have retained much gratitude in my heart, I left for another farmer (a wealthier one). It was a cold, rainy Saturday at the end of March 1943 when I went to my new employer, Jan Siedlecki. From the beginning of my stay, I slept in the room of his mother—"Grandma," as they all called her. Of course, just as at the railroad worker's place, I behaved like a devout Catholic boy. Grandma liked that a lot and often told me I was "well brought up."

Her son was not as trusting. He knew that I had no documents and yet was in no hurry to write to my home in Dubeczno, from where I had supposedly come, so that they would be sent to me. He began to suspect me, and my prior stay with another farmer in the village meant little to him. My employer, Jan Siedlecki, began to treat me with disdain, cursed me, and called me names. But because he was not particularly gentle in treating others in the household, I was not on my guard.

In reality, I should have left this farmer, left the village, as I had done many times before. Unfortunately, in occupied Poland in April 1943, a surviving Jewish boy could not freely wander around villages looking for work. Besides, I was a year older, and nobody would hire me without my showing Aryan identification papers.[2] Realizing this, I submitted to the ill-treatment, not knowing what great danger awaited me from my host and his friend Klimek. If at that point in time, in April, they had carried out their plan of examining me, as they intended, I would have lost my life.

At the end of April I began my real job. The pasture, intermingled with woods, was where I met other boys from the village, whose carefree lives I envied. I often dreamed—what if I had one of their birth certificates? I never really expected that I would realize my dream in that village.

One July afternoon, when the farmer was away, his wife, while serving me my food, began to tell me about the plan her husband and his friend Klimek had made. They wanted to lure me into the forest under the pretext of cutting down trees and to check me over. If, after pulling down my pants, their suspicions were to be confirmed, they intended to tie me up and take me to the police in town.

In further conversation, the farmer's wife asked me why I went to town so often, since I didn't have any documents. She said that if I were stopped, I could be taken for a Jew. Putting on a good face in a bad situation, I laughed and said, "But, I only go to church and sometimes to the post office to send a letter to my mother. Besides, if I did get stopped, the police could check in Dubeczno, where I come from, so everything would get cleared up anyway." My impudence may have given me courage and perhaps convinced the woman, but the danger had not passed and still hung heavily over me like the proverbial sword of Damocles.

I constantly dreamed and thought about securing Aryan papers that would help me survive. I finally was able to realize my dream, due to the fact that I slept in Grandma's room. It just so happened, simply dropped from the sky. Everybody knows that some older people like to talk a lot, and so it was with Grandma, Jan's mother, who, in the evenings, told tales about people in the village. In this way I learned about many neighbors, their families, and many stories about them. She also told me about the family of a boy whom I met every day in the pasture. This is how Jan Czerwiński, without his knowledge and against his will, realized my dream of securing false documents. Grandma particularly liked to talk about this family. She said it was a noble family, because Jan's mother descended "from nobility."

If I were to believe in the supernatural, I would say that this Grandma, like the railroad worker, had been sent to me by God himself. It was thanks to her stories about her neighbors that I got enough information to get a Catholic birth certificate. What made things easier was the fact that the parish office, located in town, served many villages. Therefore it was impossible for the priest to remember all the boys in every village.

It was November 1943. One afternoon I told my employers that I was going to the post office in town. I went to the parish office and told the secretary that I needed a birth certificate, giving all "my" data. After filling out my certificate, she sent me to the priest for his signature and stamp. After paying five złotys for this, I became the owner of an authentic birth certificate. I left my farmer after a few days. This time I followed the tracks in the opposite direction, distancing myself from the town of Gołąbki.

According to an old custom, servants were hired for the entire year at Christmastime. I knew these customs—and the work on a farm as well. In my pocket I had a safe conduct document in the form of an authentic birth certificate, so I felt safe. Therefore I requested a high price for my services.

The farmer who hired me for the year demanded that I register myself there. Because of this, besides my birth certificate, it was necessary for me to have proof that I had registered my departure from my previous place of residence. I decided to once again try my luck. To accomplish this, I needed to go to the local administrative office on the other side of the tracks, right across from the village where I took the cows to pasture and from which, according to my birth certificate, I was supposed to have come. When I arrived at my destination, I stood before the building where the local administrative office was located. I hesitated. Might the clerk know the Czerwiński family? After all, their village was located less than four kilometers away, just on the other side of the tracks. My entire future existence depended on my registering my departure, so after a moment's hesitation, I requested a document certifying the registration of my departure, paying my three złotys. Now I had all the needed documents I had dreamed about for over a year.

I soon registered as Jan Czerwiński from the village of Ustrzesz, employed as a farm worker. After filing my application for a *Kennkarte*[3] in the local administrative office at Radzyń Podlaski, I got a temporary identification card. They promised to send the actual *Kennkarte* in a couple of months to the administrator of the village in which I was staying.

In January 1944 I was again looking for a new place. I found work with a farmer called Albin, in a village about ten kilometers away from Radzyń. I began my work there full of hope that I was finally safe. Due to bad luck, before I got my *Kennkarte,* partisans came to the house. They sat comfortably on the chairs and began asking questions about family members and various things about the farm. Then, pointing to me, "What about that boy?" "That's my helper," the farmer answered. Then one of these would-be partisans said, "He's a Jew!" He then turned to me, "Come outside with us! We'll check, and if it turns out you're a Jew, then look here." He pointed to the barrel of his gun.

The "partisans" insisted that I go with them outside to check. This was the second time that being examined was to decide my life; this time at the point of a gun. But Albin did not know about my true origins, and to avoid a commotion, he came to my defense. Using all his powers of persuasion, he told them, "Come on, gentlemen! I know his family. I personally brought him from his home in a village near Gołąbki. Janek! Show them your document. Look, gentlemen, it is a temporary identification card issued by the same administrative office where he applied for a *Kennkarte.*" In the meantime, his wife brought sausages and home-distilled liquor, and these "gentlemen" got fully absorbed in it.

In February, shortly after this event, I went to the village administrator in Ustrzesz, who already had the documents for me. Thus, in February 1944, I finally became the owner of a *Kennkarte.* At the end of July of the same year, the Lublin region was liberated from German occupation.

---

1. Sobibór was a death camp five miles south of Włodawa where 250,000 victims, mostly Jews, were killed.

2. See Aryan papers in glossary.

3. A *Kennkarte* was an identification document issued by the Germans to those authorized to work and receive ration cards.

MARIA GABER-WIERNY

Born in 1929

On Romanian Papers

I have with me bitter memory
I have my smile that doesn't lie
I know that nothing can crush me any more
In the days to come

—Jonasz Kofta

I come from a poor Jewish family. I was born in Kraków in 1929. I lived with my parents on St. Wawrzyniec Street—in a room plus a kitchen, with a toilet that was shared. My mama, Salomea, took care of the house. My father, Eising Gaber, an upholsterer by profession, had his workshop on Floriańska Street, in a courtyard. He belonged to the Artisans' Guild located at St. Anna Street. He was a member of the Polish Socialist Party (PPS).

Our home was always filled with laughter. I had two sisters and two brothers. My younger sister, Eleonora, attended a Hebrew gymnasium, which was closed the moment the Germans arrived in the city. The older one, Berta, finished a dressmakers' school run by the nuns. My brother, Salo, graduated from the Industrial School in Bielsko-Biała, with the title of engineer. The other brother, Leo, worked as a bookkeeper in a cable factory. I attended the Maria Konopnicka Elementary School. I finished three grades before the war broke out. In 1938 we moved to Ujejski Street. My brother was the official tenant, because the landlord did not want manual laborers as renters in his apartment building. My father moved his shop to 25 Smoleńsk Street.

Little by little, the war began to make itself felt, first in our home, then in our hearts. The first blow for my parents was the departure of my two brothers to the USSR. Leo and Salo escaped from the occupiers. We did not have to wait long for the next step. In 1940 we were thrown out of our apartment. The Germans established the ghetto. German ruffian soldiers, paying no heed to my mother's cries and protests, threw us out of our apartment on Ujejski Street. At my mother's question, "Where should we go?" the German answered with laughter, *"Über die Weichsel"* [Over the Vistula], that is, to the ghetto.

And so began our wanderings, which lasted until 1945. We were assisted by people with great hearts and an even greater will to fight. Our first shelter was the apartment of a certain German woman, a client of my father's, who hid us for a night, concealing the fact from her husband and daughter. In the morning, my father rented a horse-drawn cart with which we moved our belongings to his shop at 25 Smoleńsk Street. There our family moved into a small, nine-square-meter space. Mother, an extremely orderly person and a good housekeeper, quickly adapted to the new conditions. On a small electric stove, she miraculously conjured up meals for the whole family.

Father, with his apprentice, Julian Harnik, continued to try to earn our keep. Times had changed, however, and so had the clients. Very often my father did not get any money for the work he did; he was only told, "Mr. Gaber, when my situation gets better, I'll pay." There was nothing to be done; the times were unjust, and the courts even more so. To this day I can picture my father in his workshop with a nail in his mouth and a hammer in his hand. He, the head of the family, knew he had to fight for its survival. My parents did not speak Polish well, especially my mother. Their linguistic shortcomings were a result of their having spent their entire youth in Żadowa Czerniowce in Romania. This page from the past came in handy during the war, because my parents spoke the German language well. Their good knowledge of German made it possible for us to stay and live in Kraków for a time. Father had obtained Romanian documents for the whole family. A notary named Dobrzański arranged these documents for us, the so-called *Bescheinigung,*[1] for a large sum of money.

In 1941, after Romania's capitulation, our papers became worthless, and therefore our existence became uncertain. The battle for day-to-day survival began. We did not want to go to the ghetto. The Germans threw us out of the workshop, leaving us with no roof over our heads. There were still people willing to help us, however.

My parents decided to go to the countryside. Father rented a horse-drawn cart, and with our modest belongings, we arrived in Bieńczyce.[2] We decided to hide there. The Świder family welcomed us into their home, where we moved into a small room. Our host, Mr. Świder, was active in the resistance movement, together with his son. One night Świder's son was wounded in a partisan action and, after suffering, died in his mother's arms.

We were not the only ones hiding in the village. We knew that our uncle's family, the Holländers, were hiding with the Bieroń family. They could not stand the tension, however, and decided to return to Kraków, to the ghetto. From there they were deported to Auschwitz,[3] and like others from my family, the Sinnreichs, they perished in the gas chambers.

The ground was beginning to burn under our feet. The Germans began hunting down the resistance fighters and their families. The village was no longer a quiet harbor where we could spend the rest of our lives. We left the Świders. We did not want to endanger our friends, who had helped us so much. We firmly decided that we would not give in; we wanted to fight for our lives. We all wanted to live. We moved to another house, with the Bednarski family. These decent people also helped us. Mr. Bednarski was also a partisan, fighting the Germans in the forests.

And the battle for survival began once again. We did not go out of the house, not to let anyone see us. The Germans hunted for Jews who had escaped from the ghetto, and then subdued the partisans in Fort Krzesławicki. Father, despite the danger, went to Kraków, because we had to have something to live on. He found work as an upholsterer with the Germans in a workshop on Oleandry Street. He started going to Kraków on foot; sometimes he managed to catch a ride on a cart. Asked at times by the Germans about his origins, he responded emphatically that he was Romanian. Fortunately, he did not have Semitic features, and besides, he spoke German fluently.

Finally, he had to stop going to work, because it was becoming ever more dangerous. We still had to have something to live on, however, so he began to do upholstery for local farmers, including Mayor Ciepiela. The mayor knew we were Jews. He helped us as best he could. His wife often gave us bread and other food. The Bednarskis shared their milk with us. We also tried to help Father. Mother made small flat cakes on the kitchen stove, my older sister sewed, and the younger, Eleonora, worked for the Germans as a secretary, because she spoke the language. She helped the locals in obtaining medical releases from work. People brought us food in appreciation.

I, as a thirteen-year-old, also wanted to help my family. I made necklaces and bracelets that I later sold. Nor did Mother let me forget about education. I studied Polish, mathematics, and German, because my provident mother had not forgotten to bring a few books, despite the turbulence of war. As a mere slip of a girl, I immersed myself in reading German novels and romances; I read A. Seghers and J. Courths-Mahler. I did not spurn J. W. Goethe, either. Father sneaked out books while working for the Germans. For instance, once he brought *Drang nach Osten* [*Drive to the East*].[4] After the war, these books were donated to a museum.

I remember one event as if it were today. Late one evening, a drunken German gendarme stormed into our home and began screaming at my father that he knew that there were Jewish girls there and that he would like to have a good time with them.

Father, keeping cool, calmly replied that we were Romanians, not Jews, and that there were only young children in the house. My sisters, terrified, hid under the eiderdown. They were shaking all over with fear. I also lay in bed with mother, tightly clinging to her. It was then that I broke down for the first time. Upon seeing the soldier trip and fall into a bucket and then try to get out of it, I began to alternately laugh and cry, not normally. At a most unexpected moment, he fell asleep. In the morning, he walked out of the room as if he did not remember anything from the previous night. We did not go out of the house. At night I would wake up screaming.

One morning another incident took place. As I was heading for the outhouse, I heard the approaching motorcycle of a gendarme. Then I heard him scream, *"Wo sind die Juden?"* [Where are the Jews?]. I ran into the room, trembling all over, and cried, "They want to catch us!" Alarmed, the woman sheltering us led us to a shed. There we slept, covered with hay. We did not know how long that lasted. Days and nights passed. I once again broke down. At last, we went out into the fresh air. How wonderful it was to feel once again the energizing fresh scent of freedom. Unfortunately, this did not last for long, because we had to go back into the Bednarski house.

My uneasy spirit did not let me stay indoors for long, however. The Osiadło family lived on the other side of the river with their children, Helenka and Julek. I often sneaked out of the house to visit my friend Helenka; her mother always treated me to whatever she had in the house. Being with Helenka and tending cows in the meadow were big attractions for me. Being a fifteen-year-old young lady, I was eager for new friendships. I sought companionship and partners for conversation.

I also met my first love. His name was Julek. He attended secret classes and seemed so wise. This was the first time I fell in love. Fortunately, war never kills these feelings. We used to meet by the river, dreaming that when the war would end, he would ask for my hand, we'd get married, have children, and live happily ever after. These were charming dreams, moments of escape from the grim reality. It could not last forever, however. One time my mother discovered us. She was looking for me, and when she saw us together, she was very upset and forbade me to meet with my boyfriend. It was painful, but I had to accept it. This is how my great, unfulfilled love came to an end.

One day my father found out that it was possible to be smuggled across the border to Hungary. A group of people arranged a meeting with a guide in Kraków. I convinced Father to take me with him, because I had not seen Kraków in a long time. I very much wanted to see my beloved city. We went to an apartment on Szpitalna Street, where we were to learn fully the plans for getting across the border. It turned out that the apartment was a trap. We got caught. The Germans put us on a truck, together with the other people, and then drove us to Podgórze.[5] We were thrown into barracks. I was scared. They tossed us some scraps of food. Every day a gendarme called out several people. We heard shots. Those people never came back.

There were only Jews in the barracks. Three SS men[6] watched over us. One was called Heindrich, another Kunde. The barracks were located in the center of the ghetto, near Józefińska Street. All the prisoners were slated for death. Every now and then an "action"[7] would be conducted that would decrease the number of prisoners. Mama, having found out that we had gotten caught, wanted to free us at all costs. She searched for contacts. She reached the German woman who had sheltered us before, asking her for help. Mama had retained, for just such a dark moment, a golden brooch, with which the German woman was able to buy us out. Saved by this miracle, we went back to Bieńczyce. There are no words to describe the joy with which we were received at home.

Finally, the long-awaited day of liberation came. I can remember it as if it were today. Russian soldiers burst into our room. They asked where the Germans were and how far it was to Berlin. We threw ourselves on their necks with joy. I was sixteen then. My hair was arranged in two long braids. One Russian told my mother that when he returned from Berlin, he would come for me and marry me. I began crying and screaming that I did not want to leave Poland and that I did not want a Russian husband. Deep in my heart, however, I was proud that this young soldier had proposed to me and not to my older sisters.

Finally, the end of the war approached. We loaded our bundles and bid tearful good-byes, very happy, at the same time, to be going home. We rented a horse and driver and rode into Kraków full of euphoria, singing, "Poland has not yet perished."[8] We got to our apartment on Ujejski Street, from which we had been thrown out. A *Volksdeutsche* named Polak, who was living there, did not want to let us into our own apartment. In the end, after long deliberations, she finally agreed to part with one room and part of the kitchen. Without hesitation, my father went to member of Parliament Drobner and asked to have the Polak family evicted. We regained the whole apartment. Father rented a workshop on Szpitalna Street, next door to the parish office of the Mariacki Church. The parish priest, Father Machaj, visited us every day.

I now began thinking about completing my education. Having finished three grades of elementary school, I enrolled in the Workers' University Association.[9] I attended the first grade of gymnasium, while my sister Eleonora was preparing for her "big" matriculation.[10] Eager for knowledge, I myself finished three grades of gymnasium. Unfortunately, the cost of living became so high that I had to begin thinking about earning my keep. My brother, then director of a power plant, got me a job in the tool storehouse. I worked there for a year. My brother tried to convince me to continue my education—to finish high school and pursue higher education. But I preferred to work; I wanted to become independent. I worked as a secretary and a librarian.

I had to interrupt my work when my mother came down with Parkinson's disease. I looked after her and our household. I was alone, because Eleonora had gotten married and moved to Silesia. Leo, Berta, and Salo, with his daughter, Lenoczka, had moved to Israel. I was then twenty-five, just the right age to be thinking about getting married. I had a boyfriend named Andrzej, a Catholic. We were developing very serious plans for our future life together. I visited his parents, who treated me like a future daughter-in-law.

However, I did not get to pick my own fiancé. My father had other plans, which he quickly put into action. When I was twenty-seven a matchmaker came to visit him one day. He said he had an appropriate candidate to be my husband. He touted him as being wealthy, as having steady work in a consignment business in Silesia. He assured my father that I would live in prosperity and that my parents—both already of an advanced age—would also be cared for. We soon held the so-called *Beschau,* the official meeting where the future couple becomes acquainted. Samuel, my future husband, was eight years older than I. When I saw him for the first time, he seemed like a fatherly older gentleman. Next to him, I looked like a porcelain doll.

Everything was arranged. I was in great despair. I cried and threatened to run away, but I was not able to gather enough courage to do so. In the meantime, I met with Andrzej. He asked me to think it over, that I should not leave him. He said that in a marriage love counted above all else. I did not know how to oppose my father's will.

Half a year later, the wedding took place in the synagogue. Everything was done according to old Jewish customs, including the *mikvah* [ritual bath]. It was quite an experience for me to enter the pool of water with only a kerchief placed on my head while a woman stood beside me reciting prayers. The wedding took place under a canopy. I wore a white dress and a veil over my head. According to tradition, the groom broke a glass for good luck.

My husband, Samuel, lived with his mother, a woman devout to excess, with old, conservative views. I could not go to Bytom to live with Samuel because of my mother's illness. I insisted that he move and work in Kraków, to share the good and the bad days with me. My husband did not want to hear about this; he came only on Saturdays and Sundays. Unable to tolerate the situation, I decided to go to Bytom to talk things over with Samuel. When I arrived, I encountered a startling surprise. It turned out that my husband had a lover. This first blow was a very difficult experience for me. But fate did not let me catch a breath, because the next day I witnessed a conversation between my husband and my mother-in-law. They spoke in Yiddish, not suspecting that I could understand every word. My mother-in-law was reproaching Samuel that I had not brought anything in as a dowry and that my father had not even paid the matchmaker. This was already too much. I could not stand it and said that I was going back to Kraków to my parents and would not set foot there again. His pleas did no good. I was desperate. I returned home. I was then already pregnant.

Father understood that this marriage was a big mistake and suffered together with me. But my parents were happy that I was with them and that they were going to have a grandchild. My husband continued to visit on Saturdays and Sundays. I soon gave birth to my son. I was happy, but not for long. . . . My husband wanted my son to be circumcised. Lying in my bed, I was totally in despair. I was afraid that my child would suffer. I did not want to hear about it. However, everything took place according to the ritual. My child was taken from me. I could hear Adam's cries from the other room. This was one more reason to hate my husband. After it was over, the crying child was brought back to me for feeding.

I brought up my son, taking care of my elderly parents at the same time. Father was already becoming ill and had to stop working. Berta, my sister, knowing of our situation, sent us letters inviting us to Israel. She wrote to my father that he and Mama would live in a luxurious home for the elderly, where he would have excellent care. Father tore up the letters, stubbornly saying he would not go anywhere, that he was a Pole and that he wanted to work here and die here. In 1962 Father died of cancer. He left some savings, which were just enough for the burial.

I understood that with his death I had lost my best protector and that nobody would shield me now. Three months later, tragedy struck again. My mother died. My sister, Lusia [Eleanora], came with her family to help me. We continued to run Father's workshop with an apprentice, but a few months later, the workshop was taken away from me, because I did not have a master craftsman's diploma. I took on work that I could do at home. I glued boxes at home and then folded them. I had to produce a prescribed quota to be eligible for support payments for my child. I glued four to five thousand boxes a day. Little Adam was then attending first grade. I sat up until late at night to do the gluing. My child often helped me in this. I then carried these packages down from the fourth floor. This is how I acquired back problems.

My husband demanded a divorce and wanted to leave for Israel with our son. We were divorced in 1969, but my son did not leave but stayed with me. I went into a deep depression. I was troubled for many years by recurrences of this illness. Hence, my frequent stays in psychiatric hospitals—until 1995. I was diagnosed with mixed psychosis, depressive-apathetic syndrome, and bipolar affective disease. My beloved son's constant visits and his concerned looks gave me the will to fight, helped me to regain my health. My love for my son helped me survive this most difficult period. My son finished his university studies, got married, and now has a small son. I have friends in the Association of "Children of the Holocaust," to which I have belonged for several years.

At home I encounter a sweet loneliness. However, there are also my grandson's visits on Sunday; together we play Wheel of Fortune and recite poems. In addition, I listen to my beloved music and write song lyrics and poems. And that's my life. . . . Is it not beautiful? I ask myself that question. Everyday I get up with a little anxiety; I wish for that day to also be as beautiful. I pray to God, I ask for my life not to change.

My Guardian Angel

When being ordinary is the greatest virtue
And normality takes on the shape of a uniform
Stand near me, like a shadow
Stand near me, like a shadow.
—Jonasz Kofta

---

1. This *Bescheinigung* [certificate] was used to certify that they were Romanian.

2. Bieńczyce is now a section of Kraków. (Author's note)

3. Auschwitz, located thirty-seven miles west of Kraków in the town of Oświęcim, began as a concentration camp for Polish political prisoners. Together with Auschwitz II–Birkenau, it became the largest German concentration and death camp in Poland. More than a million people perished there, 90 percent of them Jews.

4. *Drang nach Osten* [Drive to the East] was Germany's slogan for expansion to the east.

5. Podgórze is the suburb of Kraków where the ghetto was located.

6. See SS in glossary.

7. An "action" was a forced roundup for deportation to concentration or death camps.

8. The first line of the Polish national anthem.

9. TUR, *Towarzystwo Uniwersytetu Robotniczego,* an organization affiliated with the Polish Socialist Party, which promoted education among workers.

10. See Gymnasium and Matriculation/*matura* in glossary.

IGNACY GOLDWASSER

Born in 1932

In the Bunkers

Borysław had 13,000 Jews. The Ukrainian population gladly welcomed the Germans entering our town.[1] Right away, on the second day, the Jews felt the yoke of their enemy. The Ukrainians, mainly peasants from the countryside, attacked Jewish properties and began plundering. After the plundering, they started a pogrom. Armed with scythes, shovels, axes, pitchforks, and other implements, the peasants began to murder defenseless Jews. Three hundred were killed, and, in addition, many were mercilessly beaten. Bricks were thrown from the rooftops at escaping Jews; those who got caught were beaten with barbed wire, and cobblestones were flying in the air. After this occurred, things calmed down for a few weeks. There were now lots of poor people in town—because they had been robbed and also could not get work anywhere.

When the Germans marched in, we were living outside of town in an Aryan district on Szczepanowski Street. We were ordered to leave this district. We moved into town to our cousin's. Roundups began for digging ditches. Several days after the Germans marched in, we had to put on armbands with the Star of David to distinguish us from the rest of the town's population. We were allowed to stay out on the street only until eight o'clock in the evening. We, the Jews, were told to concentrate in one district. It became very crowded. But it was not a ghetto; the area was not surrounded either by a wall or by barbed wire. We had exceptional luck, because we moved in with our cousin where we had a room for ourselves, that is, for the three of us (Mama, Papa, and me). Father worked in an annex where bread was baked.[2]

A second "action"[3] was conducted in August by the Germans with the aid of the *Ordner.*[4] They grabbed people on the street and pulled them out of their apartments and hiding places. And this did not happen without beatings and torment. At first, everyone was assembled at the *Sammelstelle*[5] in the cinema Koloseum. They were held there without food or drink. They lay one on top of the other, that's how crowded it was. Filth, noise, and poverty prevailed. For a bribe or a favor, you could go to the toilet; otherwise you had to relieve yourself where you were. It is easy to imagine what the prisoners looked like. They were then all taken away—where to, I don't know. Five thousand people were taken in this action.

After the action was over, we came out of our hideout. When we were back on the street, an automobile filled with Gestapo police drove up and took Papa. Our despair had no bounds. After three hours, my father came back. He had been loading furniture for the Germans. We were happy to be back together again.

In September they began putting people in barracks. The Germans picked out those with a trade and placed them in a few buildings surrounded by a wooden fence. They were guarded by a Ukrainian policeman from the *Werkschutz.*[6] They had a common kitchen, from which they received soup. With it they got one-eighth of a loaf of bread without butter. Some of them did a little trading in cigarettes or tobacco and made some money that way. They bought some additional provisions from the Poles. Such trading was called the "bazaar on the bunks." A dentist named Grinszpan lived in the house next door. There he used to treat a German, the chief of the German police. Before every action the German would alert Grinszpan so he could hide.

The third action took place in October. It began at seven in the morning. Across the street from us was the building of the Ukrainian police. From it, before every action, a German came out on the balcony and summoned the Jews to assemble. Whenever he appeared on the balcony, we knew there would be an action. Grinszpan was warned by his German this time also and took us with him to his hideout. It was a small cellar. The entrance was blocked. The air was so thick that it was difficult to breathe. A match would not light. We were afraid to open the door so as not to be seen by anyone. During this action people were not taken to the *Sammelstelle* but loaded straight onto wagons. Lime had been spread inside the wagons so that people would suffocate.

That action lasted four days. This was in October 1942, and in November a fourth action took place. We left our apartment immediately. We got caught along the way and were taken to the police. There were some forty people there already. The Germans checked our papers, and whoever had a work certificate was released. Mama and I did not have one, so we were detained. Along the way, while they were leading us, I managed to escape. Farther along the way, Poles were helping Jews escape. A few dozen Poles mixed in with the Jews, and in the commotion, some of the prisoners were able to slip away. My dear mama was among them.

When I escaped, I did not know where to go. Betrayal lurked around every corner. There was little time to think about it. A sand pit was nearby, and the sand was being piled up beside it. I wanted to hide in that sand. Ukrainian boys noticed me there. They demanded ransom and threatened to turn me in to the Germans if I refused. There was no choice; I gave them my new coat, difficult though it was to part with it. The two sweaters I had on me followed the same route. When I set out to go back, a Ukrainian policeman caught me and was going to take me to the *Sammelstelle.* Along the way we passed the bakery where my father worked. He noticed me and was able to get me released with a bribe. I stayed in the bakery. Only late at night did we find out that my mother had also managed to escape.

A Pole named Luder came to the bakery. He was a good friend of Papa's. He took me and one of Papa's coworkers, Mr. Hammerman, and put us in his hideout. This was a place where formerly salt was produced. This hideout was discovered by the same Ukrainian boys who had already taken a ransom from me once before. Mr. Hammerman gave them one hundred złotys per person, and for the time being, we got rid of them. Although we were afraid to stay there any longer, there was no other choice.

The next day Mr. Luder brought Mama to us. We spent four days in this hideout. There was a pause for one day, and then an action began again, lasting a whole month. This action was conducted by Germans with the assistance of the *Ordner* and the Ukrainian police. They pulled people out of their hideouts and apartments. These people were assembled in the cinema Grażyna. The healthy ones were sent to the Janowski camp.[7] Relative peace then ensued.

The Jewish quarter was reduced in size. Around that time Papa met a Pole named Lipiński, who, for payment, took us into his hideout. When we got there, there were already two women and two children my age there. It was a pantry with a small window high up on the wall. There were two beds and a very small wardrobe. The three of us slept in one bed. We ate dinner together with the Lipiński family. We did not go hungry. For money, we were supplied with food. Papa visited us quite often. Being employed, he felt safe on the street. Before Christmas we decided to return home, because we had learned that there would be no roundups during the holidays. And we did indeed have a respite until February 15. That day, the German came out again onto his "famous" balcony, which foretold new repressions. This action has remained memorable for me.

This time Papa decided that each of us should run in a different direction. Papa went to the bakery and sent me to the Lipińskis. I had to cross a particularly well-guarded bridge. I slipped in among some boys who were going to school, and luckily, I was able to get through to Lipiński's place. There, in addition to the previously mentioned pantry, a new hideout had already been prepared. We went down to the hideout. Two hours later, Mama arrived. On the way there, she also met some boys from whom she had to ransom herself. She gave them her leather gloves and some money. Papa joined us in the evening. Mama and the Lipińskis insisted that he should stay with us. He maintained that he had been to the police and identified himself as a worker, so that there was no danger for him. In particular, he had to return because he had the keys to the bakery.

The next day some Poles came and told us that many Jews with armbands with the letter "A" had been taken. That was the kind of armband Papa had. On the third day, Mama went home. Father wasn't there. In the bakery, Mr. Hammerman didn't know anything about Papa, either. It turned out that just before the action ended, a German, standing next to the last car, summoned Papa and loaded him onto the truck. A policeman who knew Papa had tagged him with a white card, which was an *Ordner* badge, wanting to save him in that way. Unfortunately, a Ukrainian policeman came up who knew Papa and was aware that he was not a Jewish policeman, so he sent him with the others to be killed in the "slaughterhouse." That was the place where all the Jews were executed. It was a deep hole, quite long, with a wooden footbridge across it. All those doomed to die were told to line up naked on the bridge and were shot with a machine gun. There were cases when some, who were only wounded, fell into the pit and were buried alive. I can't describe my pain and that of my mother. What could be worse than to lose a healthy father in the prime of his life in such a bestial manner? He was only forty-two at the time.

After this action, the Jewish quarter was liquidated. Everyone was to be moved to the barracks. We were also supposed to go, but Lipiński came and took us to his place. We hid in a shed. Only a thin wall separated us from our host's quarters. Whenever he had visitors, we feared betrayal. We stayed there until April 1943.

We received a letter from my aunt in Drohobycz. She invited us to come to her. Mama thought a long time about whether it was worth the risk, until finally, on the night of April 12, Aunt sent a man for us, and we went with him. My aunt was in a *Lager* [forced labor camp]. The people from this *Lager* worked in an oil refinery. In addition, there was a concentration camp. The camp was guarded. The ghetto was surrounded by a wall.

Mama got a job in the *Lager* kitchen. It was not so bad for us. The commander of the *Lager* was a German named Sobotta. Whenever we found out that Sobotta was about to come to the *Lager,* we would hide—all the children and the elderly, anyone who was not working. Sobotta was known for his cruelty. There were rumors that in Sambor he had personally shot children. After a few months, Sobotta was sent to the front. A German named Mensinger was sent to us. He was much better than Sobotta. He spoke Polish. He took a liking to my cousin, Jakub Tenenbaum. He called him Jaś. When he went out on his rounds, he would take Jaś with him.

After three months of our stay in the *Lager,* the following event took place. The Gestapo and Schupo[8] arrived. They surrounded our entire camp. They ordered everybody to leave their rooms. Mama quickly stuffed me under the bed. Other mothers also tried to hide their children somewhere. While I was lying under the bed, the Gestapo came into our room, poked in the drawers, and looked under the bed. I was lying scrunched up against the wall, and by some miracle, they didn't notice me. My heart was pounding like a jackhammer. Then they took out all the mothers and children to go to a roll call. Only the children who were favored, like my young cousin, remained.

In June 1943 the ghetto was liquidated. At seven in the morning the Schupo and Gestapo arrived and began an action. All those who could work were sent to a camp. Many of those who were not workers managed to escape to our *Lager.* There was a giant cellar in our *Lager* that could hold as many as a hundred people. Some people had made bunks for themselves on which they slept. Those taken prisoner were hauled off to Bronica,[9] about fifteen kilometers from Drohobycz. There they were told to dig ditches, and later, those unfortunate people were executed. The liquidation lasted three days, after which we came out of our cellar. For a short while, it was quiet.

Next to the camp were two firms in which Jews worked.

These firms were called *Umschlagstelle*[10] and Treuben. Not long after the liquidation of the ghetto, these firms were also liquidated. Thereupon our *Lager* was made smaller, and many of those who were not workers were taken away. We had to move, because our home ended up outside the area of the *Lager.* We moved into one corner of a room. The refinery was two kilometers from the *Lager.* Next to it was a garden where, in the beginning, Mama worked. One time when a group of workers was going to work, the Schupo surrounded them. Mama was also in that group. Miraculously, she managed to escape. At that time, many people were taken to Bronica, among them my aunt.

In October Ukrainian policemen arrived with Mensinger in the lead. They grabbed all the children who were playing in the courtyard and dragged others out of their apartments. They collected about thirty people altogether, took them to the *Sammelstelle,* and from there to Bronica. It was then that they uncovered the hiding place of my Uncle Weiss and his family. They took my uncle, my aunt, and my two cousins. They were all killed. That is also when the plant that manufactured bricks and shingles was liquidated. Several dozen people had worked there. The women and children were taken to Bronica, and the healthy men were taken to work. My uncle and one cousin survived that place, but the rest of their family was killed. At the same time, the Germans were bringing in groups of thirty, forty, or fifty Poles, lining them up in the market square and shooting them. A truck would carry the bodies away.

In November the Germans announced new regulations. Before we went to work, Weintraub, our block leader in the *Lager,* had to line everyone up in rows of four for roll call in the courtyard.

After a few days, they assembled everyone. The people from our *Lager* usually waited until the people from the labor camp came in, and then they went off to work together, guarded by the *Werkschutz.* That day, the group from our *Lager* waited for the people from the camp for several hours. Finally we got news that there was a roundup in the camp. This is when people from our

Lager began running away. I had prepared a hideout. I hid together with a three-year-old boy. Mama told an *Ordner* friend where I was, so that he would know in case something happened. And indeed, the Schupo came in with that *Ordner,* looked under the beds, everywhere, except in the corner where I was. This is how I survived.

Every few weeks they conducted roundups, always taking a few people. In January we found out that our *Lager* was to be liquidated. More and more people began escaping from the camp. In March 1944 we learned that Kiev had been liberated.

Hildebrand, the chief commander of all the *Lager* in the area, came to ours. He appealed to people not to escape. He promised a transfer to Jasło, where everyone would be treated well. He said he would ensure that we would stay warm, but people didn't believe him, and escapes became more common.

At the end of March, we found out that the Soviets were very close. Several dozen people, mainly young boys, went to the forest near Borysław and built underground bunkers there. Later they would come to the *Lager* and take people back to the bunkers for a fee (several thousand złotys).

For three days Mama and I tried to catch a truck to Borysław and from there to get to some bunker. Only on the fourth day someone convinced Mama to take the train, as a Pole. We had nothing to lose; we were in danger of being deported, so we decided to go. Some woman bought us the tickets. The train was very crowded. We seated ourselves on the steps, and after many hours we arrived in Hubicz, a suburb of Borysław. Here the train stopped for a longer time. This was a disaster for us. A German noticed Mother and summoned her and me to him. He searched us. He took our documents and money and led us to the Ukrainian police. A report was drawn up, and we were taken to a cell. Mama was severely beaten there. I got a beating, too, but not till blood was drawn. Many Jews were brought in the next day. Everyone was searched again. All our belongings and money were taken. On the third day at eleven in the morning, Pel, the deputy police chief, came in and let us out. They needed people for work. We were taken to barracks in Borysław.

We got nothing to eat all those days. It was good that Mama had brought with her some bread and cheese. This saved us. We were so exhausted from the beatings and what we had experienced that we could barely stand up. Every day, when morning came, we expected to be taken away and executed. There were about a hundred of us. We lived together with some casual acquaintances we had met in the cell. We stayed there until April 12. On the thirteenth, the police surrounded our barracks. We managed to escape to a nearby sewer, which was actually only the drain from the kitchen. We hid there and deliberated on how to make it to the forest. That night the people who got caught were sent off to Płaszów.[11] People heard shots; evidently, they were firing at those attempting to escape.

Our journey was very eventful. It was night; we couldn't see the road. We kept walking into bushes or in the mud; the sound of our wooden shoes could give us away. But there was no choice, we had to keep on going. We wandered all night.

At four o'clock in the morning we smelled smoke. There was a small bunker in front of us. We entered it through a trapdoor. It was a hole in the ground. The walls were reinforced with logs. The roof was also supported by logs. Altogether twenty people could fit in there, in about six square meters of space. The walls were wet. Water was dripping down on people. There were bunk beds, and a few people had some bedding, but everything was wet. We had a tiny stove, but we could cook only at night. Every day we had to clear the outside of the bunker from snow. Those who had lived there before us had left some rye, from which we made various dishes.

A so-called forest commission or forest police was active in the forest. There were about fifteen of them, and they were armed. They knew every bunker. Each bunker had to collect five hundred złotys of ransom. The money was given to the police commander, Eisenstein. Eisenstein then used it to bribe the Gestapo. He also maintained order, making sure that people did not rebel. When escapees from the camps or *Lager* came in, the police assigned a few persons to each bunker. We were placed in the bunker of a man named Baktrog. We lived in extraordinary harmony there. Everybody shared what they had. We stayed in this bunker for six weeks, until the end of May 1944.

Not far from our bunker, there was one belonging to a man named Lubianikier. When they ran out of supplies and money, Lubianikier went to the barracks to fetch someone who was wealthy. When you had money, you could buy provisions that would allow you to go on living. Unfortunately, as soon as he left the forest, he was caught by Mensinger. Under the pressure of heavy torture, he gave away the location of his own bunker and those nearby. We found out about this, so we had to leave our shelter quickly. We headed for an area called "the Jewish quarter" in the forest (where most of the bunkers were located). Unfortunately, they didn't let us in, because there was no room.

We spent the whole day under the bare sky. Before dusk, we returned to our bunker to spend the night there. We learned that the whole forest was to be surrounded in the morning. Before dawn, we set out along the road that we had taken the previous day. We assembled on a hill. The owners of the bunkers in that "quarter" were afraid for their own lives, so they decided to take in only women and children. Therefore, the men built a makeshift shelter out of trees, which gave protection only from the rain. After a few days, we were also chased out of there.

It was terribly cold, and it was raining all the time. Things were so bad that we stopped being careful and started lighting open fires. We were tired of living, anyway. We were constantly reminded that we should not light fires, because the *Waldschutz* [forest police] could easily discover us. Besides, there were plenty of shepherds around, and it was indeed they who discovered our shelter.

Mama and I fled to a bunker we were familiar with, belonging to a man from Drohobycz. We spent barely two days there. One of the Jews had an Aryan wife who brought him food every day. The second day we were there, Szaler was supposed to meet his wife in a village called Mrażnica. The Gestapo caught him. Szaler gave away our bunker. We expected a roundup, so we went back on the road before dawn.

From a distance, we saw the entire retinue—Eisenstein, the chief of the Jewish police, Weintraub, the engineer (now living in Italy), and the Gestapo. We managed to evade them. We escaped to another forest and spent several days in the thicket. The braver ones returned to our previous place of stay and there learned that nearly all of the bunkers had been discovered. The people were taken to the barracks. Everything they had was taken away from them.

We spent six days in the forest, cold and hungry. At night the men sneaked through to the old bunkers, but unfortunately, they were all burned down. It was decided to build a new bunker. Without shovels or axes, it was a job beyond our strength. Trees had to be cut down with extreme caution, because the *Waldschutz* sometimes used police dogs to track us. Women and children hid in the bushes. During a torrential rain some shepherds discovered us, and we were forced to flee again.

We set out for the bunker of an acquaintance, Sternbach, who now lives in Wałbrzych. By chance, we encountered there Aunt and Uncle Miler and cousin Janina. After eight days, our bunker was nearly finished. As if out of spite, a heavy rain poured down. We were up to our ankles in water. Mama's legs swelled so much that she could not stand up. The first bunk was built for my mother; it was put in place, covered with bedding and other rags. This was in June. When the sun came out, we took everything outside to dry out. This was a memorable time for us.

We brought our water from a clay pit. Everyone was unhappy. Late in the evening, risking their lives, the men would go to the village for food. This state of affairs lasted for six weeks. We heard rumors of the approaching Soviet offensive. It was already very difficult for us during these final weeks. We had neither food nor money, and we had little strength left. Many people were returning to the barracks. Rumors circulated that bandits (later known as *Banderowcy*)[12] roamed the forests. They robbed, plundered, massacred, and murdered.

One day, Sternbach's son burst into our bunker and said that their bunker had been attacked by a band. They took away everything, claiming that they were partisans. He fled because he did not believe them. After a while, his father came running; he also managed to escape. He left his wife and sister-in-law to their fate. We began to panic. Where were we to run? We sent one of the men to scout around. Some people took off in an unknown direction. I stayed in the bunker with Mama. It was out of the question to go anywhere with her; she was horribly exhausted, swollen, and covered with sores.

We sat in the bunker. Suddenly Sternbach's sister-in-law burst in, all bloodied, with her blouse torn. She had managed to escape from the hands of the bandits. She told us about their cruelty. She walked around half-naked; none of us had anything to give her, nothing to cover her, as we each had only one set of clothes. She finally borrowed a coat and went to get some clothes from her bunker. On the way she managed to take with her several other people, who had survived in other bunkers. In less than half an hour, the previous band showed up and murdered everyone in a cruel fashion. Sternbach and his son watched this scene from afar; then they escaped to Borysław. Everyone from our bunker fled. Only I, Mama, and my aunt and uncle remained.

The Red Army was approaching. At the end of July a Pole named Stefan came to us with the news that the Soviets were already in Lwów. The Germans were escaping from Borysław and taking the local population with them. People from the nearby village of Opaki were fleeing to the forest along with their cattle and belongings. They camped out in the bushes and noticed our bunker. They gave the children some milk and bread. They assured us that they would not harm us, that they were refugees just like us. They said that the Soviets were in Stryj already and would arrive here any day. They said that they would come in the evening and fix some potatoes for themselves and that they would share them with us. However, after they left, we did not feel safe. Some young people ran up and shouted to us, "Run away from here as quickly as you can; the *Banderowcy* are going to come at night and slaughter you!"

We did not think about it very long. We went to Engelhard's

bunker. This bunker was very well camouflaged. We rushed in there without asking whether we would be welcome. This was our last attempt at saving ourselves. There we spent three days without fresh air, without food, and without light. Mama tried to rouse me with water; she thought I would die at any moment. I really did feel half dead; in fact, I didn't feel anything. I was like a corpse.

Engelhard did not have any place to sleep, so he went over to Ringler's neighboring bunker. That night *Banderowcy* assaulted that bunker. They ordered everyone to come out. They shot at those who tried to escape. One person was killed. We found out that before they raided that bunker, they had been to our abandoned bunker.

In the evenings we heard the sounds of tanks and shooting. My uncle decided to go to Mrażnica, and there he found out that the Soviets had already been in Borysław for three days. He came back at noon and took us to town. We were afraid of the *Banderowcy,* but the bandits had gone into hiding like mice. We kissed each other with joy.

After a few hours we reached Mrażnica. Here life was proceeding normally. I was dragging my feet like an old man. Mama was barefoot and exhausted. On the way, we met a Jew who said that Jews were being registered at the former Jewish Community office. We went to that community office. Only there did we realize what nonentities we were. Each of us got a piece of bread, which we had not seen in months. It took a long time before we started believing that we were equal to others, that we were human beings.

---

1. The Germans entered Borysław in late June 1941. See "Historical Notes."

2. *Chlebówka* was the annex where bread was baked. (Author's note)

3. See "action" in glossary.

4. *Ordner* were members of the Jewish security police [*Ordnungdienst*]. (Author's note)

5. *Sammelstelle* was an assembly place. (Author's note)

6. *Werkschutz* was the factory police. (Author's note)

7. Janowska/Janowski was a labor and extermination camp on the outskirts of Lwów (now Lviv, Ukraine) where 40,000 Jews were killed.

8. Gestapo was the abbreviation for *Geheime Staatspolizei* [German secret police]. Schupo was the abbreviation for *Schutzpolizei* [German security police]. (Author's note)

9. Bronica was a forest near Drohobycz where Jews were taken to be killed.

10. *Umschlagstelle* means transfer place.

11. Płaszów was a slave labor and later concentration camp outside Kraków where 20,000 Jews perished. It was depicted in *Schindler's List.*

12. *Banderowcy* were guerilla bands of Ukrainian Nationalists, named after their leader, Stepan Bandera. They were anti-Polish as well as anti-Jewish.

JANINA HINCZ-KAN

Born in 1926

An Unforgettable Day in Auschwitz

We were returning from our work detail extremely exhausted. The guards were walking with their dogs, somehow unusually calm. The sun was setting bloodred and threw its golden rays on our gloomy faces. It was November 1944. My aching feet, wrapped in rags, were splashing around in shoes full of holes that I had bought from another prisoner for a chunk of bread. Most of the others marched in wooden shoes. We were nearing the gate of the *Lager* [forced labor camp] over which stood the hated, deceitful slogan ARBEIT MACHT FREI.[1] At the gate of the camp we were met by an orchestra of women prisoners. They were playing a march. The sound of music in this place of death and horror, where on the average five thousand people perished every day, was one of the Germans' perverse ideas.

We quickly fell in, into rows of five. We wanted to get into our block[2] as quickly as possible to stretch our tired legs. Every day we walked fourteen kilometers back and forth. It began to drizzle, a fine, autumn rain. Standing at roll call we were shivering from the cold. Finally at a distance I saw Stenia approaching with an SS woman. We feared Stenia like the plague. She was the *Lager-Kapo*[3] for the entire camp. Sad to say, she was Polish.

After a long wait, we were counted off. We burst into our block. I quickly climbed to the top bunk and held out my hand to my mother, who had a hard time climbing up. That my mother and I were together was our only joy. I took off my shoes full of holes. The smell of rutabaga soup titillated my nostrils, nearly making me faint. The spoons clinked quickly against the tin mugs and bowls. I was then seventeen years old. I suffered the most from lack of sleep, because days in the *Lager* began very early. We were awakened at three o'clock in the morning, and we stood at roll call until dawn. During the last few days I walked, literally, as if I were drunk. Mother looked with despair at my pale face and eyes with dark circles under them. She placed under herself the wet rags that I took off my feet, drying them with her body.

The lights were turned off. I snuggled up to her. Covered with a shabby blanket, we kept each other warm. "Mama, perhaps I won't go to work tomorrow, because I feel that I'll collapse along the way." My mother's hand stroked my close-cropped hair. "Very well, child, tomorrow we won't go to work. Right after roll call I will go up to the block supervisor and ask that she leave us in the block to wash pots, and after roll call, I'll make up the bunk so as to conceal you, so you can rest."

I was dazzled by my mother's cleverness. I kissed her coarse, wind-chapped hand and fell asleep like a stone. We remained in the block according to plan, and after roll call, Mama made up the bunk with me in it. She covered me carefully with a blanket, leaving only a slit so I could breathe. She then had to wash, in cold water, six hundred bowls from the previous day's meal. Somehow, it didn't cross my mind then that Mother would have to do all the work normally meant for two people. Being together with my mother, I still felt like a child.

I slept the delightful sleep of youth for about two hours. Even such a short sleep refreshes. Suddenly, I was awakened by some noises and the sound of talking. Someone ripped the blanket off me. I jumped like an arrow straight to the ground. Luckily, I didn't trip. I rushed out of the block directly into the *Lager.* I ran without looking where I was going. I heard the patter of running feet, but I didn't look behind me. I turned behind Block II. There was an enormous wooden pallet leaning against its wall. Without much thought, I squeezed behind it, trembling with fear. I waited to see what would happen next.

My heart was pounding like a jackhammer. I listened intently, terrified, not being able to collect myself. After a while, I heard the sound of receding footsteps. I decided to peek out carefully. I saw a block supervisor walking away. Only then did I realize that it had been a bunk inspection. Every now and then block supervisors would conduct such inspections, taking everything that was hidden in the blankets. Sometimes all our possessions were in there—bread, onions, and other food articles.

I don't know how long I would have stood behind that wooden pallet had it not been for a coincidence. I heard steps, and suddenly, I felt the sun on my face. A prisoner working at the lime pit had taken the pallet, which was apparently needed for work. He bid me farewell with a pale, sad smile. I didn't know what to do with myself or which way to turn. I was afraid to approach my block, fearing that I would be recognized. The sound of SS whistles interrupted my deliberations. *"Zelle Appell! Zelle Appell!"* [Line roll call!] the block supervisors called out in their hoarse, shrill voices.

It was horrible. During those unscheduled roll calls, there was usually a selection[4] of young women, sometimes for work in ammunition plants and at other times to have blood drawn from the prisoners for German soldiers. Sometimes they made a selection intended to reduce the size of the *Lager.* One never knew exactly why a roll call was being held or who among our dear ones might depart, perhaps forever.

The full terror of the possibility of being separated from my mother flashed in front of my eyes. A moment later we were already standing in even rows, and the SS women were making a selection from among the rows. I was selected. Mother followed me with terrified eyes. After a certain time, I realized that they were not recording the numbers tattooed on our arms. The thought of escape flashed through me like lightning. When the German woman turned her back, I fell back into formation. In our blue-gray striped uniforms, we all looked identical. I counted on not being recognized.

She didn't recognize me, but after counting off those selected, she once again walked through the rows and, waving her finger, yelled, *"Komm hier!"* [Come here!] There was no other choice. I submitted to my fate with resignation. The tormented face of my mother was before my eyes. What was there to do? My feverish thoughts raced around inside my head, unable to find a way out. We were herded into the bathhouse. I was probably the youngest in the group, and with my short hair, I probably looked like a kid from a poor orphanage.

After the showers, there was an inspection by a doctor. It took place without a real examination. The degree of our strength was judged only from our looks and body build. When I stood in front of the doctor, I was seized by great sorrow, shame, and despair. I could not control myself any longer. I burst out crying, loudly and spasmodically, and folding my arms on my chest, I stammered midst my sobbing, *"Herr Doktor, ich bin hier mit meiner Mutter zusammen. Bleiben sie mir!"* [Doctor, I am here together with my mother. Please let me stay!] At the word *Mutter,* the doctor's eyes clouded over. He looked inquiringly at my miserable figure and yelled, *"Zurück!"* [Go back!] Trembling, I dressed quickly and raced to my mother. We fell into each other's embrace and cried with happiness.

That was my unforgettable day at Auschwitz.[5]

---

1. The slogan is "Work makes one free."
2. Barracks in concentration camps were called blocks.
3. A *Kapo* was a prisoner who received special privileges for supervising (often cruelly) other prisoners.
4. See Selection in glossary.
5. See Auschwitz in glossary.

TADEUSZ IGER

Born in 1941

During and after the War

It took me a long time to decide to write about all of this, because it is so difficult for me. My father, a Communist by conviction even before the war (already then he belonged to the KPP, the Communist Party of Poland), used to tell me, "Son, you can be proud that you belong to the chosen people, chosen by God."

Often I thought about this. Chosen people? For what, for maltreatment, beatings, pogroms, insults, and, in the end, being burned in crematory ovens? As a true son of my people, I had a life full of dramatic events and difficult experiences, but I am not complaining.

I was born on January 1, 1941, in Czortków, in the Tarnopol province, in our little home in Wygnanka (a section of Czortków). My father celebrated my coming into this world with his friends, starting already on the morning of December 31, 1940, although I came into the world only the next day at two o'clock in the morning. Poland's eastern regions, including our small town, were at this time already under Red Army occupation,[1] so things were not exactly merry. Despite this, I was eagerly expected and loved. My father, Joel, a dental technician by profession, and my mama, Klara, née Haker, daughter of a poor tailor, belonged to families of moderate means. In order for this marriage to take place, Father, unbeknownst to his family, had to secretly provide a dowry for Mama, and only then could he receive the blessing of Grandmother, Chaja Iger, the head of the family. (Grandfather Natan had been killed during World War I as a noncommissioned officer in the Austrian army.) But my parents did not enjoy their happiness for long.

In July 1941 Czortków and the surrounding area were occupied by the German army, and horrible things began to happen. Our Polish neighbor, a teacher, went into the forest and joined the AK [*Armia Krajowa*].[2] One night some *Banderowcy*[3] came to his home and murdered his Ukrainian wife and their already grown daughter, after having brutally tortured them, chopping off their hands and legs. The number of such incidents was increasing, because Ukrainian nationalists began to feel masters of the situation.

In June 1942 the local Gestapo organized a ghetto in Czortków. My whole family ended up there—Grandma Chaja, Uncle Natan (my father's brother), Father/Joel, Mama/Klara, Mama's parents, and also myself. Many died from hunger and disease then or because of the substantial participation of *Sich,* the Ukrainian police.[4] In 1943 Grandmother, Uncle, and Mama's parents were murdered. Those who survived were transferred to the Świdowa labor camp, where rubber was produced. There, on January 20, 1944, my mother was killed, shot by a Ukrainian policeman who had been Father's schoolmate. I survived by a miracle, tucked under the bed by my mother.

A similar miracle happened when my father and his friend, before going to work, left their little sons in a workshop under the care of a friendly shepherd. A Ukrainian policeman wandered in there. I was able to explain who my father was and ask him not to kill me. He left me alone, but he shot the little son of my father's friend. Many years after the war I often dreamed about this scene, and I would wake up screaming, all soaked with sweat and frightened.

One day a noncommissioned Wehrmacht [regular German army] officer we knew, Paweł Tomanek, a Silesian from Gliwice who spoke Polish very well, warned my father that in the next few days the SS Command was planning to liquidate the camp and that the prisoners would be shot. With Tomanek's help, Father escaped from the camp with me on his back, having made a sort of backpack out of a sack.

We ended up in Father's native village, Różanówka, where he was born and brought up and where his parents had lived and worked. The local peasants, many of them my father's schoolmates, helped us and sometimes even hid us. I remember best an elderly Ukrainian in a peasant flax shirt tied around his waist with a piece of string, who by his appearance, with a beard and long hair, reminded one of Vernyhora [a legendary Cossak]. He taught me Ukrainian songs and the language because he hated all things Polish. He didn't like it when I spoke Polish. "Tell him to give up that rotten talk," he used to tell my father. Despite this, he was an honorable man. Perhaps this was due to his attachment and gratitude to my grandfather, who had been the administrator of an estate and had treated the peasants in a fatherly fashion, helping them greatly. (After the war, in his résumé, my father described his father as a "farm worker," which amused me greatly when I learned the truth.)

Everything, however, has its limits. The people in Różanówka were also afraid. Therefore most of the time we hid in the forest, in provisional holes dug in the ground. There, once again things turned out well for me. Father was tired and wanted to make something to eat and rest a bit. He hung me up in this makeshift knapsack on a branch of a nearby tree, very close to the road, along which, as bad luck would have it, two German soldiers came riding by on a motorcycle. They stopped very close to us but, fortunately, did not notice me and after awhile moved on. My terrified father, hidden in a ditch, took this very hard.

In this way, Father and I survived the German occupation until March 22, 1944, when the Red Army once again entered Czortków.

On February 5, 1946, as part of the repatriation program,[5] Father and I arrived in Opole. Here Father became the head of the Jewish Committee. While performing this function, an unfortunate incident occurred, and he almost paid for it with his life. He was shot with a pistol by a man who came to the committee supposedly looking for help. It is unknown to this day whether it was a simple robbery or whether the act was politically motivated. Fortunately, it was only a superficial wound, and everything ended well.

In Opole, I ended up in a kindergarten (or perhaps an orphanage?) for orphans and partially orphaned Jewish children. A wild and silent child of war, I shied away from other children, keeping my distance from them. The caretakers could not handle me, either. It was the head cook who finally took me under her wing. Her goodness, a piece of chocolate here, a handful of almonds or raisins there, and her kind words slowly did their work. I grew very attached to her. I made friends outside the walls of the kindergarten, among the children of the street. I was often there, striking up friendships, exchanging chocolate for bread with lard, enjoying myself and feeling good.

Perhaps it was because of me, or perhaps not, that my kindergarten friend, the head cook, and my father became acquainted. They became friends and, in the end, got married. Elfryda Niesporek, a Silesian from Bytom, a miner's daughter, wanted to remedy what the Germans did to us, and I think she succeeded. My second mother (because after all that I owe her, I could not call her a stepmother) did everything to make me forget about the injustices and experiences of war. All that I am, I owe to her. She brought me up, was with me when I needed her, supported me through quizzes, dictations, colloquiums, and finally, examinations. She was the reason that no matter where I was (e.g., Wrocław or Warsaw), I returned home with pleasure. About my birth mother I know only that she saved my life and that she was a beautiful woman.

I once again had a father, a mother, and family warmth, as well as everything that could be called a normal, happy family. I was not an easy child. Quiet, closed up within myself, and stubborn, I often caused trouble for my parents. My friends and I once found a mortar emplacement from World War II and brought home two rounds of ammunition, nearly giving my father and mother a heart attack. On another occasion, hearing my neighbors say they were poor and going through hard times, I ran to our apartment without hesitation and took out several bundles of hundred-złoty banknotes from a suitcase under my bed and presented them with the money. Fortunately, they were honest people and gave it back to my parents. This was money meant for wages for my father's employees (there were no banks then). My parents were shocked, but they did not punish me; I meant well, I had acted like a true Samaritan.

Wandering around with friends through Opole's burned-out ruins (homes burned down by looters already after the war), we looked for things to play with. Once we found a couple of swords without handles. While fencing with a friend, I was accidentally hit in the neck. I have a scar to this day. Doctor Hołejko, the surgeon who sewed up the wound, told me, "Son, you have more luck than brains." The sword missed my neck artery, literally, by millimeters. Had it been cut, I would have surely died. How could I not believe in God?

Although I do not practice my religion and don't know anything about Jewish holidays, I do believe in God and in God's providence. My adventures with God seemed amusing. Having neither a synagogue nor a religious model of my people around (Father was not a practicing Jew), I became interested in Catholicism. As a small boy, I often went with Haniczka, an old lady from the neighborhood, to the Opole Cathedral, where the quiet, mystical semidarkness, rich decorations, and a certain mysteriousness absorbed and fascinated me. I was often found sleeping in a pew. I sought quiet and solitude in the cathedral.

When I began attending the first grade of elementary school, I once imprudently stayed for religion class. "Tadzio [Tadeusz], you can't stay during religion classes; after all, you're a little Jew," my teacher told me, sending me out of the classroom. The result of her very "educational" approach resulted, from that time on, in frequent fights and lots of aggressiveness on the part of the other boys and girls in the class. In this way I was very emphatically reminded who I was and where I belonged. Some people's version of religion didn't turn out to be as beautiful and wonderful as I had imagined. I used to come home beaten up, and the school's principal would tell my parents that it was I who beat up someone else. Father transferred me to a school run by the Society of Friends of Children,[6] which was far from home, but there I was not treated as an outsider or a leper.

My second mama also encountered a great unpleasantness. She was Catholic and very devout. One day her confessor told her she was a disgrace and had no right to set foot in the church because she had married a Jew. Many years passed before she worked up enough courage to again go to Mass and confession, where another priest, a missionary, told her that getting married and caring for a child were noble acts and that her previous confessor was a fool.

Life is full of surprises. For instance, when I was in the sixth grade of elementary school, it so happened that one of the workers repairing the central heating in our apartment went out to the kiosk for cigarettes and never came back. The militia had taken him away. It turned out that one of his victims had recognized him. While serving in the SS during the war, he had murdered many people. This was a great shock to me.

Or another case—a friend of my second mother's, a very religious woman who helped the elderly and was very kind to everybody, surprised me very much. After her death it turned out that her basement was full of wartime documents, letters, and photographs of her and her husband, an SS man. There were, for example, photographs in which her husband was holding a pistol to the head of a victim kneeling in front of a freshly dug pit, or another, where he was standing in front of a pit filled with bodies, while she held an elderly Jew by his beard, cutting it off with scissors. In yet another, she stands pressing her foot on a lying victim. In the letters were descriptions of events that made my hair stand on end. Unfortunately, all these things were later burned by the people cleaning out the basement.

I finished a general-education lyceum, then a two-year dental technicians' school, and finally, dentistry at the Medical Academy in Warsaw.

I have been working as a dentist since October 1, 1969, keeping in mind my father's words, "Act in such a way that you can sleep peacefully at night." I have tried to be dependable and honest.

After the disbanding of the Jewish Committee, my father went to work for the Union of Health Service Workers. He was head of the union within the provincial district almost to the day of his death, which occurred on March 29, 1961. My second mother, who outlived him by twenty years, died on April 11, 1981.

I continue to live here in Opole. I work in my profession, which I enjoy. I am surrounded by friendly people. Simply put, I go on living.

---

1. See September 17, 1939, in "Historical Notes."

2. See AK in glossary.

3. See *Banderowcy* in glossary.

4. *Sichovi Striltsi* [Sich Riflemen], an organization originally formed in a Cossack camp in Sich near Zaporozhe in the sixteenth century, became a nationalistic military group during the short-lived Ukrainian National Republic of 1918–20. It was reactivated during the German occupation.

5. After the war ended, eastern territories, formerly in Poland, became part of the Soviet Union (Ukraine, Belarus, Lithuania). Poles were given the opportunity to remain and become Soviet citizens or relocate to Poland and be "repatriated."

6. TPD, *Towarzystwo Przyjaciół Dzieci,* was a secular organization that operated a network of schools.

EWA JANOWSKA-BOISSE, NÉE KLEINBERG

Born in 1931

ANNA JANOWSKA-CIOŃĆKA, NÉE KLEINBERG

Born in 1936

Father Never Returned from Exile

We come from a large Jewish family that had lived in Kraków for many years. Papa's father, Wilhelm Kleinberg, owned a photography studio. His wife, Antonina, had brought up their six children—Zofia (married name Minder), Paulina (Keiner), Irena (Kirsh), Edward (Aryan name[1] Śliwiński), Juliusz, and our papa, Roman. Mama's father, Jakub Paster, worked in a bank. His wife had four children—Zygmunt, Irma (Laksberger), Alice (Kleinberg), and Rudolf. Two others had died in childhood.

Before the war broke out, we lived in Rabka, a mountain resort where Papa worked as a dentist. Our life was happy, free of care and worries. Even in 1939 nobody would have thought that the Germans, heirs to Heine, Schiller, and Goethe, would make it their goal to annihilate the Jewish people or that they would proceed to carry it out with German precision and unimaginable cruelty.

At the end of August 1939, we were at Aunt Zosia Minder's in Kraków. I [Ewa] was almost eight years old then, and my sister, Hanka [Anna], had turned three. One day Papa set out from Kraków on a bicycle with his backpack and mobilization card in order to join the army. We never saw him again.

German air raids on Kraków began. We didn't go down to the shelter, fearing that if the house were bombed, we wouldn't be able to get out from under the rubble. We assembled in the hallway, which had a Gothic arched ceiling. People believed that such an arch would not collapse.

After a few days, the Germans entered Kraków. I remember how they walked down Karmelicka Street, tired and dusty, on foot, while some rode on heavy, massive horses. A few days later, Mama, my sister, and I returned to Rabka, joined by our close relative, Lola Schifeldrim.

The Germans chased us out of our luxurious home, in which father had had his dental office, to the Rabka ghetto. We had to wear armbands with the Star of David. Mama brought from Kraków my two grandmothers, Laura Paster and Antonina Kleinberg, as well as Grandfather Wilhelm Kleinberg. (Grandfather Jakub Paster had died before the war.) It was thought that it would be easier to survive outside the big city. Things turned out otherwise.

The Gestapo went wild. In what once was the St. Theresa Gymnasium, an SS school was established. It was headed by Wilhelm Rosenbaum, who was then about twenty-eight years old. The SS officers and their wives lived on the grounds of the school. Terror, searches, and robberies became increasingly common in town. People were overwhelmed by fear and despair. On top of everything, there were also diseases. Grandma Tońcia [Antonina] got erysipelas,[2] I developed scarlet fever, and Hanka came down with diphtheria. Unfortunately, Grandma got better—unfortunately, because it would have been better for her to die a natural death than to perish later at the hands of the Nazis.

On May 20, 1942, the Nazis conducted their first so-called "action." They ordered elderly and handicapped Jews to be brought to the Gestapo headquarters. Among the elderly were our sixty-eight-year-old Grandma Laura and seventy-five-year-old Grandma Tońcia. The selection was conducted, and appropriate marks were placed beside each name; a "+" meant a death sentence, and that is what both our grandmothers received. Mama's efforts to get those "+" marks changed to "-" were to no avail.

After a few days, those who had been marked for death were summoned again. Mama escorted her mother and mother-in-law, fully aware that they were going to their deaths. The Germans crammed the people, naked (although May in the mountains is still cold), into an old shed. At dusk they led them out to the nearby woods. They shot them standing over freshly dug pits, which were then covered up. Those who were not shot were buried alive, according to eyewitnesses—Jewish workers who had been brought in to dig and later cover the pits.

Grandfather Wilhelm, by then fully aware of what was about to happen, was killed a few weeks later in another action.

Confronted with this horrible tragedy, Mama made a decision to flee from Rabka. My uncle Edward asked a relative of his wife's, a Pole, to take us out of that hell. This noble man came and took us children with him. Mama and Lola had to stay behind, because they did not yet have their false documents prepared. The man who saved our lives by taking us out of there was Marian Sikorski. He had a wife and three young children. He was a school principal in the small village of Szerzyny. When he picked us up at the train station at Skomielno in the fall of 1942, he had difficulty prying my little sister from Mother's and Lola's embraces.

The train ride lasted several hours, I don't remember how many. We got off at the station in Siepietnica and then rode in a horse-drawn wagon to the home of the Sikorskis. We children were without any papers. Along the way we stopped next to the home of the district administrator to get a drink of water. "What pretty, dark-haired little girls," the administrator said. "Little Jewish girls, surely." "No," answered Mr. Sikorski, masking his fear with a smile. "They are related to my wife." There are no words that could convey the enormity of his deed. After all, his whole family could have been shot for helping Jews. For his heroic and unselfish deed, he was awarded—unfortunately, already posthumously—the medal of the Righteous Among the Nations of the World.[3] It was accepted by his daughters, Bożena and Lidia.

It seemed to us like ages had passed before Mama arrived, but it was only about two weeks—of waiting in fear, despair, and longing. It is hard to imagine what our mama must have felt during our separation, uncertain whether we had reached our destination and whether she herself would be able to escape from the ghetto and join us. Fortunately, Mama was able to secure a falsified *Kennkarte* [identity card]. This happened at the last minute, just before the complete liquidation of the ghetto in Rabka. It turned out that the color of the stamp in the *Kennkarte* was different from the one on Mama's glued-in photograph, but it was already too late to fix anything. This was a death sentence. In desperation Mama came up with the idea to pour ink on the photograph, and if the Germans were to question her, she would explain that her children had made the ink spot by accidentally knocking over an ink bottle.

Several times during our stay in the countryside the German gendarmes checked Mama's papers. One of them, I remember, even whistled when he saw the spotted *Kennkarte.* Mama told him the story about the ink spilled by her children. He stroked us children on our heads and went away. Another time, a different German, after looking over the *Kennkarte,* made a "joke" for his own amusement, pulling out his revolver and putting it to Hanka's head. He did not shoot, just said "bang-bang," chortled, and walked away. I can't imagine what Mama must have felt then.

Not wanting to endanger the Sikorskis, Mama decided to move to the nearby village of Święcany. We moved in with a family of farmers named Szynal. Mama told the farmers that she was an officer's wife and that this was the reason why it was safer for her to live with the children in the countryside. We had instructions from Mama to bite our lips, because their natural fullness could give away our origins. Nonetheless, our black hair, which stayed curly despite constant brushing, still betrayed us. Any suspicions were alleviated, however, by Mama's beautiful blond hair and regular features.

Our living quarters consisted of a tiny room with a clay floor, which was cleaned with a broom made of tree branches. On the beds were pallets of straw, which pricked us, drawing blood.

Water was carried from the well, and Mama heated it in a small copper basin over the stove. That's how we bathed. In summer and until late autumn we bathed in the river. The toilet was outside. From this shabby little room we looked with envy upon the typical, prosperous farmstead—its big kitchen, white sitting room, stacks of lace-trimmed pillows on the beds, its barn, sty, and stable. A horse rotated the *kierat,*[4] the farmers threshed the grain on the threshing floor. There were millstones for making flour. In the evenings, the farmer's wife would spin flax yarn.

Mama had a few valuables with her, some clothes, and also some bed linens, but only as much as she could carry in her arms when leaving Rabka. She sold off these items gradually to pay for our room and food. Slowly our clothes became tattered, and the money was coming to an end. We grew out of our worn-out shoes. Mama had a local shoemaker make wooden clogs for us. The tops were made from Papa's prewar skiing gloves. We were pestered by lice, fleas, and cockroaches, as well as scabies. Our poverty began to get to us.

We children had to mind cows for the farmers in order to get dinner. The village children taught us how to walk barefoot over harvested fields without getting our feet cut—the trick was to run, making the straw stubble fold under one's feet so you wouldn't feel pain. We will always remember the difficult moments, when on rainy days, barefoot, numb from cold, hungry, with tears in our eyes, we would pray for the hour to arrive when we could drive the cows back to the barn. Afraid of the farmer's wife, we had no courage to do this too early.

The winters were cold and harsh back then. Toward the end of the war we didn't go out of the house, because we had no warm clothes or shoes. Luckily, there were various people who helped Mama in all this misery. In order to create the appearance that we did have a family, that we were not in hiding, Lola, who herself was hiding on Aryan papers, would come to visit us. Endangering her own life, she brought us money from Aunt Zosia, who by then was already in the Kraków ghetto. A priest from a nearby parish also visited us, bringing us food from time to time.

I remember that his name was Józef Wilk. Maria Wnęk, a relative of Mr. Sikorski's, who was a teacher, would come through heavy snow to visit us. She walked on foot more than a dozen kilometers to instruct us in catechism and how to behave in church.

Hanka turned six and should have gone to school. Further education for me was out of the question, because our village school had only three grades. Hanka's education ended after several days because she was always crying, whether she was separating from Mama, staying in school, or even returning home. She was terribly afraid that when she got back, she would find Mama and me killed by the Germans. This fear didn't leave us even for a moment. There were days when Mama would tell us to hide in the nearby woods, because she would get a tip that German gendarmes were coming into the village. At such times we were dying of fear, wondering whether we would still find Mama alive when we returned.

In this village, Mama met a man from Sieradz who had escaped from a train that was taking him to forced labor in Germany. His name was Władysław Nogala, an exceptionally good-hearted and noble man. He helped us, bringing us onions so that "the children wouldn't get scurvy." He also gave us chickens and whatever else he could obtain. Władysław Nogala was respected in the village and was involved with the partisans who were active in our area.

One day the village administrator, knowing that Władysław was friendly with Mama, told him that "people are talking that Mrs. Janowska is a Jew, and I will have to report this to the police." Władysław Nogala replied, "If you do, your head will lie in this dunghill." After this encounter the administrator was silent. The heroism of Władysław Nogala was tremendous. After all, he could have brought disaster upon himself, on us, and upon the farmers with whom we lived.

Finally, January 1945 arrived. One day we heard shots. The Russians were entering the village. The shooting lasted all night. Mama, the two of us, and the farmer's whole family hid behind a big stove and sat there through the whole night in the middle of resounding gunfire. By morning things grew quiet. We could see that the windows were full of bullet holes. At first, the grown-ups, then we children, stepped outside and saw Russian soldiers running from a nearby, snow-covered hill after the fleeing Germans, yelling "Hurrah!" Mama stood on the threshold and cried. We cuddled up to her. In my childlike naïveté I couldn't understand why Mama was crying, since the nightmare had ended. I didn't know then that you could cry from joy.

But our happiness wasn't complete. We still didn't know the fate of our papa. All through the war, our mama and we constantly thought about him and prayed to God for his return. But this did not happen. His fate after leaving Kraków unfolded tragically. At first, he made his way to Lwów. From there, desperate letters arrived about his fruitless efforts to return to Poland, letters filled with great worry and anxiety for us. Then the correspondence ceased.

After the war we learned that he had been sent to a *łagier* [Soviet forced labor camp] in the Yaroslavl *oblast* [district].[5] It is known from eyewitness accounts how inhuman the work and living conditions were in those *łagry* [camps]. Nevertheless, Papa survived this period, was released, and wandered around the great expanse of Russia in order to join the Polish army of General Anders.[6] He never reached there. Exhausted by the camp, he came down with typhus and then pneumonia. He died in the Kalinin *sovkhoz* [state farm] in Uzbekistan on January 7, 1942, at the age of thirty-nine. He was a handsome, good man, full of joy for life; he worshiped Mama and us. He was buried in a refugees' cemetery in grave number nine, of which undoubtedly no trace remains. The news of our father's tragic fate was reported to us by Mrs. Emilia Czternastek, a nurse who was present at his death. She said he died with our mama's and our names on his lips. She also passed on to us photographs of us and fragments of his last letters from Mama.

This was not the final blow. News reached us of the tragic fate of the majority of our large family. Aunt Zosia Minder perished in the Stutthof[7] concentration camp, while her husband, Izydor, died in Russia—just like our father. Their son, Jurek, a young, talented writer, survived the hell in Russia, went to Palestine with the Anders Army, and then on to England—but there he died of tuberculosis, which he had contracted during the war. Uncle Julek, with his wife, Sabina, and son, Eryk, died in an unknown location in the Podhale region. Aunt Pola survived the war in Russia with her son, Olek, as did Aunt Irena, who escaped to England through Romania. From Mama's family, Aunt Irma and her daughter, Ada, who now lives in Israel, survived the concentration camps in Płaszów[8] and Częstochowa.[9] Her husband, Rajmund, died in Buchenwald[10] on the eve of its liberation, while her son, Jurek, survived this camp and now lives in America. Uncle Zygmunt also died somewhere in Podhale with his wife, Mala, and lovely daughter, Anita, who was the same age as Hanka—not even a grave remains. Uncle Rudek [Rudolf], too, died in an unknown location. One can easily see that the count is tragic, but we had to go on living.

Władysław Nogala contacted our mama several months after the end of the war. Their common experiences during the war brought them to join in marriage. He was a good father to us and gave care and support to Mama, just as during the war. From this marriage was born a son, Jacuś, but he died after two weeks. This was also a tragic result of the war and Mama's frail mental and physical health. We had enormous sympathy for our stepfather, who was not to have a son of his own after all the love he had bestowed on the children of someone else.

Our further fate was commonplace. We remained in Poland because our closest family was here, and here we were educated and started our own families. We worked professionally and were appreciated and respected in our work and in our circles. We did not experience any unpleasantness because of our origins. However, our tragic childhood did leave its mark. Hitler had devised a horrible fate for people. Everyone experienced hunger, cold, disease, fear, as well as separation from and the loss of their loved ones. This suffering remains in memory; we have all been wounded, regardless of our age during the dark days of Nazi slaughter, or no matter by what miracle our one and only life was saved. It doesn't matter whether we survived in a ghetto, a camp, in hiding, or in inhuman conditions in Russia, nor is it significant how long we suffered—for a day, a month, or for years. It is impossible to measure this suffering by the amount of time or the sort of repression experienced.

In conclusion, we would like to pay homage to all the victims of the war, to those who helped others to survive, and most of all to our splendid mama—who, unfortunately, is no longer with us. Having two small children in such inhuman conditions, she held out courageously until the end of the war, despite the tragic loss of her own mother and the constant fear for her own life and the lives of her children, as well as for the fate of her husband and the rest of her family. When we asked her how it was possible, she modestly answered, "Necessity awakens the power within us. Besides, I always believed that a miracle would happen and that this hell would end." She was right; our survival was indeed a miracle.

---

1. Śliwiński was the adopted Polish name of Edward Kleinberg.

2. Erysipilas is an acute streptococcus infection of the skin, similar to cellulitis; also called Saint Anthony's fire.

3. Righteous Among the Nations of the World is an honor awarded by Yad Vashem in Israel to non-Jews who saved Jews in occupied countries during World War II.

4. A *kierat* is a mechanical device powered by a horse harnessed to a rod walking around in a circle. It was used to drive farm machinery such as a small thresher.

5. The Yaroslavl district is in northern Russia. During the Soviet occupation of eastern Poland (1939–41), many Polish citizens were deported to Siberia or Soviet labor camps. See "Historical Notes."

6. See Anders Army in glossary.

7. Stutthof was a concentration camp near Danzig (Gdańsk) where approximately 65,000 people perished.

8. Płaszów was a forced labor and later concentration camp near Kraków.

9. In and near Częstochowa were several forced labor camps, mostly in armament factories.

10. Buchenwald, located five miles north of Weimar, was one of the largest concentration camps in Germany. More than 40,000 prisoners perished there.

JAN KLAPPER-KARPIŃSKI

Born in 1930

My Nanny

I was born in Kraków on January 27, 1930, into a middle-class Jewish family. My father was the business manager of the Solvay soda factory in Kraków. He was an orphan, brought up in a children's home. Starting as a messenger, he advanced to this position through his own efforts. Mama, whose maiden name was Blausstein, was from Lwów. After World War I her parents lived in Vienna with Mama's younger brother. Mama had two other brothers, one of whom emigrated to Belgium in the thirties and the other of whom, Uncle Lolek, lived in Łódź.

There were three of us at home—my eldest half brother, Alfred, born in 1915; the middle one, Rudolf, who was born in 1921; and me, the youngest one.

On September 3, 1939, when the German forces were nearing Kraków, Mama took all three of us, and we fled to Lwów. Father remained at his post in the factory.

We lived in Lwów until the German-Soviet war broke out. In the first days of July 1941, in commemoration of the assassination of Petlura,[1] there was a roundup in which Mama and Rudolf were caught. All trace of them vanished. Alfred and I were left all alone.

After the formation of the ghetto in Lwów, we moved within its confines, to Janowska Street. The situation within the ghetto was becoming increasingly difficult; hunger loomed. My brother decided to send me back to my father in Kraków. On Christmas

Day in 1941, he put me on a train with wounded German soldiers returning from the front.

In Kraków I found shelter on the Aryan side with my nanny, Katarzyna Żołna, who had always lived with us. I stayed there until September 1942.

Father lived in the ghetto and visited us often, protected by ironclad documents issued to him by the firm Solvay, which also paid his salary. Despite this, during an "action" in the ghetto in May 1942, Father was caught and sent to one of the death camps—where he was killed. In September 1942 my nanny received the news that my older brother, Alfred, was killed in a similar way.

I was left alone without any resources, supported by my nanny who was living off her pension. The danger grew. The people from whom my nanny was renting her room were afraid to hide a Jew, so I was forced to move to the ghetto. I lived with, or rather found shelter with, acquaintances of my parents', who helped me a little. At the same time I was trying to earn a living by selling cigarettes on the street. I was able to survive several liquidation roundups, thanks to help from a Jewish policeman, a friend of my hosts, who used to take me out of the ghetto while an action was in progress.

While on the Aryan side, I camped out in the park area surrounding the old city. My nanny helped feed me. After the action was over, I would sneak back into the ghetto.

In the middle of March 1943, the Kraków ghetto was liquidated. The Germans sent all those able to work to the camp in Płaszów. The rest were to be liquidated. I tried to squeeze my way into the column of people going to the Płaszów camp, but my short stature betrayed me as a child. An SS man chased me out of the column with a club. I was wandering through the streets when suddenly, a wagon driver whom I didn't know pulled me up onto the platform of his cart, hid me under a pile of bedding, and drove me outside the barbed wire of the ghetto.

On the Aryan side I jumped off the cart and contacted my nanny. The situation seemed hopeless, because she had no place to keep me. I decided to go to Warsaw, where my Uncle Lolek, Mama's brother, was hiding. I had the address of his brother-in-law, a Pole. I sneaked aboard a night train full of smugglers (the more crowded it was, the safer) going to Warsaw. In the morning, after I got off the train, I was nabbed by some blackmailers. I had nothing and couldn't ransom myself. They handed me over to the Polish police at the station on Jerozolimskie Avenue. The police checked my origins[2] but let me go free, warning me that I'd better not show up in that area again.

I found my uncle, who arranged to get me a false birth certificate and a school identification card. Having these papers, I began my life on the Aryan side, often changing my place of stay. Once I was hiding at Hotel Pod Różami, where I was caught by the vice squad. But once again they set me free, only admonishing the owner to never allow any Jews there again. Thanks to some help, I once again found a new place and stayed there until the beginning of the Warsaw Uprising.[3] I took part in it, serving in fire-fighting squads.

After capitulation and the expulsion of the population of Warsaw, I hid in the rubble around Napoleon Square.[4] This is where liberation found me on January 17, 1945.

Summarizing my wartime adventures, I believe I survived only thanks to good fortune (why did it happen particularly to me?), a convergence of various coincidences, and help from noble people to whose memory I dedicate these recollections.

---

1. Simon Petlura, a Ukrainian Nationalist leader, was assassinated in Paris on May 25, 1926, by a Jew. With the encouragement of the Germans, the Ukrainian police carried out the so-called "Operation Petlura" in late July and early August 1941, presumably to avenge Petlura's assassination.

2. They examined him to see if he was circumcised.

3. See Warsaw Uprising in glossary.

4. This square, located not far from the main post office, is now called Plac Powstańców Warszawy [Insurgents of Warsaw Square].

STELLA KOLIN, NÉE OBREMSKA

Born in 1926

From a Camp to the Aryan Side

For Ludka — my sister and savior

Prologue

There comes a time when one can no longer remain calm and silent. There comes a time when obligations take precedence, even at the cost of reopening old wounds.

From time to time I feel that something is tormenting me. It's an impulse to write about the tragic past. When we, the survivors, are no longer around, our children and grandchildren, wishing to learn something about the Holocaust, will have to plow through documents and memoirs. As long as we last, we have to bear witness to the horrible events that were our lot.

And so, insofar as possible, I have tried to present fragments of what I experienced. Let this be my modest contribution to the holy cause of preserving "the Memory."

My Unwritten Diary

I come from Warsaw. My parents were owners of the well-known Obremski footwear company. They had six shoe stores and a tannery at 15 Walicôw Street. I attended the F. Mirlasowa private school in the Simons Arcade. During the occupation we found ourselves in the Warsaw Ghetto. My mother was caught in a roundup on September 10, 1942, and deported to Treblinka.[1]

My father, my two sisters—Ludka and Rózia—and I were captured during the ghetto uprising and deported to the concentration camp in Majdanek.[2] No one from my family, other than myself, survived. I couldn't write a diary like Anne Frank. There was nothing to write with, or on, in the death camps. I was waging a difficult battle to survive, and that absorbed me completely. Nevertheless, each moment has etched itself in my memory and will haunt me till the end of my days.

MAJDANEK, MAY 1943

This was a horrible day. I saw my father on the other side of the barbed wire separating the women's camp from the men's camp. He seemed so thin and frail. I wanted to embrace him, to be close to him, but we were separated by an electrified double fence.

I wanted to give him what was dearest to me—my daily ration of bread—even though I was so very hungry! I shouted to him, and with all my might, I threw my piece of bread in his direction. But I was too weak. The bread landed short of its goal and bounced off the wires, setting off a piercing alarm that could be heard throughout the entire camp. Almost immediately I was surrounded by guards. They dragged me in front of Hermine Braunsteiner, the worst of the camp's beasts. She sentenced me to twenty-five lashes and looked on as one of the guards carried out the punishment with a bullwhip. I fainted after the ninth stroke.

I am lying on my bunk half-dead and bleeding. I am scared that if I don't go to work tomorrow, they will send me to the gas chamber.

SKARŻYSKO-KAMIENNA, *WERK* [WORKSHOP] C, SEPTEMBER 1943

I still cannot comprehend what happened and how my sister Ludka managed to do it. After a thorough medical examination, she was slated for a transport out of Majdanek. She had been declared healthy and able to work. I, however, had been rejected. Ludka exchanged our clothes—and our sewn-on numbers. When her number was called, she pushed me to the front of the ranks. I could hardly walk after my beating, but my friends helped me get to the train. Miraculously, I was out of danger.

There in Skarżysko[3] I recuperated a bit. What bothered me the most was the news from people who arrived with the next transport from Majdanek. They told me that Ludka, still healthy and strong, was taken somewhere. She was wearing my name and number. She was not able to convince the SS men that she had not yet gone through the selection. Only God knows whether we will ever see each other again.

SKARŻYSKO-KAMIENNA, *WERK* C, AUGUST 1944

The Russians must be close already. We could hear the artillery fire at night. The Germans have become very nervous. There are rumors that they want to kill us off. They said that they would take us to Germany, but nobody believes them.

I heard that some of the *Kapo*s[4] have escaped. I don't know what to do! If they ran away, it must be that we are about to be killed. I have to escape, but how? We are surrounded by a heavily guarded, two-and-a-half-meters-high, electrified, double barbed-wire fence. And where would I go without money or friends on the other side?

I mustered enough courage to make my way through the fence. It happened in the dead of night. There was a hole in one part of the fence.[5] Without thinking, I squeezed through to the other side of the barbed wire and in no time reached the woods. My flesh was torn all over from the barbs.

Right away I chanced on the bodies of two men lying in the woods. One was already dead, but the other, whom I knew, was still alive. His name was Jurek. Suddenly, I heard German voices close by. I lay down on the ground next to Jurek, pretending to be dead. The Germans approached and kicked the prostrate bodies with their boots. Neither Jurek nor I gave any sign of life. The SS men thought we were dead and went on.

I lay in this way for a long while until I heard shooting, shouting, and the roar of vehicles from the direction of the camp. The evacuation had begun. Suddenly, I felt shudders going through

Jurek's body—the agony of death. The sight of a man dying was horrible. Meanwhile, the forest lived its own life. Birds began singing, welcoming the new day.

I was completely covered with my own and Jurek's blood. Walking through the forest, I tried to clean myself up. I got to some kind of road. I met two small girls who showed me the way to the nearest train station. In the lavatory there, I found a cracked mirror and a newspaper. I wiped the remaining blood from my face and combed my hair with my fingers. I boarded the first train and immediately locked myself in the lavatory. From time to time people knocked, but after a while, they went someplace else. I couldn't get out, because not having a ticket, I was afraid of the conductor.

ST. MAGDALENE'S CONVENT, CZĘSTOCHOWA, AUGUST 1944

When the train stopped in a larger station, after several hours, I left my hiding place and got out. The station sign told me I was in Częstochowa. On the next platform there was a train surrounded by guards and filled with people in civilian clothes. They must have been prisoners taken during the Warsaw Uprising[6]—which had broken out some weeks before—on their way to concentration camps. Not far from me stood a nun talking to a young girl. From bits of their conversation, I realized that the girl had escaped from the transport and that the nun wanted to help her. After a while they both left the station.

The train started slowly to move. I wanted to avoid an encounter with a patrol walking by, so I started walking out in the direction of the city. I noticed another nun sitting on a bench, looking as if she were waiting for someone. "I am in trouble, Sister," I whispered to her. "Confess everything to Jesus, and He will help you," was her reply. I told her I had just escaped from the transport and that I was afraid of the Germans.

The nun took me by the arm and led me toward a nearby convent. There I found myself face-to-face with the mother superior. Right off, she asked, "You're from the Warsaw Uprising? Tell me what's happening there." Luckily, while still in Skarżysko, I had heard about the outbreak of the Warsaw Uprising. But I also had memories of the earlier uprising in the Warsaw Ghetto,[7] in April 1943, which I had witnessed personally. So I told her about burning buildings, people jumping from windows to escape the flames, and how the Germans dragged people out of their bunkers and shot them.

Mother Superior was clearly shaken. She gave me a rosary and announced that I could stay in the cloister without fear and work for my upkeep. I was fed and given clothing.

Then, misery me, I made a terrible mistake! Did I have to give in to an impulse to confess the truth? In the convent I felt safe, especially after I became familiar with a prayer book and learned the "Hail Mary" and other daily prayers by heart. The days passed peacefully, and I felt so good in their caring, protective hands. Because of my loneliness and the sense of decency instilled in me, I felt an irrepressible urge to get out of this situation. I wanted to find consolation from the hands of those who had the calling to do this, even though I was only a Jewish soul, not one of them. This was a kind of test for me and for the bonds of friendship that had grown between me and those who were helping me. I felt that I was deceiving them by hiding the truth. Looking at the Virgin Mary's radiant smile on a painting in the chapel, I really believed that it was also intended for me.

How foolish I was! Unfortunately! One day, during confession, I told the priest that what I wanted to confess was a very serious matter. "Jesus will listen to you, my child," he answered, adding, "Whatever it is, it's a matter between you and me and God."

"Father, I am a Jew," I confessed as quickly as I could. Then I told him about everything that had happened to me during the recent months. The priest was clearly troubled. He told me not to worry but I should tell Mother Superior about everything.

A few days passed. I didn't find enough courage to go to confession again. But during a chance meeting, the priest asked me whether I had told everything to Mother Superior. I told him that I had not as yet. The next day, she summoned me into her private sanctuary. She told me that I could no longer be together with the others under her care. I had to move to a dreary room next to the laundry and do the wash from then on. There was no radiant smile on her face. She spoke in a stern tone and no longer reminded me of the Virgin Mother in the painting.

The days that followed were a nightmare. My hands were chapped and covered with blisters from the harsh gray laundry soap. I washed the linens by hand from morning till night. I felt that I could no longer bear the strain. I complained to Mother Superior, to which she replied, "My child, the harsher one's fate on earth, the greater the reward awaiting in heaven."

REFUGEE CENTER, KRAKÓW, OCTOBER 1944

I couldn't stand it any longer. One day, after delivering the washed linens to town, I hid and ran away. After many mishaps, I made my way to Kraków. I ended up in a refugee center, not knowing what the next day might bring. How much I regretted what I had done! I'll never share my secret with anyone again.

In Kraków I experienced an awful scene. I was working as an attendant in a hospital at the time. One day, on my way to work, I chanced upon a roundup. I was herded in together with the others, taken to some kind of school, which was already filled with many people. There was a rumor that a German had been killed and we had been arrested in retribution as hostages. We sat in a large hall for a long time. More and more people were being brought in. We were watched by Germans and by blue-uniformed [Polish] police.

After a while, I felt the need to use the toilet. I approached a policeman, together with some older woman, and we asked him to let us out. At first he didn't want to, but I finally managed to convince him, and he let us out, first me—"for five minutes"—saying he'd let my mother (so he thought) out after my return. Looking for the toilet according to the policeman's directions, I ran to the basement and opened the door to some closet used for storing buckets and brooms, which had a small window. There was also a ladder there. Not thinking too long, I hid behind the ladder and covered myself with rags. I stood there for some time.

Suddenly, I heard the tromping of army boots and horrible screaming. I abandoned my hideout and put the ladder to the window to see what was going on. I saw the courtyard where the Germans were herding all the prisoners. Suddenly, I heard machine guns. My heart almost stopped beating. I was so scared I trembled all over. All I saw through the little window were people being shot. Blood all over. I was paralyzed. I could have been among them.

After a while, which seemed like an eternity, some men arrived. I think that they were prisoners picking up the bodies and placing them on trucks. I probably fainted then, because when I opened my eyes, it was dark and quiet outside. I slowly came out of my hiding place, crying softly. I was so tired, still not believing what I had seen, thanking God for my not being one of the executed.

Then I had a stroke of luck. Pretending to be a Christian Pole, I got a job as a maid at the home of a German doctor. He and his wife were nice people. The doctor even took care of me when I fell ill. Once again I felt the need to tell these people who I was, but I held my tongue; I have learned something already!

LEIPZIG, APRIL 1945

The year 1945 was approaching, and the Russians were coming closer. My German employers were evacuated by a military transport to Dresden, and I was forced to go with them. This was a time when heavy Allied bombing was turning the city into an inferno. Planes were systematically dropping bombs on one section of the city after another. In the general confusion, I slipped away from the doctor's family. I saw that the low-flying airplanes were bombing clusters of buildings, passing over open spaces. Instinctively, I ran to a large park and hid among the trees. I also thought that if I had to die, I wouldn't want to be buried in the same soil with the Germans; I'd rather be there among the trees!

The heaviest air raid of World War II finally ended. I was once again alone, in the middle of the ruins of Dresden. I couldn't pass for a German, and I couldn't stay by myself in a foreign city for long. I didn't know what to do with myself. Suddenly I saw a column of Polish-speaking people. I joined them. I knew that as long as no one recognized me as a Jew, I had a chance of surviving.

The group of about two hundred men and women was taken to Leipzig and put in an underground bunker. Suddenly, soldiers in unfamiliar uniforms burst into the bunker. One of them pushed me toward the exit with all his might. *"Schnell, schnell!* [Quick! Quick!] *Out!"* he yelled. Other soldiers, using gestures and shouting, were also trying to empty out the place as fast as possible. Literally, a moment after the bunker was emptied, there was a powerful blast that threw us to the ground. It turned out that the Germans had placed time bombs in the bunker with the intent of blowing it up along with the people inside. Our liberators, the Americans, found out about this at the last minute and managed to save everyone. The soldier who led me out gave me a piece of bread. To me, he seemed like God himself. What else could I have asked of the Almighty had he appeared before me? He saved me from certain death, gave me bread, and announced that the war and our misfortunes had come to an end!

For the first time in many years I didn't feel hunger. I was free!

After a period of recuperation, I returned to Poland. In Wałbrzych, I met my husband, Michał Kozłowski (now Kolin), who survived the war in the USSR and fought the Germans in the ranks of the First Polish Army.[8] We were married in 1946. In 1947 I gave birth to our son, Ira. In 1950 we came to the United States. Our daughter, Marlene, was born in 1955. We now have five grandchildren—Brian and Laurie, the children of Ira, as well as Matthew, Andrew, and Zachary, the sons of Marlene. We all live in New York.

A few years ago I had the opportunity to meet Hermine Braunsteiner Ryan, the bestial SS woman from Majdanek, during hearings on her deportation from the United States. Thanks to testimony from me and others, she was deported to Germany, where she was tried and convicted of crimes against humanity.

Postscript by Jakub Gutenbaum

In 1993, on the occasion of the fiftieth anniversary of the Warsaw Ghetto Uprising, Al Gore, the U.S. vice president, came to Poland. During his meeting with the Jewish community in the Jewish Historical Institute, to which I had been invited as the representative of the Association of "Children of the Holocaust," I noticed a woman whose face seemed familiar. After a short exchange of words, we fell into each other's arms. It was Stella, with whom I had worked in the same factory room for more than a year at the forced labor camp for Jews in Skarżysko-Kamienna, in the so-called *Werk* C. We had arrived in Skarżysko from the Majdanek concentration camp, to which we had been deported from the Warsaw Ghetto during the uprising in April 1943. We had parted more than fifty years before; she had escaped from the camp the day before it was evacuated and now lives in New York, while I was taken to the concentration camp in Buchenwald[9] and now live in Warsaw. We knew nothing about each other. Neither of us knew that the other had survived the war and the Holocaust.

I asked about Adela with whom Stella was friendly. It turned out that she was no longer alive, having recently died of cancer. Adela was the only person from *Werk* C whom I had known from Warsaw. She was an orphan, adopted before the war by two teachers, a married couple, friends of my parents. She was goodness incarnate. Many times she gave courage to me and others in difficult moments. Optimism—genuine or pretended—was an exceedingly rare commodity in those cruel times. The unexpected meeting with Stella reminded me of an event involving her and Adela, which in my consciousness is encoded under the name "Sugar Cube."

In Skarżysko, lice were eating us alive. Exhausted, starved prisoners were being decimated by a typhus epidemic. In March 1944 I also came down with it. I got a high fever and not being able to go to work had to report to the doctor. In the infirmary barracks, triple-tiered bunks stood crowded together. The sick were lying two to a bunk. It was dark, crowded, and the stench was unbearable. The only place to be found was on the top tier next to a man already lying there. It did not take long to figure out that my neighbor had diarrhea and was defecating under himself. I knew that at *Werk* C one did not survive in this condition. And indeed, the next day, my neighbor died. With great effort, I threw his excrement-soiled blanket to the floor.

Several days in a row I lay ill with high fever on bare planks, in tattered clothes, in stinking barracks, to which it required heroic self-discipline just to enter. Suddenly, one day, I couldn't believe my own eyes; above me I saw the smiling faces of Adela and Stella. I don't know if anything like this had ever happened in the entire history of this stinking place of death; a sick person had visitors! But this was not the end. Adela gave me a tiny package. I unwrapped the paper, and I saw a *sugar cube!* I had not had such a delicacy in my mouth for more than four years. And here, at the very bottom of this camp inferno, I saw a real piece of sugar and two good souls above me! I don't know how they got it, how many sacrifices it had cost them. I only know that never in my life had I gotten such a marvelous gift. I'd say even more, that this visit by Adela and Stella and that piece of sugar saved my life!

---

1. See Treblinka in glossary.

2. Majdanek was a forced labor and death camp located on the edge of Lublin where Jews, Polish and Soviet political prisoners, and Soviet prisoners of war were interned. Close to 250,000 people were killed at Majdanek.

3. Skarżysko-Kamienna was a forced labor camp located between Radom and Kielce, where 23,000 Jews lost their lives.

4. See *Kapo* in glossary.

5. The day before evacuation the SS commander of the camp, bribed by Jewish camp functionaries, promised that he would remove the guards and let them escape. As it turned out, it was a trap. Armed guards waited for the escapees, most of whom were shot. A few were able to escape. Many prisoners knew about the planned escape. (Author's note)

6. After the collapse of the Warsaw Uprising (see glossary), residents of Warsaw were forcibly removed from the city to the countryside or to concentration camps.

7. The Warsaw Ghetto Uprising was an uprising in the Warsaw Ghetto by the small population remaining after the deportation of some 400,000 Jews to the Treblinka extermination camp. Organized by the Jewish Fighting Organization (ŻOB), it began on April 19, 1943, and continued until the burning of the ghetto in mid-May.

8. The First Polish Army was a Soviet-controlled Polish army formed in the Soviet Union in 1944 under the command of Polish General Zygmunt Berling.

9. Buchenwald, located five miles north of Weimar, was one of the largest concentration camps in Germany. More than 40,000 prisoners perished there.

JADWIGA (WICHER) KOTOWSKA, NÉE BRAUN

Born in 1934

The Little Smuggler

I come from a family of tradespeople. Before the war, my grandfather owned seven hackney carriages. He lived on Grzybowska Street in Warsaw. I most likely lived on Twarda Street, but my grandfather had his stables on Grzybowska. Grandma—as much as I remember of her—wore a wig. Grandma and Grandpa were Hasidic Jews. They were religious people, for sure. I lost my mother as a young child, before the war. I don't remember her at all. On the other hand, I remember our maid well; I remember her extremely well. She became my mother, but that was later. At first she was the maid for my grandparents, but then when Mama died, she came to us. She was a country girl—simple, but good. She must have been good if I liked her. I became a child of the streets only because of the war. After all, I remember that Papa used to spend a lot of money; I took piano lessons and had a governess for French. That means we could afford it.

They established a ghetto. Just before the war broke out, Papa had bought a house; we lived on Stanisławowska Street in Grochów.[1] Then the war started, and later, they set up the ghetto and we had to move to the Jewish quarter. I don't remember the move itself; I was too young. I do remember the wall and the corpses. I find it difficult to talk about this even today. I was there from the beginning until January 1943. I was a smuggler. I supported the whole family; everyone waited for me to bring something from the Polish side.[2] They wrapped me in various things—shirts, blouses, sweaters, and they bandaged me. With these on I stole across the wall. If the guards at the checkpoint were nice, they let us through; if they weren't, well, then they wouldn't.

In a TV movie I saw, there are several children in the Little Ghetto.[3] We sneak past the guard post. At that moment we get caught by a Jewish policeman; that is the scene. Having had no idea that such a film had been recorded, I recognized myself in it. The Jewish policeman, beating me with his club, dumps out the potatoes and flour or sugar—at this point in time, it is difficult for me to say which. That's one scene. Well, I am more than sure that it was me, with a group of other children. In the second scene, my aunt and I are in the middle of the ghetto. This is the Little Ghetto. We are begging, asking for alms.

I used to arrange to meet our maid somewhere near the center of town. She would always promise, "Jadzia [Jadwiga], don't worry, I'll come to get you."

My uncle—my father's brother, who was eleven or twelve, perhaps sixteen, well, I don't know—used to go with me. Something very important happened. I crossed over, but he got caught by a Polish policeman on the Aryan side. The policeman was hitting his head against the curb for so long—blood was pouring out—that for sure he killed him. He opened the sewer and threw him inside. I saw this with my very own eyes; I was watching from a hideout. It is difficult to talk about it. . . . I was sure he had died. He'd been crossing over with me to the Polish side for quite a while. I knew everyone was dying, but I wanted to live. I felt that in me. Nonetheless, I was convinced that I wouldn't survive, that I simply would not be able to last!

I had a very large family. Grandma didn't want to take any food for a very long time, because it wasn't kosher, but then she started to when she got weaker. She didn't get out of bed (if you didn't eat, how could you walk?). . . . Later she began to eat but still couldn't get out of bed. We knocked out a hole in the cupboard. We hid there during an "action," but Grandma wasn't with us, because we decided we wouldn't be able to take her along. She was killed during the action.

This was 1942 already; the summer was hot. Difficult memories. There are wounds that don't bleed anymore, but when one talks about it, these wounds start bleeding again. It's tough then. Everything appears before one's eyes. One sees and feels everything—all over again. Whenever I have any stress, any worries—the corpses come back, even more so because I saw so many uncovered bodies. In the morning, I was supposed to go out when they hadn't yet had the time to take them away, or even cover them—unless the snow covered them. At night I dream of eiderdown, so much down, and I see that down on the streets, in houses, on staircases, in courtyards—everywhere. I remember a lot of down in the ghetto—on roofs, in attics, in hideouts, wherever.[4] Sometimes I wake up with the fear that my pillow or comforter has been ripped open and the down is pouring out. At first I very often had these dreams—and would wake up at night. As the years went by, things began to calm down.

Back to smuggling. I was afraid, I really was afraid. Other children did it; I saw them do it, but I didn't take the initiative. I simply think that Papa agreed with our former maid that I, as a child, would have the best chance of getting across and bringing something back. Not only I went; Papa also used to go over to the Polish side. In fact, in the meantime, he was trying to get us Aryan papers. I was the main supplier. Other children used to go as well, in groups of four or five. Some wouldn't come back again; we didn't wait for them. Of course, whenever there was an opportunity, we went through. The next day, looking around the courtyard, we knew that some of the children had been caught, killed, bludgeoned to death, or taken during an action. These weren't fixed groups. I always had arrangements to meet with my "mother," meaning the maid, who always waited for me on the Aryan side and would lead me to the apartment of her friends, the Dworakowskis, I believe.

I was only a smuggler. Nobody thought about educating me. I suspect that my family wasn't all that rich. The best evidence is that I started to take out rags brought to me by others, from other homes or apartments where three or four families lived together. Perhaps I carried valuables, too, but I didn't know anything about it; they just wrapped me in bandages, and I sneaked out looking like a little barrel. At first I used to sneak out through the Little Ghetto. I remember that bridge clearly, but I don't recall who tore the bridge down. I used to run. . . . At the beginning, we even played games there—as children do. I don't know how that bridge later disappeared, or in what way; that bothers me a bit.[5] I would like to see that bridge, those steps, lots of steps.

Our former maid supplied me with provisions. When I used to cross over to the Aryan side, I sometimes rebelled, especially if I got caught and beaten. That happened three times. Of course, no one from my family forced me to go out of the ghetto. I had a large family. Most likely no one survived. I have already lived my life. I now have children and grandchildren. But somewhere, in the secret part of my soul, I'd like to have one of my loved ones.

Back to smuggling again. Things were getting worse; it was harder and harder to get through, more difficult to get anything. The hunger was terrible. We sneaked past the guard post and went through some hole. Sometimes we slipped through the Court House,[6] though rarely, because we were somehow strangely afraid of the courts. I was supposed to cross over to the Polish side. There were four or five of us. They simply rounded us up on the street, a bunch of children, and we were on our way to the *Umschlagplatz.*[7] It was an action aimed at children. I suspect (but can't be sure) that this was at the time when Korczak's orphanage[8] was being liquidated, because there were lots of children. It was in 1942 that I got caught, if I am not mistaken.

I must mention that Grandpa had a horse, already his last horse, and he had the right to go everywhere to pick up corpses. I don't know how Grandpa knew—whether he spotted me, or perhaps guessed it. He never told me, but at one moment, I felt someone pick me up by my coat and sit on me. He drove with me under the driver's seat, among corpses, out of the *Umschlagplatz.* He took me out and passed me on to my mother (our maid) and told her, "Bronia, if there is a God, if you say that you love Jadzia and care for Józek (meaning my father), remember, I am going to die. Rózia (my grandmother) is already gone. Remember, you must protect Jadzia; she can't go back to the ghetto again." I can't remember anymore, however, whether I went back to the ghetto at that time or not.

I know of this conversation between Grandpa and Mother from my mother's lips. That Grandpa drove me to the Jewish cemetery and that she was there, that I know for sure. A strange resentment remains from the ghetto—those restaurants and stores full of food and us begging on the street—so repugnant. Today I certainly look at some things in a different light . . . well . . . but the fear was terrible, it was indeed terrible. When later in 1943 my father led Grandpa and me to the Aryan side, I was no longer Jochewed or Jadwiga Braun, just Jadzia Zalewska. I was simply given the maiden name of our servant, and she became my mother. I wasn't very old then—eight, nine, at the most. I kept on trading; I still had to support my mother. She had a child, a boy, that is, my stepbrother. Somebody had to stay with that child.

I got caught by the Gestapo, denounced by someone. They took me to Szucha Avenue[9] and beat me terribly. I have marks on my back to this day.

I knew I was a Jew. I don't know how, as a child, I was able to do it, how I managed not to say that I was a Jew! They must have checked. They were at Mrs. Zalewska's, my mother's house, and they checked. Yes, but she told them I was her illegitimate child and that she had nothing to do with any Jews. I was released after three days (it must have cost a fair amount of money), beaten and black and blue all over. I lay sick for six weeks, couldn't move either a hand or a leg. I don't know how I got back from Szucha Avenue to Stalowa Street. I don't know how it happened at all. I only remember the "streetcar"[10] in which they kept me. Those benches with the torturers sitting on them back-to-back. But as to the faces, they've become completely blurred. Besides, it wasn't just one person who interrogated me or just one person who beat me! To this day I have marks on my back.

I had a birth certificate in a little bag made to wear around my neck. I wore it on a piece of string. We only had enough money for my papers; my father also needed papers for himself. Well, my father, as a tradesman had many connections (before the war we had stores, kiosks on the Kercelak Bazaar and at the Mirowski Market). He thought that somehow he would be able to get the money for himself, one way or another, maybe he would borrow it from his friends. He had lots of them; they respected him very much and knew him well. Unfortunately, it happened that one colleague pointed him out. This happened near the Mirowski Market. Father ran in the direction of the Saski Garden.[11] He was killed. I was told about it. I didn't see it myself.

He was lying with half his face resting on the spot where the slab of the Tomb of the Unknown Soldier is today (that slab wasn't there then, of course). Papa lay there nearly a whole day. Then his friends came and brought my mother and took me in their arms so we could see Father one last time! He lay covered with newspapers. I started screaming. Father's friends held me in their arms, covered my mouth, and took me to some stairway. They were simply afraid that I would run up to my father. This was my final farewell to Father. He couldn't be buried as a Pole, because he didn't have any documents. A truck arrived, he was thrown on it, and they drove off. We don't know where he lies. This was already 1943.

I couldn't accept it; I knew it, but I didn't believe it. I kept thinking that the door would open, and he would walk in. I remember how Father was leaving the house on that last day. I remember very well what he wore, but his face has grown dim. One thing I know for sure; he was bald, completely bald. He was stocky, of a stocky build, and I see him, I see how he walks out of the house, but what eyes he had, his mouth, his nose . . . I don't know.

It is very difficult for me because I don't know where my loved ones lie. I would very much like to have at least one grave in order to honor the memory of all of them, my entire family. Very often, when I am alone at home (lying or reading), in a flash, the times of the occupation come to mind. I think of the ghetto, about that childhood of mine, about this family, about the joyfulness that reigned, and then I start crying, because I miss them. I would like so much to at least have the graves of my dearest ones, meaning my aunts and Father, not to even mention the more distant relatives that I remember. For me this is a tragedy, that is why I mourn them to this day.

Right after the liberation, I went straight to the ghetto, that means to the ruins of the ghetto. All of Warsaw was one big ruin, but I, as a Warsaw newspaper girl, went to the ghetto. Something was smoldering inside me, that somebody would be there, that somebody would be alive. Being a child, I slipped through with a government delegation crossing the pontoon bridge. This was in January. Somehow, I strongly believed that someone would be there. It didn't enter my consciousness that nobody from my family would be there. I wouldn't admit it. I knew that there was a place called Treblinka, but I didn't imagine at all that people could be finished off like that. (I wasn't in the ghetto during its final liquidation.) Besides, some inner feeling told me that somebody would be there. Anyway, I kept waiting. All the time. If anybody unknown moved about the courtyard, I expected . . . that maybe it was for me . . . that they were looking for me. I was waiting for that moment.

I know that the ghetto was cleared of rubble. I worked there so passionately as a child. The Jewish youth and I—my picture was in the newspaper. I believed that I would find something under that rubble; I believed it so strongly. The most likely place to find me was in the ruins of the ghetto—with newspapers, soda water, rolls, anything I could sell. Jews took me from the street with my bundle of newspapers, and, well, as a child, I was impressed by their respectable clothing and new shoes. First, the Central Committee of Polish Jews assigned me to a children's home in Śródborów, near Warsaw. They wanted me to be a child, but, of course, I was no longer a child. I already knew what money was and how to spend it. I knew how to hustle, trade, and swindle. I was eleven. Why would I suddenly want to be a child? So I ran away from Śródborów.

Instinctively, I did not want to be a Jew and had already somehow transformed myself into being a Pole. In general, it was a tragedy for me that I had to go to a Jewish orphanage. That's why there were all those escapes.

Later they took me to Bytom. I stayed there a week, maybe. I ran away at night, barefoot. I rode in the lavatory compartment of a train, without a ticket, from Katowice to Warsaw. The police dragged me out of that lavatory. They took me to the Central Committee of Polish Jews. They put me in some home. I was supposed to have been transferred to another children's home, but of course, I escaped, as usual. I couldn't be a child, I didn't know how to be one. So I ended up in an orphanage in Chorzów. Again I ran away. Again the police. After two escapes from Chorzów, I didn't try a third time, because I was beginning to feel good there. The orphanage in Chorzów was closed, and we were transferred to Bielsko. There, slowly, slowly, I regained my childhood; then came the most beautiful years, which I recall with pleasure to this day.

When I wanted to call other children names, I called them "Jews." Whether we were playing volleyball, *palant,*[12] or *dwa ognie,*[13] if I didn't like something, I'd yell, "You dirty Jew!" I was simply scared to be a Jew. (Let someone else be a Jew; why should I be a Jew?) I was no longer Jochewed; I was already Jadzia. "They" were the Jews. I was not a Jew. There were four of us children who knelt and said our Catholic prayers in the evening.

Then came a moment in the orphanage when I took my prayer book to the principal. I told her, "I'm not a Christian any more." It was the other side of the coin. When I gave back that prayer book—because I didn't need it (although I didn't want it to be destroyed)—I immediately became a Jew.

Later, in 1950, the orphanage was closed. I was taken to a dormitory in Warsaw at 28 Jagiellońska Street. I was the only one from the teachers' lyceum there; everyone else was a university student, except two who were already working. Nobody was interested in me. I was left alone. I didn't have money for textbooks or notebooks. I was hungry. I gave up school and returned to my former profession—street trade. I started selling ice cream. And so I began being a grown-up again. All alone. I think that the Jews made a big mistake by leaving me all alone. Why did they give me those few carefree years? If I had stayed on the street with my bundle of newspapers, I wouldn't have experienced the taste of something better. Mother (i.e., our maid) didn't want to take me in with her. Once again I had no roof over my head. Again I stayed in parks and attics.

I met my husband, with whom I had two children—two daughters—who are grown up now. We had a single room on the third floor. You had to carry water up and carry it back down. I never hid my being Jewish from my children. Both my husbands also knew. It didn't bother the first one; there was no problem. Only when he was drunk or was trying to annoy me, he would call me a Jew. In the 1960s and at the beginning of the '70s, my husband and I applied several times for emigration to Israel, but we were refused each time. I wrote everywhere I could, but we were always refused.

My husband and I decided that I would go with the children. He agreed that the children could go. We counted on the fact that I would then try to bring him over, so that there we would again be reunited. Well, in the end, we got divorced, and there came a moment when I received permission to go to Israel and a notification to pick up my passport. My husband took me on the staircase, started to cry terribly, and said, "Listen Jadwiga, I'm not worth much anyway, and when you go, it'll be the bottom of the pit for me. I'll never see my children again. I'm afraid I'll never be allowed to leave." And I was really moved by that. After all, I did have children with him. I felt sorry for him, and I gave up my plans for leaving.

I consider myself a sick, morally broken person. I regret that my life did not evolve as it should have, because of the war and the ghetto.

I've had a very difficult life.

As told by Jadwiga Wicher, current name Kotowska, to Katarzyna Meloch in an interview for the Kestenberg Foundation in 1994.

1. Grochów is a district of Warsaw on the eastern side of the Vistula River.

2. Children were able to slip in and out of the ghetto more easily than adults.

3. The Little Ghetto was the southern part of the Warsaw Ghetto, bound by Wielka, Sienna, Żelazna, and Chłodna Streets, connected to the Big Ghetto by a wooden bridge over Wolska Street. (Author's note)

4. Down pillows and comforters were a favorite place for hiding valuables. Seeing down flying in the air meant that there had been a search and they had been ripped open.

5. The bridge between the large and small ghettos was torn down when the Little Ghetto was eliminated.

6. The Court House on Leszno Street had two entrances, one from Ogrodowa Street, on the side of the ghetto, and the other on the Aryan side; this passageway was used for illegal exit from and entry to the ghetto. (Author's note)

7. *Umschlagplatz* is a square on Stawki Street that was used as a transfer point where people were assembled for deportation from the Warsaw Ghetto to the death camps. (Author's note)

8. Janusz Korczak, real name Henryk Goldschmidt, was a famous physician, writer, educator, and director of a children's home before the war and later in the Warsaw Ghetto. He refused asylum on the Aryan side and accompanied his young charges to Treblinka, where they all perished. Revered by Poles and Jews alike for his courage and dedication.

9. Szucha Avenue was the site of Gestapo headquarters.

10. The "streetcar" was the nickname for a long corridor with benches at Gestapo headquarters.

11. The Saski Garden is a large public garden in central Warsaw.

12. *Palant* is a game similar to baseball, played with a stick and a small rubber ball.

13. *Dwa ognie* [two fires] is a ball game in which the opponent is attacked from two sides.

ALFRED KRÓLIKOWSKI

Born in 1928

Helped by Żegota

I was born on January 8, 1928, in Kraków, as the son of Zygmunt Leopold Szancer and Zofia Szancer, née Haber. Following family tradition, I was given the name Alfred after my paternal grandfather.

My father, born on April 5, 1902, in Vienna, was the son of Alfred Szancer and Margareta Szancer, née Strakosch. My mother, born in Kraków on July 5, 1904, was the daughter of Wolf Wilhelm Haber and Alta-Schaindla Salomea, née Pechner.

Before the war we lived in Kraków—until 1935 at 31 Kazimierz Wielki Street and from 1935 to 1939 at 3 Chopin Street, Apt. 5.

In 1934 I started elementary school at St. Wojciech's Public Grammar School, No. 2, which had seven grades. In June 1939 I completed the fifth grade at St. Florian's Public Grammar School for Boys, No.7.

My father worked as manager of the purchasing department and also as the deputy director of a cable factory in Krakow. My mother did not work.

After the Germans occupied Kraków, Father remained in his position as manager of the purchasing department until October 1940. Due to his excellent knowledge of German (he had been brought up in Vienna until age nine) and his familiarity with the operations of the plant in which he had worked since 1929 in the same position, it was difficult for the new German management to replace him. The manager of the factory at the time, a German, Dr. Cappenberg, tried to keep him in his job as long as possible. However, Father was dismissed when the plant was designated as *Rüstungsbetrieb* (a defense plant), which was followed by a change in the character of the factory and its management.

At about that time we were thrown out of our apartment on Chopin Street. This street, as one of the more modern ones, became part of the German quarter. At the same time, we were also deprived of most of our belongings, such as furniture and household goods, which we had to leave for the new German tenants. For a brief period we stayed at 13 Potocki Street; from there we were resettled to Rzeszowska Street. This time, during the move, they took away from us all that remained of our personal articles and household goods. A *Volksdeutscher*[1] by the name of Balko, who lived nearby, oversaw the loading of our belongings onto a truck, which he dispatched, with the help of gendarmes he had summoned, to a storage depot called the *Treuhandstelle* [trustees' place].[2]

We were never able to get anything back from there. We lost not only the rest of our furniture, antiques, paintings, porcelain, and crystal but also our personal belongings—such as clothes, underwear, and bed linen—as well as a valuable stamp and coin collection that my father and I had assembled. The only things saved were a briefcase with some documents (which were later hidden by the janitor from the factory, who offered to help Father), Mother's purse with money, and some valuables—thanks to which we were able to survive those periods during the occupation when Father could not earn any money.

It was impossible to live in the empty apartment on Rzeszowska Street because of the expectation that it would later be included in the ghetto area, and my father was determined to avoid being enclosed in the ghetto. Thus he made contact with a former classmate, Father Stanisław Proszak, a parish priest in the village of Biały Kościół, eighteen kilometers from Kraków, in the direction of Ojców. This priest helped us a great deal, giving his guarantees on our behalf when we rented a room at a local farmer's, and later, by recording in the parish books a fictitious baptism of our entire threesome (Father, Mother, and me) and issuing us certificates of baptism. At that time our given names were also changed for the first time—Father's to Stanisław Zygmunt, Mother's to Jadwiga Zofia, and mine to Jerzy Alfred. According to our thinking then—somewhat naive, as it turned out later—this was supposed to disorient the Germans in case they discovered our escape from Kraków.

On the basis of these documents and thanks to Father Proszak's connections, we received temporary identification documents from the local administration—which we used as evidence of our identities for a brief period of time. For a time, Father, unable to make a living in the village, worked in Kraków at the Władysław Klimek Iron Foundry, owned by a friend of his, and on Sundays, he rode his bicycle to Biały Kościół. This lasted until the spring of 1941, when Father was warned—I don't know how and by whom—of the necessity to flee further.

Our next stop was Słomniki, near Kraków, where Mr. Klimek had a little house in which he gave us shelter. The three of us lived there in a little room without any conveniences. We had to carry our water from a spring a half kilometer away. This was particularly difficult in winter. My father was able to earn some money by writing applications to various authorities and institutions in German and Polish for local people. He devoted the remainder of his time to teaching me languages—which he knew thanks to his innate abilities (he knew German, English, French, and Italian)—and helped me, as much as he could, to go through high school level material. There we survived the extermination of the Jews of Słomniki, who were herded out of their homes one night, assembled in the surrounding fields, and then, in the morning, taken to the train station for deportation. We were saved by an *Arische Wohnung* [Aryan living quarters] sticker on the door of the house and our host's verbal assurances, which we heard clearly through the door to the hallway, that there were no Jews living there.

In the spring of 1943, Father's reputation as someone who wrote applications in excellent German had spread too far. He was called in by the *Kreisleiter* (regional administrator) in Miechów, where he was told that with a name like Szancer and such a knowledge of German, he must either come from a German family or he was a Jew. In the first case, he should fill out an application to be placed on a *Volksliste.*[3] That very day, after Father's return to Słomniki, we left for Kraków, taking with us—once again—only a briefcase full of documents and Mother's purse—with whatever still remained in it—as our means of support. Then, that same night, we boarded the first train to Warsaw.

Once there, Father went to see an old friend of his, Mr. Jerzy Bielecki, who gave us shelter in his apartment. Mr. Bielecki, it turned out, was a very active member of the Home Army[4] and of Żegota.[5] He had plenty of contacts, thanks to which he got us false documents with new names—Edmund Królikowski for Father, Joanna Królikowska, maiden name Kozłowska, for Mother, and Alfred Jerzy Królikowski for me. Arrangements were also made to provide us with a temporary place to stay. For security reasons, we were all placed separately, especially since the Warsaw Ghetto Uprising[6] had broken out at that time. My parents were placed in various hideouts in the Warsaw area, while I was placed with the family of a member of the organization, the Borysiewiczes, in Radość, near Warsaw (at 18 Kościelna Street). This again was a tiny room, a caretaker's cubby, without any conveniences. In return for my room and board there, I helped with various tasks in the house and in the garden.

There, despite the general restrictions on my leaving the hideout, I attended secret courses along with the Borysiewiczes' son, Adam. These courses, conducted by several teachers under the direction of Mr. Adam Tatomir, covered secondary school level material. The teaching took place at irregular times in various apartments made available by the parents of the course participants, mainly the Borysiewiczes and certain other trusted families. These were selected from among the acquaintances of the organizers, mainly people involved in the AK. As for me, after several dangerous run-ins with the Polish police and German patrols, earlier in Słomniki and later in Radość, I was rarely and only reluctantly allowed to leave the house.

I stayed in Radość until the arrival of the Soviet Army and the First Polish People's Army[7] on the last day of July 1944. When in September 1944 the front moved to Praga,[8] our secret courses were converted into a private gymnasium and lyceum in Radość, where I finished the third grade of gymnasium.

After liberation I returned to Kraków, where I met up with my parents. Father tried to return to his job at the cable plant and to reclaim our apartment on Chopin Street. We also resumed using our last name, Szancer. However, it was not possible to recreate the prewar situation. Father encountered an extraordinarily negative attitude from his old acquaintances, particularly the new management of the factory, which consisted of prewar lower-level employees promoted to management positions during the occupation or immediately thereafter. He also encountered resistance from the current residents of our apartment—which had been taken over immediately after liberation by a professor from the Academy of Mining and Metallurgy in Kraków. Also, despite the trial and sentencing of Balko, the *Volksdeutscher,* we failed to recover any of the things pilfered from us. Neither were the city authorities forthcoming with any help in reestablishing our lives.

After the well-known Kielce pogrom,[9] Father decided to return to his wartime name of Królikowski and to move to Silesia. In Katowice he took the position of director of the Association of Zinc Industries and, subsequently, as director of a scrap metal center. After several job changes and a great deal of harassment in the 1950s as a result of his "intelligentsia class origins,"[10] he died in Katowice on November 6, 1953.

In Katowice I finished the fourth grade of gymnasium and then a general education lyceum in an accelerated program. I passed the matriculation examination in June 1947.

In 1949 in a streamlined process, my parents and I succeeded in legalizing our name change [to Królikowski].

From October 1947 to December 1952, I studied at the University of Wrocław, named for B. Bierut,[11] in the Mathematics, Physics, and Chemistry Department, from which I received a master's degree in physics. However, due to my irregular secondary school education, I was never able to fill the gaps in my education and general knowledge. I was able to compensate for this only by my knowledge of foreign languages. This did not allow me to take up any highly advanced work in my specialty, and later, it caused turmoil in my professional career, in which I alternated between being a teacher and an administrator.

On March 28, 1950, I married a university colleague, Halina Antonowicz, born on July 5, 1929, in Białystok, a philo-Semitic gentile. We remain in a happy marriage to this day. Despite her young age, my wife was a partisan during the war and is a veteran of the AK. Of course, the ordeals of that time left their mark on her health, and she is now classified as having a group one disability.[12]

We have two daughters, Ewa and Anna, and three grown grandchildren.

As a result of the purges of 1968,[13] I was dismissed from the State Office for the Utilization of Nuclear Energy[14] and returned to work in secondary education.

In 1956 my mother emigrated to Australia to join her brother, Henryk Haber, who had left immediately after the war and had settled in Sydney together with his wife, Irena, and son, Ryszard. My mother lived and worked there until August 1990, when, seriously ill, she returned to Poland and moved in with us in Warsaw. She died on June 12, 1991.

My mother's brother, his wife, and their son were the only other members of her family who survived the occupation, first, hiding out in Poland, as we did, and later, interned in a camp in Hungary.

Father's younger sister, her husband, and their son, Rittigstein-Rapaczyński, also survived. After her husband's death and her son's dismissal from the university in 1968, she emigrated to the United States, where she later died.

During the war, the following members of my closest family perished:

Father's mother—died of a heart attack on September 2, 1939, upon hearing the news of the outbreak of war.

Father's uncle, Eugeniusz Szancer—taken during a roundup in November 1939, died in Auschwitz.

Mother's brother, Dr. Marek Haber—fell in partisan combat. His wife, Maryla, and son, Wilhelm, as well as my mother's mother, all perished during the liquidation of the Jews in Limanowa.

---

1. See *Volksdeutscher* in glossary.

2. *Treuhandstelle* [trustees' place] was a storage depot for confiscated Jewish property.

3. The *Volksliste* was a list of Poles of German descent who had declared loyalty to Germany.

4. See Home Army in glossary.

5. See Żegota in glossary.

6. See Warsaw Ghetto Uprising in glossary.

7. The Polish People's Army [*Ludowe Wojsko Polskie*], formed in 1944 when the Soviets re-entered Poland, was a combination of the First Polish Army (see glossary), formed in the Soviet Union, and the People's Army [*Armia Ludowa*], a leftist resistance movement operating inside Poland.

8. Praga is a district of Warsaw on the eastern bank of the Vistula River.

9. See "Historical Notes," July 1946, for Kielce pogrom.

10. The Polish government favored "workers" and discriminated against the intelligentsia.

11. Bolesław Bierut was the first postwar Communist leader of Poland.

12. Beneficiaries of disability pensions are classified into three groups and receive pensions according to the severity of their disability and suffering.

13. In 1968 there were student demonstrations in Poland against government censorship. They were crushed by the Communist regime and blamed on "Zionists" (*some* of the students and professors who backed

them were Jewish). A wave of anti-Zionism and anti-Semitism followed. Jews were accused of not being loyal to Poland and were often demoted or summarily dismissed from their jobs. At this time about 30,000 Jews who had survived in Poland or returned to Poland after the war emigrated.

14. State Office for the Utilization of Nuclear Energy—*Biuro Pełnomocnika Rządu do Spraw Wykorzystania Energii Jądrowej.*

RACHELA MALINGER

Born in 1927

The Beginning of Hell

It was the night before the Germans were expected to march into Łódź. The city had previously been shelled with artillery fire and bombarded. The shelling had gone on without interruption, so for a long time we couldn't leave the cellar, which had been quickly converted into a shelter. When things finally quieted down, we moved from the fifth floor, where we lived, and where the danger seemed greater, to our neighbors' on the ground floor. Fully dressed, holding in our hands bundles that contained only the most essential items (needed in case our own apartment was destroyed by a bomb or a shell), we lay on the floor, waiting for further events to unfold.

That night, knowing that the German army was already just outside the city, was the worst. The Germans were to enter Łódź the next day. What should we do, escape from the city or stay?

We had one night left to make the decision. It had to be made right away; the next day would already be too late. Those who decided to escape began to gather in the courtyard, loaded down with their household "treasures." "We'll go toward Warsaw. It's the capital, after all. They won't let the Germans in there," some people said, trying to convince others, but mainly themselves, that they had made the right choice. "Fools, what are you doing?" said the ones who decided to stay. "Can there be an effective defense against the Germans, with their technology and armaments?" Both sides were haunted by doubts, but there was no time for deliberation. After the farewells, tears, and despair, those who decided to escape moved out toward the gate in a long line.

Mama decided to stay. She was afraid that Papa might come back and not find us. Our courtyard on the Eleventh of November Street[1] reminded one of a large square-shaped well, surrounded by four six-story apartment buildings. An iron gate led out to the busy street, one of the four radiating out from Kościuszko Square. There were two grocery stores, one on each side of the gate. On the day the Germans entered the city, the shutters of the stores were closed, and the people who decided to stay looked at the Germans through the bars of the closed gate, trying to figure out what those people in bluish-gray uniforms were bringing them.

The Germans, seated in even rows on trucks, or riding on motorcycles, drove by our gate in the direction of Kościuszko Square, throwing fleeting glances at us. Some, having noticed the lovely face of my eighteen-year-old sister, smiled at her with unmistakable desire. These smiles gave some of the onlookers a wrong impression. "Well, they're people like anyone else," they said, and pitied those who had gone east into the unknown. "Look, they're smiling. They're not all beasts, after all," they repeated, wanting to convince others of that which they themselves wanted to believe. But we were soon convinced that human beings are always the victims of force and cruelty.

Those who went east on that horrible night, hoping for rescue, made a costly mistake. The long column of people, plodding along toward Warsaw with their "treasures," their children, and the elderly, were cruelly machine-gunned by Nazi warplanes. Not many were left alive. Having lost their relatives and loved ones, they returned to their deserted apartments in Łódź. We then learned from them about these dreadful events.

Soon we, too, the ones who had stayed in the city, found out that the soldiers' smiles did not mean anything good for us. Those smiles were not meant for us. Those were the smiles of victors, who took pride in having power over millions of defenseless people. The next day, as usual, I went to school. But changes were taking place there already. Classes in some subjects were forbidden, and after a week, the school was closed entirely. Why bother to educate children doomed for annihilation?

Soon the Germans issued an order that all Jews, including infants in baby carriages, were to wear a yellow Star of David on the left arm. Mama carefully sewed this emblem on our clothes. We children, not yet understanding the significance of this symbol, squabbled over whose star was prettier.

The streets became dangerous. One time I saw an old woman marked with a star sitting on the sidewalk selling some trifles, and a soldier kicked her in the face. Another time I witnessed a scene in the courtyard of the command post. Soldiers were tormenting a group of bearded old men who were standing in line; they had come in response to an order to surrender all bicycles and radio sets. They made them squat, jump, and crawl on the cobblestones. And on another occasion, there was the sound of a windowpane being broken in a store where not so long before Papa had taken me to buy sandals. The storekeeper had tried them on me while I sat on a high chair—pair after pair, until he found precisely those white ones that I had always dreamed about. And now, through the broken window, they were plundering and destroying the store, while a crowd of Aryans was laughing and egging them on against the Jews.

Day by day our living space was shrinking more and more. We were forbidden to walk on the main streets, but we still had to get food, and since we lived in the center of the city, we had to move about through courtyards and small alleys. Roundups were a great danger. They would grab everybody who happened to be on the street at that moment, load them on a truck, and take them in an unknown direction. People would come back from such roundups badly roughed up or would disappear altogether.

Once, while standing behind our gate and watching such a roundup near our house, I was horrified to see my sister among those captured. My sister, whose beautiful face made even the passersby take notice, used to take great pains to mask her good looks. She disheveled her black hair, smudged her cheeks with soot, and dressed in old, worn-out dresses. This helped a little. But who knows how this roundup might end for her? I ran home to report what I had seen. Mama immediately ran out into the street, and paying no heed to the danger of being caught herself, grabbed a soldier by the sleeve and began saying something quickly to him in German. The Fascist evidently got confused by the sight of a woman with a yellow star speaking in his native language. In a second, Mama pulled my sister out of the crowd. "Run away," she whispered to her. The gate was right there, and before the soldier knew it, both of them had disappeared. Thus, knowing the enemy's language turned out to be a salvation.

Life in occupied Łódź was becoming increasingly difficult. The general poverty brought people together. Our neighbors, who had at one time been divided—into the rich in their comfortable apartments on the lower floors, the middle-class on the fourth or fifth floors, and the poor in the basements and attics—became equals after having been marked with the Star of David. The results of each roundup—the stories of the lucky ones who returned home, the fate of the ones who didn't—all this concerned everybody in our building. What we heard often surprised us. Some people came back from these roundups roughed up, with their beards cut off or simply ripped out, and with other signs of cruelty and humiliation, while others returned with small bags of flour or groats as payment for their work. The impression that was created was that the Germans had not yet received definitive instructions from "above" about how to treat people in the occupied areas. Thus, while general rules in keeping with Fascist ideology were followed, what actually took place depended on the "amateurish creativity" of the occupiers. Poland was the site then where they were testing how to carry out their theories in practice.

One evening, we heard loud knocking at our door. We were terrified—it was past curfew, so it couldn't have been any of our acquaintances. The knocking at the door was persistent and ever louder. Mama pushed my brother and sister out on the back stairs, and taking me with her to the foyer, opened the door. A German soldier rushed in, showering us with curses, and calling us *verfluchte Juden* [cursed Jews]. "Where's your husband?" he asked. "He's not here; he was killed at the front," she answered. "And where's your son?" The soldier must have had information about our family from someone. "He went to Warsaw, to relatives," she lied. The uninvited guest began to loot the apartment, looked in the kitchen, and kicked Kajtuś, my favorite little cat.

Mama understood from his behavior that this was not a planned assault but rather an amateurish act of an occupier who chanced upon us, looking for something to eat. "Maybe you could use some money?" she asked gently, to make the question sound polite. But there was no need for courtesy. "Give it to me, give me the money," the robber in the Wehrmacht uniform readily agreed.

That time we ransomed ourselves with a modest sum, because it had only been a small private venture of one Fascist. But the occupier's policies were taking on a more incomprehensible and ever more terrifying form. Increasingly, our vocabulary began to include a word uttered with horror—*ghetto.*

---

1. "11-go Listopada" [11th of November] is a street named in honor of Polish Independence Day, first proclaimed at the end of World War I on November 11, 1918.

MARIA ORWID, NÉE PFEFFER

Born in 1930

Father

Sometimes when my fellow psychiatrists, especially Germans, ask me to what extent and how my traumatic childhood influenced my attitude as a psychiatrist, my banal response is that in my professional work, I place the greatest value on human dignity, the dignity of the patient. I've often wondered why it is that dignity is so important. It is probably due to many reasons—mainly to what my father instilled in me during my childhood. One situation in particular has etched itself in my memory. It is a short story about my father, already from the time of the Nazi occupation. My father's name was Dr. Adolf Pfeffer. He was an attorney in Przemyśl who had studied in Kraków and Vienna. He was born on January 31, 1894, in Przemyśl and died of tuberculosis on May 17, 1943, in Lwów—on Aryan papers. I was with him then.

As long as I can remember, we had this custom in Przemyśl that every evening we would all gather at Grandma and Grandpa Weinstock's. Toward the end of June 1941, right after the German attack on Przemyśl, I was walking in the evening, as usual, to my grandma's, this time across Kolejowy [Railroad] Square. I noticed a commotion in the square. I came closer and saw that a man was lying on the ground, while German soldiers were kicking him with their boots and screaming something at him. A small crowd looked on. I walked up even closer. The man on the ground—it was my papa. I froze with horror and fear.

After a while the soldiers stopped and headed toward the train station—they were going to the eastern front. They were full of fury. Papa got up with difficulty. He brushed himself off and wiped his hands on his clothes. He was very pale and didn't say anything. Suddenly, he saw me. He immediately put a finger to his lips, which meant, "Don't say anything." He walked off toward Grandma's house, with me following, in total silence. When we got to the door, he said, "Kitten,"—he usually called me that—"not a word about this." I nodded.

When we walked into Grandma's house, he went to the bathroom and washed his hands for a long time. He was still very pale. At Grandma's that evening, there was an acquaintance, a very beautiful, elegant lady, the wife of an attorney. When Papa reappeared from the bathroom, she was just saying, "Oh, what luck that those primitives (the Soviets) are gone, now we have *Kulturträger;*[1] they can't do us any harm. Perhaps things won't be all that good, but at least we'll be dealing with people of culture." (This lady perished in Auschwitz.) Before I could think, Papa grew even paler and said to me, "Come, Kitten, let's go home." We walked out, leaving Mama at Grandma's. She didn't know what it was all about and got upset.

We lived very close by. We walked side by side, this time in complete silence. I don't remember how Papa behaved that evening and what he told Mama. The next day he was silent. I watched him with anxiety. I knew how he felt. In the morning he sat down at a little table between the windows, with his back to us, and began reading Shakespeare. He read and read for an entire year, until July 1942, when we had to move to the ghetto. All that year he didn't say a word to Mama or to me. He ate very little, and only when some food was handed to him. He just read Shakespeare the whole time.

Years later, when I was already a psychiatrist, I began doubting my memories and the adequacy of human recollection, and I got into a quandary. Did all this really happen? Or did I just make it up, using a child's imagination to glorify Papa even more? I never asked Mama about it, because I didn't have the courage to confront this possibility.

Only recently, these doubts were cleared up for me quite unexpectedly. My cousin, ten years my senior, the late Gustaw Pfeffer, unexpectedly asked me, "Do you remember how your father sat all year and read Shakespeare?" I reacted with joy and disbelief, "It's true then; I didn't make it up?" My cousin didn't understand and answered, amazed, "Naturally you didn't make it up. It was I who, a few months before, had brought your father the *Collected Works of Shakespeare;* he'd always been fascinated by him." The doubts were dispelled. Thus, the drama that Papa had experienced was confirmed. I had understood him well! Despite everything, I felt happy; my papa had defended his human dignity.

---

1. *Kulturträger* (German) means "carrier of culture." (Author's note)

ALINA PARZĘCZEWSKA

Born in 1934

A Good Hiding Place

I am not describing the events chronologically but according to the impact, the depth of emotions that remain in my memory.

When in May 1945 the bells were ringing, announcing the end of the war, Mama and I fell into each other's arms. Mama burst out in violent sobbing and couldn't calm down for a long time. I had never seen her in such a state before; even in the most difficult moments, she was always composed. Now I understood that out of our whole large family in Poland—from Odrzywół, Przysucha, Warsaw, and Łódź—we were the only two left alive. But even two was a lot!

When I found myself in the Association of "Children of the Holocaust" in Poland, I understood that I was very lucky, not only because I had survived, but because I *knew* my parents, grandfathers, grandmother, and cousins. I have no prewar photographs, but long ago, in school, I attempted to re-create a likeness of my father on a postcard that had a picture of Juliusz Słowacki—by changing the poet's hair, the shape of his mustache, his collar. . . .

I know that during the war I was a witness (perhaps the only living one) to several events, which I want to describe. I want to depict the atmosphere of those times when there was a ghetto in Warsaw and an Aryan side, to recall people whom no one else will remember. Sometimes I recall the image of Ewa-Agata, who, in a manner known only to herself, constantly traveled back and forth between the two sides. She brought back secret addresses of Poles who were willing to take in Jews from the ghetto for an appropriate payment. This applied mainly to women and girls who had "Aryan looks" or to very little children, of whom there were few left. She helped many people, including me.

Sometimes I remember sixteen- or eighteen-year-old Janusz, who was at one time put to work cleaning up *Umschlagplatz,*[1] and his eight-year-old brother, Hermuś, crying at night with his parents. . . . I cannot forget Tosia, a girl rescued from *Umschlagplatz* by mistake. . . .

But first I want to describe the shock that split my life in half (well, maybe not exactly in half). After it, I would talk about "this was before *that*" or "this was after *that.*" The event relates to my own personal "Snow White" and a Hebrew language textbook.

That day I was sitting with some women, our neighbors, at a long table in a large apartment on Muranowski Square in the ghetto. We settled in this apartment after getting out of *Umschlagplatz* (I'll write about *Umschlagplatz* another time). The apartment was nice, with beautiful old furniture. I don't know who had owned the apartment or the furniture and the other things that were left behind in a great rush. There were some Hebrew books and newspapers, and Mama even found some kasha in the kitchen. I found a strange piece of a chain with geometric patterns and circles and a piece of coral stone of a strange shape topped with a dome-shaped wire screen. Later, on the Aryan side, I was told to throw it out because it was "some kind of Ashkenazi Jewish piece of work." What do you know! Even a chain was "Jewish!"

Getting back to the subject, that day—it was February or March—the morning sun was shining brightly. Besides me, there were two neighbors sitting at the long table; an older one, with black hair fastened in the back of her head, was playing solitaire, having put her coat and purse on the chair next to her. She wore a wool scarf on her shoulders. She hadn't gone to the "shop"[2] with her husband that day, because she wasn't feeling well.

The other was a girl with dark, wavy hair. That morning, her parents had gone to work in the shop. Unfortunately I can't remember her name, but in my thoughts, I call her "Snow White." Behind us there was a large, dark cupboard, and in it were tablecloths, dish towels, and napkins, carefully folded by the previous owners. In the drawers were silver dinner knives, small knives, big forks, dessert forks, tablespoons, and teaspoons. On top there were lovely little porcelain pitchers, which Ewa-Agata exchanged for carrots, beets, or potatoes. In the corner of the room was a large grandfather clock, and scattered beside it, in disarray, were children's toys, books, coral necklaces, a ball, and a doll's baby carriage—with the comforter folded back but no doll inside. While cleaning up, Mama superstitiously avoided that corner with its toys that had belonged, not so long ago, to a little girl. I, too, was afraid to touch that empty little carriage. . . .

The apartment had one great advantage: after looking around a bit, we found a great hiding place in case of a blockade.[3] This was not some room behind a wardrobe, where I had a scarf tied over my mouth and was taught to hold my breath so that not even a heartbeat could be heard. This hiding place was out of the ordinary—through a little window in the kitchen or the bathroom, I don't remember which, one could get over onto the roof of a lower building next door and hide behind a chimney!

The neighbors had come to our room that day because of that hiding place. They sat and talked, while the girl filed her fingernails with a small file. On her slender wrist she wore a bracelet, and on her finger, a lovely ring. On her other wrist shone a little watch. In front of her, by her cuticle stick and small scissors, lay an open, worn-out book—it was a children's textbook for learning Hebrew, with large pictures of various animals, little horses. I sat next to her and looked at pictures in a large book about Snow White, then at those in the Hebrew book, back and forth. The girl was tall and slender and had her hair pinned up just like Snow White, except that instead of a ribbon, it was pinned with two little combs. "You're like Snow White," I told her. She laughed, touched the tip of my nose with her finger, and said, "And you're Dopey!"

The neighbor beside us mumbled something. She was getting more and more upset; her solitaire game wasn't going well, so she picked up the cards and laid them out again. I could hear Mama in the kitchen as she shuffled pots, opened windows, and went out on the stairs. She was on the alert whether a blockade was coming. Everything was cold in the apartment. We couldn't even leave warm water in the teapot. In case there was an inspection during a blockade, everything was to look as if no one had been there, that everyone was at work in the shop. I remember that Snow White leaned over her book, pointed to something with her finger, and said "And what's a *sus*?"[4] when Mama ran suddenly into the room and yelled, "They're already here!" Each of the women grabbed her things, I buttoned my sweater, and we all crowded by the little window.

The neighbor with the cards went out on the roof first and hid behind the chimney so she wouldn't be seen. Next, the girl slipped out through the window and lay down behind another chimney. Mama pushed me out, crawled out herself, and pulled the curtain over the window. I was very scared, but the girl held out her hand from behind her chimney, as if to beckon to us. Pushed by Mama, on all fours, I got to the chimney behind which the girl was sitting. We sat off to the side, so that we couldn't be seen from the apartment window. I heard yelling, greatly intensified by megaphones. Mama leaned sideways against the chimney and put her free arm around me. We were all safe; we couldn't be seen from the windows in the apartment.

Suddenly, close by, I heard German being spoken. I looked up and saw two helmets and two gun barrels high up at the edge of the roof of our building. They were screaming something. From up there they could see only me and Mama, because we were sitting at the side of the chimney and not behind it. All of a sudden, a shower of golden, tiny, pointed cylinders fell all around. These were shells, shining in the sun like golden pellets. Sometimes when they hit the roof, sparks would fly. Mama and I sat, silent and still. I didn't look up anymore. The sun was shining harshly, and there were more and more of these little golden pellets. They jumped around and rolled off the roof. I thought that after the shooting ended, I would pick them up and show them to the children in the courtyard.

And then a piercing thought reminded me, "In what courtyard? What children?!" There were no more children in the courtyard, and in a short while, I would also soon be gone. "Dear God," I prayed silently. "Dear God, don't let these golden pellets hit us." I didn't see, but I heard and sensed it as the neighbor ran out from behind her chimney and, running toward the window, yelled, "Let's go back, they'll kill us here." Later, they said that this woman's nerves couldn't take it; she ran, zigzagging back to the little window. She didn't make it. There was a horrible scream, a thump, and, for the moment, everything fell silent.

We both sat as if turned to stone. From above, they were screaming something. I heard "*Donnerwetter, verfluchte . . .*" [Damn it, cursed . . .] Later, Mama, who knew German very well, told me that they were berating themselves for shooting so badly. Their ammunition was running out, but none of them wanted to bother going down to get more rounds. Besides, the blockade was over. Only they and we were left on the roof. They decided to shoot more accurately with the last few remaining bullets. Again they yelled for us to come down from that roof. One was particularly loud, yelling and cursing terribly. He cursed us, his buddy, and even himself for having missed so badly; he cursed everything and everyone. More golden pellets fell beside me. Suddenly blood spurted out, my arm and leg were red; blood flowed under me, I felt I was sticking to the roof. The red spots grew larger on my white sweater. Mama held me tight, and we didn't move anymore. My last thought was that I had just died, but I didn't make a sound.

When I opened my eyes, I was standing in the middle of some courtyard in a basin of water. Mama was sitting in a chair beside me. The blockade was over. A woman was taking my sweater off, wiping me with a towel, and kept saying with wonder, "She's not even scratched."

A ladder that was used to get us down from the roof stood nearby. The courtyard was full of people who had come back from the shop. Two young Ukrainians in German uniforms and a group of men stood off to the side. One of the men spoke briefly with Mama, then took things out of various pockets of his coat and vest and handed them to the soldiers, so they wouldn't take us away. They looked perplexed at the girl lying nearby. Then they approached her, "How did that happen?" one asked. They hadn't seen her when they were shooting, and she wasn't the one they were aiming at. It turned out that in that moment the girl had leaned out, as if to see something or to speak. Her head was then behind my arm and leg. The shots hit her in the neck.

In the end, both German soldiers rode off on a motorcycle. The husband of the neighbor who had been killed stood silently over her body. Her tousled hair stuck out from under the covering. The dead girl lay a little closer. Her father stood over her with clenched fists, her mother crying. And I, looking at her, suddenly began repeating, "What's a *sus*? What's a *sus*?"

Shortly after this, at almost the last moment before the ghetto uprising began, Mama and I got out through the sewers to the Aryan side. It was dangerous there, too, but I can't write about everything in one breath. Some other time.

---

1. See *Umschlagplatz* in glossary.

2. A "shop" was a forced labor workshop in the ghetto where shoemakers, brushmakers, and tailors worked for the Germans. (Author's note)

3. A blockade was the closing off of streets to prevent escape while all the inhabitants were rounded up for deportation.

4. *Sus* (Hebrew) means horse, one of the first words of elementary Hebrew. (Author's note)

EDMUND RUDOLF DE PELLIER

Born in 1931

First in Line to Go to Heaven

Fragments of Memories

We were children of happiness and joy, my twin sister, Ida-Joanna, and I. Our mama—Luiza, née Sprecher—had a degree in pharmacy, while Papa—Jan—was a physician.

Our mama's family was among the wealthiest in Lwów. We had many factories, hotels (including the famous Hotel George), apartment buildings, movie theaters, etc. The Sprechers were also active in charity work for the poor, whether for Jews, Poles, or Ukrainians. They built a hospital for Jews on Kurkowa Street and continued to support it. Gifts to the poor were distributed from our chocolate factories (called Branka and Hazet), while our pharmaceutical company, Lancon, provided assistance to hospitals and drugstores.

We lived together with Grandpa and Grandma, the parents of our mama, at 2 Akademicka Street, across the street from our Hotel George. We occupied the sixth floor. The building was eight stories tall and was the tallest structure in Lwów. People called it "the skyscraper." Outside (and inside) the walls were covered with light brown marble. The building was beautiful and modern and had an iron-reinforced concrete structure and a high-speed elevator.

In 1936 my sister and I entered first grade at St. Kinga's School. It was a large and beautiful school. Grandpa used to take us to school in a very pretty Fiat or a Mercedes or sometimes in a *bryczka.*[1] Once a week after school we drove around with Grandpa and Grandma to our family's different enterprises—to the Branka chocolate factory, to the Lancon pharmaceutical company, to the hotels, and to other properties. On Mondays the children at school always waited for us because we used to bring lots of candy and pastries. On Saint Nicholas Day we would go to school in the *bryczka,* and Saint Nicholas would ride with us with packages for children—poor and wealthy, Polish, Jewish, and Ukrainian, for everyone who went to school with us.

Each year Grandpa would take one of the poor children on vacation with us. We went to Gdańsk, Berlin, and Paris.

We spent the years from 1936 to 1939 without a worry—studying and going on family trips. We studied very diligently and had a tutor at home who did homework with us and taught us good manners—proper behavior both in school and at the table, as well as respect for every religion and for older people and also love of family.

At times, I close my eyes and can see our carefree childhood of those years. Like a dark night, everything is gone—it is not a dream, it is the tragic truth.

It was 1939, and antiaircraft drills were being conducted on the streets. The threat of war was hanging over us. We children paid little attention—we didn't understand the danger. Everyone at home was issued gas masks, and Grandpa ordered a shelter prepared in our iron-reinforced concrete "skyscraper." The cellar had two levels, and within a few days four rooms were furnished like salons; they differed little from the rooms above. There was so much food gathered in the pantries that we could have lived off it for two years without going outside. Grandpa, Uncle, and Grandma said that no bomb could touch us there, because it was a genuine bunker.

In the first days of school in September 1939, our Polish language teacher, Mr. Wójcicki, told us, with tears in his eyes, "Dear, beloved children, in the next few days we will certainly have to interrupt our lessons, and perhaps we will never see each other again, because this is war. Do not forget God and the Fatherland."

And then it started. During the first air raid, bombs fell on the Mikolasch Arcade and the railroad station. The blast was so powerful that our whole house shook. We started crying and cowering in our parents' arms. We understood that something terrible was happening, but this was only the beginning of the war.

Everything that was beautiful in our family—happiness, joy, wealth—were all nothing in the face of war; they all vanished. It is difficult to describe all of it, but life became a road of torment. The war of 1939 lasted only a very short time. I remember, as if through a fog, that there were always guests in our house, even during air raids. These were officers, magnates, manufacturers, all deliberating what to do. My papa and mama had American passports and hoped that this would save us.

September 17: In Lwów there was a great shock, because the war was with the Germans, but it was the Soviet army that marched into Lwów. From a window in our skyscraper, we watched how crowds of people greeted the Bolsheviks. We also noticed that the Polish higher-ranking officers had changed into civilian clothes.

This was the first blow for our family, because the Bolsheviks mainly looked for factory owners, bankers, and other rich people. We were at the top of the list for deportation to Siberia. We thus thought about going into hiding. We had to watch out for certain Jewish neighbors whom we knew to be Communists. In our whole family there was panic and fear—what will become of the children? Nobody worried about our possessions anymore.

For a few days there was dead silence. One day my sister and I were in Hotel George, across the street from our skyscraper, because all sorts of valuables there were being packed up. When we went out of the hotel with our uncle, we saw that there were two Russian cars and a large army truck in front of our house. Uncle tried to convince us that we should wait on the street until they went away or go back to the hotel, but we insisted that we wanted to go to Mama and Papa. It turned out that the house was full of guests. These were high-ranking Russian officers, and we later found out they were Bolshevik NKVD [Soviet Secret Police]. We did not sense any fear at home; Mama was lively, and the officers were very courteous. This whole crowd was brought to us by a Communist named Ari Zusman, who came from a poor Jewish family and not so long before was still selling lemonade at the market.

Mama was delighted when we arrived. There was plenty of food and wine on the table, and Zusman behaved as if he were in his own home. We were told that we were in no danger and that although the Soviet government would take over our properties, Papa would still remain in charge. The feast lasted until late into the night. Nobody believed Zusman, and the family decided to escape, as far from Lwów as possible.

I remember, as if it were today, that very late at night in November 1939, the NKVD came to our house accompanied by several Jews we knew (because formerly, they had been our employees), dressed in Russian uniforms. These Jews were very aggressive. My mama was very beautiful, and as I recall from a subsequent conversation between my grandparents, two of these Jews with the NKVD wanted to rape her. An officer calmed them down.

They demanded that the documentation of the factories, hotels, movie theaters, and other property be turned over to them. "You are no longer the masters; the Communist authorities now rule," they said. My parents remained calm and asked them to sit down and have some tea, but they said they would make it themselves and walked around the apartment, opening drawers. The Russian officer told them not to touch anything. An argument ensued; the officer told them he was in charge and took out his pistol. The situation became dangerous. He put them at attention and told them to get out.

The house was filled with fear. The officer received all the documents; he even made out a receipt and said, "Now, my host, give us some vodka." There was plenty of that dreadful stuff in our house. They got food and drink. There were three of them, and they even sent for those who had been told to get out. They ate and drank their fill, and each got several bottles of Baczewski vodka[2] and plenty of food for the road. But these Jews who had worked for us and were now in Russian uniforms in drunken condition insisted that the NKVD officer take us this very day to prison. Once again it nearly ended in shooting. In the end, the officer telephoned military headquarters, which quickly sent some people who handcuffed those four Jews collaborating with the NKVD and took them away in their car. As we found out later, they were shot to death in the jail on Jachowicza Street.

This didn't change much, only postponed the verdict. As members of the bourgeoisie, we were doomed anyway to be deported to Siberia or killed on the spot.

We survived the Bolshevik invasion. Our family consisted of twenty-nine people. Nearly everyone avoided the Bolshevik deportations to Siberia, except for one uncle, my mother's brother, who committed suicide in 1940. We were in hiding with our good friends. We were completely safe and living in very good conditions, divided into five groups. In 1941 the Bolshevik Army was decisively defeated and fled. After the Germans arrived, we came out of hiding. We returned home unimpeded. However, the situation soon repeated itself. One day Germans came to our house. They behaved elegantly—they said they knew about our holdings, that we were in no danger. They said a separate district would soon be set up in Zamarstynów, where all the Jews would live and work. These visits by German officers recurred several times.

From the time the Nazis entered Lwów, Papa and Mama were employed in our Lancon pharmaceutical plant at 6 Zamkowa Street. They wore green armbands with the Star of David, designating them as workers at a military plant.

We experienced much ill treatment from the *Judenrat*[3] and the Jewish police. This happened later, in the ghetto, but for the time being, we lived on the Aryan side, except that we all had to wear armbands with the Star of David. Once again, there was danger and fear, because it was clear that this would be the end for us. People who did not live through this horrible nightmare and know it only from stories will never understand. As I remember it, I was living in constant fear and dread.

Later, an announcement appeared saying that all Jews and their families had to move to the outskirts of Lwów. There we were to make our homes and live—such was the order of the *Stadthauptman* [commander] of the city of Lwów. We were enclosed in a ghetto. There was an unceasing commotion—shooting, fires, inhuman cries. My twin sister and I took all of this very hard. Papa used to give us some kind of medication so we wouldn't cry or be afraid. We were completely numb to everything. As long as our parents were with us, we got the medication. After they were gone, we were left alone and had to hide like mice. We had no medication, and we experienced this whole horror in its full intensity.

But God's hand protected us. Before the liquidation of the ghetto, we were taken in by an Aryan family who knew our parents from before the war. They saved my life, but my sister perished. This was a very decent family, linked to the AK. I owe my miserable life to them. Mr. Stanisław Grabowski, with whom I was in hiding, received recognition by the Jewish Historical Institute in Warsaw and the medal of Righteous Among the Nations of the World from Yad Vashem in Jerusalem. His family received four such medals.

I was brought back to Poland[4] by Dr. Smerek, who handed me over to the Kędzierski family in Przemyśl. Dr. Kędzierski, in turn, placed me with his relatives in Kraków, a physician couple, Maria and Eliasz Kędzierski.

This was in 1946. I was a wreck, and I was placed in a hospital. I spent about three months there. A certain nightmare torments and haunts me all the time—fire, screams, fear, no place to hide. But it passes and then things get better.

I constantly receive medications, and when I don't forget to take them, things are quite good. I live like a cosmonaut, but I live. Because of my illness, I couldn't work anywhere. When my condition deteriorated, I was treated at a mental hospital. I am presently receiving outpatient treatment at a mental health clinic. When I take my medication, nothing bothers me. I am not afraid; I don't feel any anxiety or fear. But the memories sometimes return, and then my world collapses. The doctors tell me I shouldn't think about those years and that when something haunts me, I should immediately take my medication.

The things I went through on this earth will remain in books, in films. I should be the first in line to go to heaven for all that I have gone through, for our suffering, abuses, and humiliations.

---

1. A *bryczka* was an open, four-wheeled, horse-drawn carriage with a retractable top.

2. Baczewski was a well-known brand of vodka produced in Lwów before the war.

3. The *Judenrat* was the Jewish council appointed by the Germans to interface with the Jewish population and carry out German orders.

4. After the war was over, Poland's borders shifted west, and Lwów was no longer in Poland; it became part of Ukraine.

MARIA PERLBERGER-SCHMUEL

Born in 1933

"They're Jews, Don't Look in That Direction!"

We lived in Wieliczka.[1] Everything was ready—school supplies, book bag, and new and freshly starched smock. But on September 1, all those things were quickly forgotten. War! A strange, ominous word, but in some demonic way—fascinating. Everyone at home was busy taping the windows, but I was most interested in the flashlights with darkening glass filters on them (you could change the colors to yellow, green, and blue). In a word—a great toy!

I was walking on the street with Papa—suddenly we heard muffled explosions, as if someone were opening soda pop bottles one after another. It was an aerial battle. Several airplanes were circling—and at first, nothing. Only there were these white puffs of smoke around them. Suddenly one flipped over and, like a bird that had been shot, began spiraling downward. Smoke was coming out of its tail. And so it fell, trailing a plume of black smoke behind it. Two others calmly flew off. Already on the first day of war German airplanes were flying over our city.

I don't know and I don't remember what all happened after that. Some conversations, deliberations, should we run away—or should we not—and suddenly, we too, like the others, found ourselves on the road. Our first stop was a peasant's cottage. Plenty of others like us were there—refugees. Whether we were there a week or only a day, I don't know. Mama decided to return with me to town; the men, including Papa, continued on. The roads were full. Carts, bundles, horses, and crowds; masses of people were walking, everybody headed in a different direction, just to keep moving, to escape. Suddenly, an airplane appeared in the sky, dove low, and simply began strafing this human mass with its machine gun. Nearby, a soldier in a dirty, wrinkled uniform began to shoot (from a regular rifle!) at the airplane. People began screaming at him that he was endangering everyone, so he stopped. Mama dragged me down into a ditch, and we lay there, curled up. The airplane flew off as suddenly as it had appeared.

We returned to our apartment. At about that time, the new authorities issued an order to hand in all radio sets, weapons, etc. The penalty for not turning over these things was severe. Mama decided not to give up our radio. She hid it (how naive!) behind the wardrobe. The deadline for turning in radios had already passed long ago. One day someone rang the doorbell. They were German soldiers. "You haven't handed in your radio," they said in German. Without a word, Mama took the radio from behind the wardrobe (in their presence) and handed it to them. They didn't yell; they even said, "Thank you"—and left.

Suddenly, the mood at home became secretive. I was not allowed to enter the bedroom, and then Mama sent me off to my aunt's. Eventually, the mystery was solved. Papa had come back from his attempt to escape, but nobody was supposed to know about it. This was a time of uncertainty. For the time being, Papa decided to leave town, where everyone knew him, and move in with his sister in Kraków. Mama rented a peasant's cart, Papa was covered with straw, and in this way, he was taken to Kraków.

A few days later Mama told me that I, too, would be going to Kraków, to Grandma's. I was also taken in a peasant's cart; by then Jews were not allowed to travel by train. Mama returned home, and I stayed with Grandma, alone without my parents for the first time. After a few weeks I returned home.

I attended our local school. That part of Poland was then already called the General Government.[2] Schools were under the control of the German authorities. There were only two or three of us Jewish girls in the class. One day, our teacher told us that she would take us (i.e., the Jewish girls) home personally. The rest of the class was bursting with envy. "Well, those Jewish girls are really in good with the teacher!" We went home. Our teacher talked to Mama for a long time in the sitting room.

After she left, Mama told me that the schools were probably going to be closed for the winter, since after all, it was war, and there wasn't enough fuel. That's exactly how it was during the First World War when Mama herself was a pupil. During the following days, girls from school came over and reported what they had been studying that day. "How can they be learning, if the schools are closed?" It was only then that I found out the truth. The schools were not closed; it was only that Jews could no longer attend.

At that time, we still had with us our Catholic maid—Józia. This Józia often took me with her to church, even bought me a rosary and a prayer book. She told me that any Christian could baptize anyone who really wanted it. Because that was just what I wanted, I convinced her to baptize me in church. She sprinkled me with holy water, and from that time on, I considered myself a genuine Catholic.

Once I ran into a group of children, who, as usual, began to call me names, "Jew, Jew!" I told them that I wasn't a Jew anymore, because I had gotten baptized, but I asked them not to tell my parents. From that time on I had no peace. One of the girls constantly followed me, demanding that I give her dolls, books, and toys, saying, "If you don't, I'll tell your mama that you're a Catholic now."

Around that time, the Germans requisitioned one of our rooms as quarters for one of their officers. He turned out to be a relatively peaceful man. He held long conversations with Papa. Once he said that all Jews would be shipped off to Madagascar. He was later transferred, and no one else was assigned to us afterward.

Days, weeks, and months passed. Rumors spread that the Germans were going to establish a ghetto in Kraków where they would confine all the Jews. At that time, many Jews from

Kraków and vicinity came to our town to avoid being enclosed in the ghetto. All these new arrivals tried to find a place for themselves to live. There were lots of them everywhere.

Suddenly, Mama's whole family—my grandparents, her two sisters, and their families—descended upon us. We turned over most of the apartment to them; some of our furniture was moved to the attic. The apartment, once spacious, became overcrowded. The atmosphere was poisoned. There were no open quarrels, but each person looked askance at the other.

It was 1941 already. The Germans then ordered all Jews twelve years old and over to wear armbands with the Star of David. Because this order did not yet apply to me, I could continue to walk freely about town. I had only one concern—that my family might find out that I was going to church. One time Papa asked me, "Marysia, what's the story about this church?" but that was the end of it.

One of our neighbors was a certain Mr. Grzywacz. A large white plaque proclaimed, CERTIFIED SURVEYOR, FELIKS GRZYWACZ. I didn't know then what "certified surveyor" meant, but it sounded important and impressive. Out of the blue, the surveyor declared himself a *Volksdeutscher.* Germans were constantly hanging around there, the Grzywacz family were always throwing noisy parties, and finally, some German officer was quartered there. This one hated Jews—not only in theory and along propaganda lines. When he saw a Jew, he would simply go berserk, foam at the mouth, scream, yell, and curse. Getting through the stairway then became a real problem. We had to sneak through quietly, look all around, and only then, when we succeeded in going down and out the gate or in and up the staircase without running into the beast, only then was it possible to breathe freely until the next time.

Around that time I found a real friend, Wanda Duszczyńska, whose mother was my parents' friend. Wanda was from Warsaw and had been living in Wieliczka with her mama and grandma only for a short time. Her father had remained in Warsaw.

Wanda lived in a neighborhood called Zadory, in a small house with a garden that served as an excellent place to play.

When winter came, the Germans ordered the Jews to surrender all the furs they owned. We only handed in our fur collars and gave all our other furs to Mrs. K., a doctor's wife, for safekeeping.

Spring came. Again, Wanda and I played in the garden. I was about nine then; Wanda was about a year older. We were interested in very "adult" and forbidden subjects—that is, such as how children came into the world. The theories we then came up with were indeed original! But in the end we didn't solve the puzzle. We exhausted the subject, and, bored with it, we went back to our dolls. These weren't just ordinary dolls—they were cut out of magazines, with fantastic, impossible names—but the possibilities for play were endless. We used to leave all those other "real" dolls at home, forgotten. However, when I turned nine (this was my last birthday at home), I was delighted with a gift from my parents. It was a doll, a beautiful "prewar" doll. She had blond hair, a blue dress, and closed her eyes and said, "Mama!" She was so beautiful, it was a shame to take her out of the box. I never had another chance to play with her.

It was then that I discovered the world of books. I kept company with *Anne of Green Gables,* I was sold and chased, together with the black slaves from *Uncle Tom's Cabin,* and I traveled from the Apennines to the Andes with an Italian boy, the hero of a story in the book *The Heart.*[3]

The summer of 1942 arrived and with it, vacation. Mrs. Zapiórowa, my teacher, gave Mama a report about my progress in studies. She even told her that I was at a higher level than other children my age (of course, she didn't say this in my presence, but I already had big ears then). This was about the time when rumors of an impending "action" against Jews began circulating. When the rumors became widespread, we decided to make a hideout for our family on Papa's side. The courthouse building belonged to us. One of its wings had been empty since the beginning of the war. At that time, one of Papa's sisters, who had come from Kraków to avoid being closed up in the ghetto, lived there with her children. Some of her furniture was moved into one of the empty rooms of the building. It was decided to convert this room into a hideout. Its tall door was to be covered with a huge cupboard. The court beadle, who lived downstairs, was to try to get food for everyone hiding there.

We all gathered there, and the door was barricaded with the cupboard. It was awful. It seemed like there was no air, that the room was overcrowded, even though there weren't that many of us there. It was the blocked door that intensified the feeling of overcrowding and fear. The fear of the adults also infected us children. Everyone talked and talked, and I listened without understanding. They said something about the possibility of shooting, of the building being set on fire—the fear stuck in my throat and choked me. The men began practicing jumping out of the window that faced the orchard—where I used to play. After a few practice jumps, they came to the conclusion that if the building were surrounded, it would be of no use. There, outside the window, the sun was shining, bees were buzzing, and here, this fear, so terrible.

In the evening, the beadle came and said that we had to leave the place immediately or he would denounce us to the Germans. We all went to our respective homes. Mama wanted to ensure my safety somehow, so we went to Aunt N., one of Papa's sisters. Deep despair reigned there. They paid no attention to me and talked about things I shouldn't have heard, about poison having been prepared, about the fact that they were ready to take it.

My aunt's son, Rysiek, was twenty already, so he was likely to be taken for forced labor. (Did they know by then what fate awaited those who weren't taken for work?) Mama pleaded with him to take me with him as his own daughter (at the beginning, children of these workers were issued "cards of life").[4] Nobody was thinking logically anymore, because even if Rysiek had had children, then it certainly couldn't have been a nine-year-old daughter! Because this plan seemed uncertain, we went back home. The streets looked so normal, like on any other day; the weather was beautiful, but here, in our hearts, were feelings of helplessness, despair, and—fear. From then on my family began saying that it would be safer to hand me over to a Polish family for "safekeeping" (like our furs?).

Wieliczka was the county seat. A few days before the action, all the Jews from nearby towns assembled there, as ordered by the Germans. There was no time to lose. It was decided that I would go to Mrs. Duszczyńska and she would take me from Wieliczka to another town.

It was the last day before the planned action. Large posters plastered all over town proclaimed that all Jews should gather at the assembly point at a given hour. Anyone who stayed behind at home would be shot. Whoever hid a Jew would be shot. Whoever helped a Jew in any way would be shot. Mama prepared little pouches for the whole family, to be worn around the neck, and put some money in them. One of my aunts and her daughter had Aryan papers. All through the war they had moved about and traveled freely, but now, all of a sudden, they decided not to use those papers. Everyone was overcome by despair and completely resigned. It was already getting light outside when suddenly someone rang the bell. It was Mrs. Duszczyńska.

The Germans had reinforced their patrols and posted them all over the center of town. There, they gathered all the Jews from the other streets. However, my parents decided to remain in our apartment until the end. Papa broke down completely and began sobbing loudly. He no longer spoke, only cried. Mama, still trying to convince him to change his mind, pleaded with him.

I don't know when I found myself on the stairs. Mama was leaning over the handrail and kept repeating, "Well, go already, go!" But I turned around one more time and exclaimed (but in a whisper), "Bye, Mama, run away!" "Yes, yes, we'll run away, but go already, go!" and that was all. I managed to get out; nobody saw me. The streets were empty, not a soul anywhere. And then I started to run. I didn't know that I was starting a new game—a game of hide-and-seek with death.

It was decided not to delay but to take me to Kraków early the next morning. I couldn't fall sleep. It was quiet outside, but from time to time, I heard single shots—one, two—and then silence again. Only the dogs were barking, a regular canine concert. "What's happening there?" I kept thinking. "Why this shooting?" My heart pounded like a jackhammer. Finally, exhaustion prevailed, and I fell asleep.

Early the next morning, Mrs. Duszczyńska woke me up. "My mother will take you to Kraków. We'll dress you up like Wanda. She'll stay home, but if any of the neighbors see you, they'll think it is she who is going to Kraków with her grandma." We were about the same height, only my braids were longer, but we had the same auburn-colored hair. My braids were shortened. They dressed me in Wanda's coat and her little hat. (It was good that the hat covered my eyes and nearly half my face!) We had to hurry. We were to take the first train to Kraków. Wanda's grandmother took me by the hand, and we set out on our way.

It was a long way to the station. The streets were still almost empty. Suddenly, on another street, around the corner, I saw a mass of people, so dense that it almost didn't seem to be moving. There was something unreal about it. No sound was coming from there, but when I looked more closely, I saw that this mass was moving, heading in some direction. I could even make out individual figures of women, children, and men, their bundles and suitcases. I didn't understand what it was, so I asked Wanda's grandmother. "They're Jews, don't look in that direction," she said. So these were Jews, and I was not supposed to look in their direction. Obediently I turned my eyes away and didn't look "there" anymore, even though the streets ran parallel.

Meanwhile, we were approaching the station, the traffic was increasing, people were rushing to the train from all directions, going to work. After all, it was a regular weekday. "They" were herded toward the freight train station. Then the streets diverged, and I couldn't see them anymore. (From that day on "they" were the Jews, and "we" were the Poles, Christians. . . .) It didn't even occur to me that my parents might be there among them—after all, Mama had promised me that they would both run away.

Wanda's grandmother bought us tickets, and we entered a compartment. Fortunately, there wasn't anyone there who might have known me. The train started moving. I crossed myself. What I had done in secret at home now became a necessity. Wanda's grandmother made the mistake of asking, "Do you know how to cross yourself? Cross yourself!" It's a good thing nobody heard.

One day, Mrs. Duszczyńska said that the birth certificate was ready and she would soon be taking me to Warsaw. The certificate (such an unimpressive-looking piece of paper) attested that Maria Teresa Nowakowska, born in Pińsk to Jan and Ludwika, née Gajewska, was baptized and inscribed in the parish books of the church of the Most Holy Virgin Mary in Pińsk. These were details I had to know by heart and be able to recite whenever asked. The day before leaving, Mrs. Duszczyńska came over, as usual, but started whispering secretively with the landlady, who looked at me with pity and sympathy. Later, I learned that Mrs. Duszczyńska told her my mother had died. She did it to somehow explain the fact that I was not going back home but rather to my aunt's in Warsaw.

The train to Warsaw was to leave that evening. Mrs. Duszczyńska told me to call her "Aunt," because "Mrs." might raise suspicions. However, the word "aunt," for someone who was not my aunt, stuck in my throat, so I addressed her as little as possible. Night fell. At some station, a bunch of German soldiers crowded onto the train. They took all the empty seats in our compartment. I was tired, my head was wobbly, my eyes wouldn't stay open. Mrs. Duszczyńska propped me up in the corner, when suddenly, one of the soldiers said that I would be better off on one of the luggage shelves. "And how do you say 'little girl' in Polish?" he asked. He tried to repeat it, but it came out garbled. Then, concerned that I might be cold, he took off his military overcoat, wrapped me in it, and lifted me onto the shelf. I smiled at him as a sign of appreciation. Oh, if he had only known who I was! And so I fell asleep. Mrs. Duszczyńska breathed more easily. Her dangerous ward slept wrapped up in a German soldier's overcoat, and that meant a safe trip all the way to our destination. In the morning the train arrived at Warsaw Central Station.

Mrs. Duszczyńska took me to a certain family in the Praga district. These were friends of Mrs. K., one of our neighbors in Wieliczka. I then found out that Mrs. K. would be the one to decide my fate from then on. I wasn't happy about that; I had grown attached to Mrs. Duszczyńska, but I couldn't choose my guardian. After a quick farewell with Mrs. Duszczyńska, who after all had to return, I was left alone once again.

Meanwhile, I had to get used to my new surroundings. The family consisted of an elderly woman and her two daughters, both single (and not very young). Out of the three, only one of the daughters, Wacława—who many years earlier had been Mrs. K.'s schoolmate—knew about my origins.

The apartment was spacious, furnished in an unpretentious style and—to my delight—there was even a piano in it! Right away, the very first night I spent in Warsaw, there was an air raid. Loud bangs and explosions rocked the air; the entire house shook in its foundation, while I trembled from cold and fear. With every new explosion, I yelled, "Jesus! Mary!" (I thought that this way I would prove myself as undeniably "Polish.") Eventually, things got quiet, and we all returned to the apartment. The first remark I heard from Miss Wacława, said in a sharp, accusatory tone, was "Polish children don't yell like that!" (because in her eyes, I was not a Polish child).

One day I told Miss Wacława that it was a good thing my first name, at least, didn't have to be changed, because I was always called Marysia. To this she replied, "Really? And I thought your name was Sara, or maybe Rachela!" From that time on she began taunting me by mocking the way Jews butchered the Polish language. At first I "swallowed" these remarks; later I tried to defend myself by saying that in my family we spoke good Polish, not Yiddish, and that I didn't even know one word in that language. Nothing helped. On the contrary, she didn't believe what I said and kept repeating her "attacks" in various ways.

Meanwhile, it became clear that I hadn't learned to lie well enough yet and missed giving myself away only by a hair. Some woman came to visit. I was introduced, of course, as Marysia Nowakowska. "Oh, I knew the Nowakowskis; perhaps it was your father. The one I knew was named Jan," she said. I replied, nearly joyfully (my memory didn't fail me—the birth certificate said "born to Jan . . ."), "My papa's name was also Jan!" So she said, "Yes, but that one had a brother." I wasn't prepared for this—I didn't know yet how to improvise on the spot. I fell silent. Miss Wacława broke in, "Well, did you have an uncle?" "I don't know," I replied, nearly in tears. After the woman left, I got scolded. "You can't hesitate, you have to be sure of yourself; answer quickly, no matter what!"

After that time I began to attach a great deal of importance to food (perhaps out of boredom?). I was simply hungry, which never happened at home, even during the war. There was a canary there, an ordinary yellow canary. Every day they placed a sugar cube between the bars of its cage. Once while I was alone in the room, that sugar cube began to tempt me. I took it out carefully, licked it, bit into it, and put it back between the bars of the cage. From then on, I bit off a piece of that poor canary's sugar every day, until one day, Miss Wacława said, "Somehow, recently, the sugar of our canary has been melting in a strange fashion." Naturally, I never touched the sugar again.

I waited. I knew someone would appear and take me from there. Perhaps I would be together with Mama? One day someone rang the doorbell, and—before they even opened the door—I knew it was about me. A woman with a pleasant expression on her face came in. She wanted to speak to Miss Wacława. After a few moments, I was summoned. "So this is the girl; she doesn't look it." (No, I didn't "look it"; "not looking it" in those days meant not looking like a Jew.) "My name is Irena Ch. I have a daughter who will help you with your lessons. I am sure you will like being with us."

When we walked out on the street, I gave my new guardian my hand, and for the first time in many weeks, I felt trust toward a stranger. We traveled through all of Warsaw by streetcar, from Praga to Koło. There was something nice in just the sight of the little, light-colored two-story houses there. The war, bombing—all that seemed quite far away. Built shortly before the war, this was a military neighborhood. Most of the homes were owned by officers like Mrs. Ch.'s husband, who, as a major in the Polish army, had been taken prisoner by the Germans.

We were welcomed by Wanda, Mrs. Ch.'s sixteen-year-old daughter, and Mrs. Zawadzka, her mother, an elderly woman whom I will from now on in this account call "Grandma." Wanda dug up a thick volume of *Płomyk,*[5] and with that she won me over completely. The autumn sun was still beating down. I sat on the stairs leading into the garden and read. I felt good. The next day I was introduced to all the neighbors. "The more relaxed you are, not avoiding people or acting afraid, the less they will speculate or suspect anything," Mrs. Ch. told me.

There were two apartments in our building. We lived on the ground floor, while on the second floor the Cz. family lived with their two sons, one of whom, Janusz, was Wanda's age, while the other, Zdzich, was a few years older. Their father, called "the Major" by everyone, had a bushy mustache, a deep voice—with which he reprimanded his sometimes unruly sons—and rather poor hearing. In the house next door lived a Mrs. G. with her eight-year-old daughter, Basia, who immediately invited me to play with her. That woman's husband, an officer, was also a prisoner of war, as was the husband of another neighbor, Mrs. Kamińska, who often visited Mrs. Ch. Not one of these neighbors questioned where I came from, nor did they pry into who I was. I quickly became friends with Basia; we were constantly together.

A few days after I arrived in Koło, one of our more distant neighbors appeared in our house. She attacked Mrs. Ch., saying,

"You are keeping a Jewish child! Yes, don't deny it, I had a good look at her while she was playing; she made such Jewish gestures with her hands!" Mrs. Ch. kept her composure. "But, my dear woman, don't say that! The other children won't want to play with her!" The woman, taken aback by such a response, said nothing more and walked off.

Mrs. K. regularly sent money transfers for my upkeep. The winter passed. The snow melted; nature, paying no heed to storms stirred up by people, was waking to new life. It was April. Gentle spring breezes brought with them the joyful atmosphere of spring and the approaching Easter holidays. Once again I played with Basia in the garden.

Suddenly, news of the uprising in the Jewish ghetto broke out. The surrounding streets were blocked, and streetcars didn't run near the ghetto wall anymore. Shots and explosions could be heard. The first plumes of black, dense smoke began rising over the ghetto. The underground press published reports confirming that the Jews were putting up armed resistance. There were even words of respect for the handful of diehards, but it was obvious that their struggle was hopeless. We went up on the roof but couldn't see anything besides smoke. At night there was a huge red glow in the sky. The fighting in the ghetto lasted several weeks (the underground press gave regular accounts of the situation). Gradually, the smoke began thinning out and finally cleared completely. The fighting was over. Suddenly, the rumble of an explosion shook the city. The Germans had blown up the synagogue on Tłomackie Street, which was not even within the boundaries of the ghetto. This is how they sealed their "victory."

I remember conversations and remarks made by people who visited us. These were mostly relatives of Mrs. Ch., occasionally acquaintances. Discussions would start about the then current Jewish topic. Somebody once said, "After the war we'll have to forgive Hitler all the harm he did to the Poles. Just the opposite, he deserves a monument, because he freed Poland from the Jewish plague." Mrs. Ch. disagreed, saying that what the Germans had done with the Jews was barbaric, an inhuman deed. "It was the only way to solve the Jewish problem—nobody else would have dared to do it; a strong hand was needed. Hitler, he's a genius, perhaps an evil one, but a genius!" That was the response she got.

I listened and didn't say anything—children didn't take part in adult conversations. But from what I heard, I concluded that if I also talked like this, I would clear up any suspicions anyone might have regarding my origins. An opportunity soon presented itself. I was at a friend's house. We were playing, when her mother came in and started talking about Jews, about how terrible it was when the Germans were burning the ghetto. Because no one talked about these things with children, I understood she wanted to find out who I was. In an indifferent tone, I responded, "Oh, they reproduce like rats; there will still be plenty of them left." It helped.

One time our neighbor, Mrs. Kamińska, came over. She was very agitated. She told Mrs. Ch. something in a whisper and kept repeating, "Whoever heard of a nine-year-old child slashing his veins? It's beyond human understanding." After a while I found out what it was about. Between Koło and Żoliborz there was a young forest, planted just before the war. Children used to go there to play, and that day they found a little nine-year-old Jewish boy there, who had somehow managed to escape from the ghetto. The children were in for some fun! What a great game! They began taunting and threatening their victim with the Germans. They called him names—after all, they had been denied such "pleasure" for so long! The little Jew tried to run away, but the circle tightened. The bolder ones threw the first stones. He stopped running, sat down, took out a razor blade and slashed the veins of his wrists. The blood oozed out slowly and sank into the sand in big drops. Only then did the children back off—they ran back home to spread the "news."

At that time Mrs. Ch. took in a boarder. It was an elderly lady who almost never left her room and even took her meals alone. Despite this, I managed to see her. I was struck by her ugliness.

Her large nose and wide, down-turned mouth, with a protruding lower lip made her look like a frog. Days passed. Our boarder sat by the window under which I passed as I went out to the garden. One day she invited me into her room. She asked me whether I'd like to play cards with her. I tried to get out of it, but in the end I stayed. She taught me how to play "War" and "Sixty-six." I, in turn, taught her the rules of the "Maritime Game." From then on, a game with our boarder was part of the daily program.

Once, when I came in, I noticed she was reading a prayer book. At the first opportunity I said, "Our boarder is a Jew!" I apparently said it as a statement of fact, not a question, because Mrs. Ch. didn't even attempt to deny it. She only asked, "How did you know?" To which I answered, "I saw her prayer book; it's completely new, and 'grandmas' like her have well-used ones."

The woman had a son who was hiding somewhere else with his wife. Sometimes they both came over to see her, but these were short, dangerous visits. Then she'd again be alone for long days and weeks. In time I grew to like her; I even got used to her ugliness. The poor woman always tried to prolong our card games, but I was drawn to the outdoors to play.

Summer and vacation time arrived. In September I was supposed to go to school. A religious problem appeared—confession and first communion—all of this so I could later participate in school retreats. I told Mrs. Ch. the story of my baptism. She decided it was enough. However, as for confession and communion, it was decided that it would be safer if I received the sacraments in another parish. Here in Koło the priest knew everyone and also taught in the school. Indeed, I, too, was to become his student. I wrote my sins down on a piece of paper and went with Mrs. Anna to St. Alexander's Church in Trzech Krzyży [Three Crosses] Square. It was dimly lit, quiet; there were burning candles, flowers, and the smell of incense. The priest patiently listened to my naive, childish sins, and, in the end, told me, heart to heart, not to sadden God by sinning. I decided that after the war I would convince my parents to also accept the Catholic faith. After all, this was the faith that had saved us!

One day I found Wanda and Mrs. Ch. conferring about something together. Suddenly Wanda turned to me and asked, "Marysia, would you like to join the girl scouts?" My heart quickened with joy; I couldn't speak but nodded eagerly. Scouting! It was a part of the "real" underground, because scouting activity was secret and illegal. And so began new days, full of meaning. Scout meetings were held in a different place each time, so as not to arouse suspicions.

A traveling amusement park came to Koło. Mrs. Ch. gave me money for the merry-go-round. The place was swarming with children. I took my place in line to buy a ticket. Suddenly, a man pointed his finger at me and said loudly and emphatically, "And this, ladies and gentlemen, is a mixture of Semitic blood!" What was I to do? Go back home? That would have confirmed his words! Feign surprise? Begin to defend myself? Now that would have raised real suspicion! I decided to pretend not to understand what he was talking about, that it didn't concern me at all. The music played. The merry-go-round spun faster, faster. But the man stood off to the side, and pointing me out with his finger, stubbornly repeated, "This, ladies and gentlemen, is a real mixture of Semitic blood!" Finally, he got bored and walked off. I returned home and reported what had happened. "It's good he only said 'a mixture' and not 'pure Semitic blood,'" Mrs. Ch. said. "But perhaps you shouldn't go to the merry-go-round anymore."

I remember well those scorching last few days of July 1944 in Warsaw. Everyone knew that any day, any hour, something decisive was going to happen. From the direction of Praga,[6] you could see columns of German soldiers streaming westward. They weren't the same cocksure, confident Germans but dusty, tired remnants of what had once seemed an invincible army. Huge posters appeared on walls of buildings, appeals by underground organizations to the people of Warsaw, stating that although difficult days were still coming for the city, the moment of liberation was drawing near. The artillery fire at the front could already be clearly heard. Warsaw gossips were already telling each other that Russian tanks had previously been spotted in the area of Grochów.

The scouts were conducting alarm drills and checking equipment. A fragment of the song "Hey, Boys" took on a new relevancy. "Who knows whether tomorrow or the day after tomorrow, or already today, will come the order for us to go?" Crowds poured out into the streets to look at the retreating German army. "Look at the Krauts running away!" people laughed. "Hope you don't make it to Berlin; hope you croak on the way," a woman yelled. "They'll put fire to your asses, you scum, you Antichrists!" But the Germans walked on, not looking left or right. Even if they didn't understand, they must have known what kind of farewell they were getting.

On the first of August, one sensed something unusual hanging in the air. It wasn't noon yet when Wanda told me to carry a letter to Iśka (also a girl scout), to Chmielna Street, but she warned me to hurry and get back home before five o'clock. I didn't take it too seriously, however, and, as usual, took my time. I didn't find Iśka at home. Luckily, I met her on the street, so I handed her the letter, and happy to have fulfilled my assignment, I returned to the streetcar stop. As if out of spite, the No. 1 left just as I arrived.

I waited a long time for the next one, and when it finally came, the conductor announced that it would only go to Młynarska Street. He smiled mysteriously as he said it. As we passed Żelazna Brama [Iron Gate] Square, we heard the first shots. The streetcar rode on, not stopping anywhere. There were still quite a few people on the streets, but frightened by the shooting, they sought shelter in entryways. Everyone thought it was one of the frequent street roundups. The streetcar, as the conductor had announced, reached Młynarska Street.

I was waiting for the next one, when suddenly, shots rang out around the corner. "It's begun," some woman said. "My husband went already this morning," added another. Then I understood that it was the [Warsaw] Uprising. Taking advantage of the fact that I was alone and nobody was watching me, I took off along the street to see what "it" looked like. I had barely walked a dozen steps when suddenly—bzz, bzz—a bullet whizzed right by my ear, then another, then a whole series. I ducked into some entryway. It was dark there, but it turned out that the place was full of people seeking shelter. Everyone was talking about the situation.

The uprising had already been going on for a couple of hours.

The news from the city was not good. The Germans had brought reinforcements into Warsaw to quell the uprising. It was now a battle (how uneven!) for every house, courtyard, or patch of street. The Germans called the insurgents "bandits" and treated them as such. There was no talk of any rights or consideration for prisoners—those who fell into German hands were shot to death. Stories were circulating about terrible "wardrobes" (projectiles capable of blowing away entire floors of a building). Their grinding noise reminded people of the sound of a wardrobe being dragged; that's how they got their name. There were reports that the Bank of Poland building was burned down with its defenders inside.

Another week passed. Suddenly the streets of Koło swarmed with German soldiers. A van stopped at the corner. *"Achtung! Achtung!"* a voice rang out from the megaphone. "Attention! Attention! All Koło residents are to leave the quarter immediately!" Once again the streets of Koło filled with people heading into the unknown. This time there were already fewer of us, as some people had not returned after the previous deportation.

Suddenly, like a bombshell, came news that the uprising had collapsed. General Bór[7] had negotiated with the Germans and obtained their assurance that the insurgents would be treated like a regular army and, in accordance with those rights, would be taken prisoners of war. Mrs. Ch. inquired wherever she could which way the prisoners would be led out. She wanted to find out something about Wanda. She took me along with her, and so we walked through various roads, asking people whether they knew which way the Germans would be leading the insurgents out of Warsaw. It was drizzling. We walked around like this every day, returning home tired and wet—and without results.

Finally someone told us, "They're taking them along the road leading to Ożarów!" We went immediately in that direction. Already from far away we saw a crowd on the road; it was the insurgents! They walked proudly, white-and-red[8] armbands on their sleeves—soldiers of the underground! The uprising had collapsed, but their spirit was triumphant. They were guarded by only a few Wehrmacht soldiers, who seemed tired and more disheartened than the prisoners they were supposed to guard. Just then the column stopped. We slipped into the ranks and asked about Wanda, who'd been a liaison. "What is her pseudonym?" This question threw us off. After all, we had no way of knowing what her insurgent's pseudonym was.

We searched like this for many hours; they kept walking by while we stood in the middle of the road, straining our eyes. In the evening we went back home. The next day, however, we went back out on the road. Crowds of insurgents kept on moving. Then suddenly, we heard a call from the crowd, "Marysia! Mama!" It was Wanda. A flood of words began. "Wandzia, run away, run away! They aren't guarding you that closely, after all! We're at Mrs. Cz.'s place!" Wanda hesitated. "I wanted to be taken prisoner like Papa." "Yes, but we need you so much," Mrs. Ch. pleaded. In the end, Wanda relented. She said she would run away before nightfall.

We got back to our place. Now began the hours of waiting and tension. Would she manage to escape? Late in the evening she arrived. That night nobody slept—we all sat around and listened to her stories about the uprising.

Now events began to evolve rapidly. Mrs. Ch. decided to take her mother and Wanda to her family. However, they couldn't take me with them. It was decided that along the way we would stop in

Kraków, and Mrs. Ch. would go to Wieliczka and reestablish contact with Mrs. K. (contact had been interrupted at the outbreak of the uprising). Before leaving, my braids were cut off, because, after all, there was no way I could take care of them. The trip was difficult. The passenger trains no longer ran on time—German military transports had priority. We had to transfer countless times. Sometimes we were pushed away from the wagons.

We reached Kraków. Mrs. Ch. immediately went to Wieliczka, while we stayed in the waiting room of the train station, which was full of travelers. After a few hours, Mrs. Ch. returned. Mrs. K. promised to come to Kraków the next day to take care of me. In the meantime, she sent me a note with a certain address. That was the place where I was to wait for her.

It was already past curfew, so I could no longer go out into the town. Mrs. Ch.'s train was to leave in another hour, so I would have to spend the night there alone in the waiting room. I wanted something to delay the departure of that train, but it so happened that it arrived on time. A quick farewell, and they got into their compartment. Wanda stood in the window. Tears began to choke me again. "Well, Marysia, take care of yourself," were Wanda's last words to me, and the train began moving.

I was left alone in the crowd. The minutes, which sped by so mercilessly before their departure, now began to drag. The whole long night was ahead of me. I found a corner in which I could prop up my head against the wall and doze off until morning. I dragged my little backpack there and wrapped myself in my coat but couldn't fall asleep. Suddenly, a Ukrainian in German service came up to me. It turned out that he spoke fluent Polish. He began questioning me about where I was coming from and where and to whom I was going. Then he asked me what school I had attended recently and what I had learned; he always posed the questions so that I couldn't answer evasively. He kept returning to the same questions over again—where I lived, where my parents were and why I was alone, whom I was going to visit, where I went to school, and so on, over and over again. This is how I spent the night.

When normal street traffic began, I decided to leave. But, there was my Ukrainian again! I could feel him approaching, grabbing me by the arm. But he walked by. Only then did I realize that it was someone else entirely.

I went to the address indicated on the note and rang the bell. A woman opened the door, looking at me suspiciously from head to toe. "Mrs. K. asked if you could let me wait here for her. She should be here shortly," I mumbled. She let me into the kitchen. Again, I was flooded with questions. To avoid them, I enthusiastically began telling her stories about the uprising. Hours passed, and Mrs. K. still hadn't come. Finally, she arrived. We walked out on the street, and she began an angry harangue. "What am I going to do with you now? Couldn't Mrs. Ch. have taken you with her? If I can't find you a place, there will be no choice. I will go and hand you over to the Gestapo!" "No!" I responded.

She finally found me a place with a certain family. Nobody there knew who I was except for the daughter of the lady of the house, Miss Franciszka. She reminded me a little of Miss Wacława. Like her, she was a friend of Mrs. K.'s, was unmarried, and like Wacława, made similar remarks about Jews. I had to help with the housework and, what is worse, share the bed with Miss Franciszka. As for my education, it was naturally out of the question.

After a few weeks, further instructions arrived from Mrs. K. She indicated a certain address in the district of Podgórze where I should be taken because "her mama is there." I wasn't celebrating yet, but I did believe in the impossible. I thought that perhaps Mrs. K. couldn't find another place for me and decided to take the risk and send me to where Mama was hiding.

We finally reached the specified address. Once there, emotions overwhelmed me. I kept quiet, but my heart was pounding. In a moment, I was going to see Mama! The door opened. We were led into a room where a nice-looking older woman greeted us. Miss Franciszka said she had brought me at Mrs. K.'s request. Mama was nowhere in sight. I pulled Miss Franciszka by the sleeve and asked in a whisper, "But where's Mama?" Miss Franciszka turned to our host, "Oh, yes, we were told that her mama was here, too," but the woman denied it and added, "But if you pray ardently and sincerely, you'll surely find her."

Miss Franciszka left. Only then did I take a good look around the room. On all the walls and all the tables were holy pictures, crucifixes, and statuettes, because Mrs. Bereżyńska was very religious. She was a widow and lived with a housekeeper who was just as pious as she. And so I became more devoutly religious than ever before. I knelt and prayed ardently before going to bed. Until then nobody had really paid much attention to it, but here it seemed there was never enough of this praying. And so I prayed and read about the lives of saints, selected especially for me by Mrs. Bereżyńska.

Suddenly one day we were told to go down to the shelter immediately. The Russians were just outside Kraków. A few artillery shots and—silence. Suddenly, the rumble of an explosion shook the air. And again silence. The Russians had captured the city. This explosion was the retreating Germans blowing up all the bridges on the Vistula River. In the shelter, people were talking and talking. Suddenly someone said, "So now that the Russians have arrived, the Jews will probably come back." And to this some "lady" responded in a high-pitched voice, "Ah, yes, I completely forgot that we'll be seeing those sidelockers again."

But the subject died out, because at that very moment, a German soldier dashed into our shelter! For a moment panic set in, but it soon turned out he had simply come in looking for shelter and a hiding place from the Russian soldiers. He trembled and stammered with fear. Somebody who understood German translated what he said. He had been called to the front against his will and had never wanted this senseless and cruel war. He had known from the beginning that the Germans would lose. In a word, he was the personification of justice. He begged us to give him civilian clothing and to hide his uniform and gun, shaking like a leaf the whole time. But nobody wanted to hide a German soldier, his uniform, or his gun. In the end, he was simply forced out of the shelter. He walked out, and immediately we heard a single shot.

We returned to the apartment and to prayer. The streets were full of Russian soldiers, loud and clumsy-looking in their padded jackets. Meanwhile, Mrs. K. hadn't shown up. Transportation for the civilian population was not yet fully operational. A pontoon bridge was built across the Vistula. Crowds streamed across in both directions.

One time I was walking with Mrs. Bereżyńska when suddenly, I heard someone calling, "Marysia, Marysia! Marysia Perlberger!" I stopped. It was my cousin. Mrs. Bereżyńska stopped a little farther on, ostentatiously turning her back. Meanwhile, this cousin, Henek, asked where I was staying and with whom. Seeing that I didn't want to answer, he gave me his address, adding that another cousin had survived and was living with him. He asked me to visit them. "You'll come, won't you?"—he wanted to make sure. "All right, I'll come," I said and walked on with Mrs. Bereżyńska. "What did he want from you?" she asked. I told her that he wanted me to visit him. "Very well, go, but I must warn you; Jews poison every child who has converted to the Catholic faith. They would rather see the child dead than converted. To such a child they give tea with poison in it."

For several days I hesitated. Should I go or not go? In the end, I thought I might find out something about my parents, and that shifted the balance. I decided to go. I rang the bell. Henek opened the door. "Oh, Marysia! How good that you've come, come in!" I didn't want to go in right away, so I stood at the threshold. And he began asking me, "Marysia, where do you live? Who has been taking care of you this whole time? And with whom did your mother leave her jewelry? How about her furs? Well, come in, I'll make you some tea." When I heard this, I was gone. Henek, leaning over the handrail of the stairs, yelled after me, "Why are you running away? At least leave the address where you're staying!" But I kept on running and didn't even turn my head. "So that's how it is," I thought. "First they ask where my mama's jewels are, and then they want to poison me with tea!" Mrs. Bereżyńska was very happy with this turn of events. She only said, "You see, I was right. You shouldn't go there any more. Pray and you'll see that all will go well for you."

One day Mrs. K. appeared. I thought she would give me some news about my parents or take me with her to Wieliczka. But she responded impatiently and brusquely, as usual, "Your parents have not yet returned, and I can't take you to Wieliczka. The Germans could come back at any moment, so it's better if nobody knows you're alive. I can't take care of you now or pay for you, so I'm going to leave you at a children's shelter here in Kraków, and later we will see."

Mrs. K. took me to a shelter for homeless children. I was led into a room. The noise and confusion that reigned were indescribable. Against the walls stood bare bunk beds, pieced together from rough boards. The place was full of children—on the floor, on the bunks—boys and girls of various ages. They were all horribly dirty and dressed in a strange manner—sleeves too long, shoes too big, sometimes even unmatched. Everyone was playing cards or with knives. There were no adults supervising them. This was a rabble of children from the lowest layer of society.

"Oh, look, there's somebody new. Probably a Jew!" "I'm not a Jew," I denied. "Then look for a place on this side." Because on the other side stood the bunks of the Jewish children. They were indescribably thin and weak. They didn't move at all from their place, and only their large, dark eyes gave evidence that they were living beings. But what did I care about Jewish children! A certain girl agreed to accept me on her bunk (each bunk was occupied by two and sometimes even three children). Bed linen was out of the question. They all slept in their clothes and covered themselves with a coat (if they had one).

It was a bad situation, but I didn't even think about going back to the Jews. If my parents came back, they would find me through Mrs. K. Other Jews I regarded with disgust.

One evening, a family stopped by for the night. They were on their way from Warsaw to Łódź and, by a strange coincidence, happened to stop in Kraków. They were directed to our shelter for the night—they were to continue their journey the next day. They noticed me, asked me a few questions—and asked whether I would like to go with them. They seemed nice, so I agreed. In the office of the shelter they made no objection—my name was simply crossed off their roster. And thus I set out with my new guardians on the way to Łódź. Mr. and Mrs. Stoliński (that was their name) had a little daughter, perhaps two years old. They promised that I would become their older daughter, that they would send me to school and perhaps even adopt me later.

Outside, it was March weather—windy and sleeting. I felt I had a fever; my head was spinning, and my ears hurt. We waited a long time at the station. The child cried from hunger, and I felt a strange dullness, most likely caused by the fever. In the end, we managed to get a place in a freight car. The train crawled along and stopped every few moments. A day later, we reached Łódź. The Stolińskis lived there before the war, but their apartment had been taken over by Germans and they'd been resettled in Warsaw. Now they were returning to live again in their old apartment.

After a few days my ears stopped hurting, but I went deaf, absolutely and completely. Mrs. Stolińska didn't believe me at first, thinking I was pretending, but she was finally convinced. In order to communicate with me, she began to write. But a doctor was out of the question. Mr. Stoliński returned to his old prewar job as a civil servant. Weeks passed. Then suddenly I regained my hearing but remained weak and tired. At night I slept curled up on two armchairs pushed together, which, with my every move, slid apart. To make things worse, Mr. Stoliński typed in the same room where I tried to fall asleep. My bones ached, and the clacking of the typewriter bothered me.

The promise of sending me to school was not fulfilled. I was told to take the child for walks and perform various household chores. Mrs. Stolińska constantly asked me whether perhaps I was a Jew. I stubbornly denied it.

I decided to return to Warsaw. Mrs. Ch. has probably returned to Koło by now, I thought, she'll surely be happy to see me! And if she's not there, I'll try to get a place at the cloister of the Sisters of the Immaculate Conception and become a resident there. That would solve all my problems. Not thinking long, I packed my little backpack and told Mrs. Stolińska about my plans. She expressed surprise that I wanted to leave them but gave me money for the trip. After many complications, I arrived in Warsaw. In front of me was a forest of ruins.

I returned to Koło. Mrs. Kamińska began questioning me whether I wanted to go back to the Jews. I was astonished and taken aback by the fact that she knew who I was, but I didn't want to hear about returning to Jews.

I wrote to Mrs. K., letting her know about my plans. She wrote back angrily, "What has gotten into your head? Upkeep at the Cloister of the Immaculate Conception costs one thousand złotys a month! You're doing things independently without permission. If you had stayed in Kraków like the other children, you would be going to school by now."

The 1945–46 school year had already started, and there was no room in the cloister. But, in the end, I got a place! It was not at the Immaculate Conception but at St. Ursula's, and so I achieved my goal! I thanked Mrs. Kamińska for her hospitality and immediately set out on my way. Then, all of sudden, among the ruins of Warsaw, I met Wanda! She managed to write down my new address at the cloister, and we parted (the local train I was taking was just about to leave).

I got to Piaski. All around were empty fields. From afar I could see a few houses. I asked about the Ursuline cloister, and someone pointed the way. It turned out to be a white building, rather nice looking from the outside, which was surrounded by a stone wall. I was led into the mother superior's office. She was short and very round, and her plumpness gave her a semblance of gentleness. I turned over to her all my documents.

I was sent to the kitchen for lunch. I was hungry; I hadn't had anything to eat since early morning. The dinner I was given reminded me of the food at the shelter in Kraków—the same kind of banged up tin plate and the same contents—a little watery soup with a few sparse cabbage leaves floating in it. A few girls came in from school. They were served the same dinner. They ate greedily; I could see they were starved. A nun took me to a room. It was tiny. The beds, made up with white sheets, were arranged tightly, one next to the other. Judging by their number, I thought there would be four of us staying there, but by the time evening came, I found out I was mistaken.

A bell rang. I thought it was time for supper, but it was a call for evening prayers in the chapel. It was dim, but unlike in a church, there was no smell of incense in the air. The prayer was long and monotonous, conducted in a low voice by one of the nuns. Finally, it ended, and we were taken to the refectory for supper. We were served barley soup for a change, also watery. I tried to cheer myself up thinking that perhaps the next day, on Sunday, the food would be better.

December came. Snow, early that year, covered the ground. I found no joy in it like the other children. The snow was now my enemy. Everything I had to wear was falling apart, and getting anything new was out of the question. On top of this, while walking along, snow stuck to my wooden clogs and after a few steps formed thick clods that had to be knocked off by force. Thus the walk to and from school lasted twice as long.

I was assigned to a room with the older girls. Every morning I observed the same scene with amazement. A nun woke us up, but I was the only one who got up obediently. These "elders" hid in a wardrobe to avoid going to Mass. Then they calmly went back to bed. When the nun reproached them, they answered impertinently and without fear. I was tempted to follow their example and get a full night's sleep for once, but I was afraid. "What if they think I'm a Jew?" I thought, "Then they would throw me out of here, and where would I go to school then?"

The Christmas holidays approached. In the school it was announced that the charity committee would invite children who had no homes to which they could go, to a modest Christmas Eve celebration. I signed up, despite the embarrassment. After all, I was hungry, and I had no home. The celebration took place after class. Packages of sweets were distributed to us. By the time I returned to the cloister, the contents of my package were gone. I walked slowly, not rushing. However, this time a surprise awaited me. I was called into the office, and—I saw Wanda! There was a man with her whom I did not know. It turned out to be her uncle. They came to take me for the holidays! Mother Superior gave her permission, and we were on our way.

We drove up to a villa. It was a home for children of fallen soldiers and officers. We found ourselves in a brightly lit hall. There were children all around. Preholiday commotion reigned. I was introduced to the director, who, in turn, introduced me to the children as a "guest who will spend the holidays with us." Wanda and her uncle left, and I remained alone in the midst of strangers again. However, I was immediately looked after, and someone brought an additional set of angel wings so I could take part in the Christmas pageant.

A bell was sounded for the Christmas Eve supper. The food was tasty and plentiful. Nobody there looked hungry. Later, we all returned to the common room, where we sat around the Christmas tree and sang carols. Then the Christmas play began. The roles, which were sung, were amusing. Not lacking were a peasant and a Jew.

The peasant sang:

Jew, Jew, a Messiah is born,
So it behooves you, it behooves you
To welcome him!

And the Jew responded:

And where is he,
And where is he,
I would be glad to see him.
We'll bow down,
We'll bow down,
If it's becoming!

And so they sang, one after the other, until the peasant started battering the Jew with a stick, and the Jew ran off the stage, hopping around comically and singing, *"Oy vey, gevalt!"* So a comical figure of a Jew was always a highlight of those plays.

After some time, I found myself in a children's home near Opole. There we lived in a thirteenth-century castle. For school we went into Opole. One day, during lunch, the director suddenly asked loudly, very loudly, "Marysia, what's this about an aunt of yours called Schenker?" All eyes turned toward me. I was struck dumb. I shrugged my shoulders. I really didn't remember such a name. However, the director went on, "They are summoning you to Kraków. I think you should go and clear up what it's all about." The next day I was on my way to Kraków.

It was a drizzly autumn day, and my spirits felt the same. In Kraków, I went to the specified address without delay (to have it over and done with quickly). I rang the bell and stepped over the threshold. The apartment was in a state of predeparture chaos. There were suitcases everywhere—parts of clothing, shoes, some papers, letters, and photographs. An elderly woman and several other people were busy packing. I stood there without a word.

Then the elderly woman's eyes fell on me. "Marysia!" she shouted and hugged me warmly. "Marysia, so you did come after all!" At first I didn't react. She was an aunt I didn't know at all, my grandfather's sister, someone from the older generation. I first wanted to figure out whether this new aunt would suit me, but, after a moment, the ice was broken. Aunt said she had nothing against my being a Catholic, that I could continue to go to church. Naturally, I immediately announced that I had come for only one day and that I wanted to get back to the children's home as soon as possible. (I was already trying to figure out how I'd convince everyone that it had been a mistake when I returned.) What does the name Schenker have to do with me, Maria Nowakowska?!

All of a sudden another woman in the room broke in, "Well, all right, let her go back. She evidently doesn't want to know about her family. In that case, the family wouldn't want to know about her." The word "family" had a magical power, and that's what shifted the balance. I stayed. However, the aunt was supposed to leave to go abroad in a couple of days. For the time being, therefore, she decided to leave me here in Kraków until she could arrange for me to join her. I learned how she had found me. She had survived the war in Russia. Recently, she had returned to Poland and begun to search for surviving members of the family. She got my address from Mrs. K.

My aunt left. I was once again in a children's home; this time it was a home for Jewish children. I looked at my new surroundings with distrust and even with a measure of disdain. The dark, curly hair and Semitic features of the children bothered me. Weeks went by, and I slowly grew accustomed to my new surroundings, but I never went to town with my new friends, who looked Jewish. From time to time I still went to church, but then, all of a sudden, I discovered it didn't attract me as much anymore.

I waited for news from my aunt, but it turned out I also had other relatives. An unexpected letter arrived from an uncle in Belgium, who was my mama's brother. Suddenly, and equally unexpectedly, someone appeared who had been sent by him, and, before I realized what was going on, I was on my way to Cieszyn where I was taken across a bridge to the Czech side.[9] There, my uncle was waiting for me.

I was on the other side.

Maria Perlberger-Schmuel has been living in Israel since 1947. She wrote down her wartime experiences shortly after leaving Poland in 1946. Her memoirs, entitled "W chowanego ze śmiercią" ["Playing Hide-and-Seek with Death"], were published in Israel and reprinted in Poland (*Więź,* Issue 357, No. 7–8 [1988]: 185–224). We are publishing them here, somewhat abbreviated, with the permission of *Więź.*—Katarzyna Meloch

1. Wieliczka is a village on the outskirts of Kraków, well known as a tourist attraction because of its salt mines.

2. The General Government was the area of Poland occupied and gov-

erned by the Germans but not formally annexed to the German Reich (as were territories closer to Germany). It was divided into four districts—Warsaw, Kraków, Radom, and Lublin.

3. *The Heart* was a popular book by Edmondo de Amicis.

4. "Cards of life" were identity cards that gave the bearer certain rights—to get food and not be deported.

5. *Płomyk* [small flame] was a children's magazine.

6. Praga and Grochów are districts of Warsaw on the eastern side of the Vistula.

7. General Tadeusz Bór-Komorowski was the commander of the AK [Home Army]. See glossary.

8. Red and white are the colors of the Polish flag.

9. Cieszyn is a divided town, half of it being in Poland, half in the Czech Republic (then Czechoslovakia). It served as a passage for illegal immigration to Palestine.

JANINA PIETRASIAK

Born in 1934

I Am One of the Lucky Ones

This is the story of one human being, one of so many touched by the war to a greater or lesser degree. I realize that I owe my life, and those of some of my family, to a chain of people of good will. Without their great sacrifices, heroism, and exceptional courage, I would have been gone from this world long ago.

My parents were Józef and Rozalia Feldman (née Zwanziger). Father came from Tarnopol, Mother, from Przemyśl. They both completed their studies in pharmaceutics at the Jagiellonian University in Kraków. Their first apprenticeship was in a pharmacy in Kraków. Later, they leased a pharmacy in Grodziec, in Upper Silesia, with a four-room apartment above it. They ran it together, alternating shifts all through the day. They also treated the local population; in small communities pharmacists were authorized to do this.

My sister, Ewa, and I were born in Upper Silesia—Ewa in Chorzów in 1932 and I in Królewska Huta in 1934. The most wonderful years of my childhood were spent in Grodziec. We had a large, beautiful apartment, servants, and plenty of assistants in the pharmacy; we frequently took wonderful trips to the mountains—to Żegiestów, Zawoja, Zakopane, or some mountainside village. I, as the youngest, was doted on and loved by everyone. The children's room had white furniture, beautiful toys, and dolls. We played with the neighbors' children every day and often visited the pharmacy, where there were so many treasures to play with.

The war came; I was five years old. The Germans chased us out of our apartment. We had to leave everything behind. The war found Mama, my sister, and me in a mountainside village. We did not return to Grodziec. Instead, we went to Kraków. And so my entire good and congenial world collapsed. In Kraków we moved in temporarily with my grandfather—Papa's father—at 11b Sebastian Street. From there we were all taken to the ghetto, right after it was formed in Kraków.

Terribly difficult times followed. Father worked there as a paramedic, while Mother was taken to work every day at a brush factory (her hands always had cuts from the difficult work). After two years of vegetating in the Kraków ghetto, right before its liquidation, my father, together with a group of other men, walled in the three of us, together with a number of other people, including mothers with children and some old people. Father thought we could be saved in this way. The place in which we were hiding was crowded, dark, and had no sanitary facilities or water. Penetrating cold and hunger were ever present (it was a severe winter). Moreover, complete silence was obligatory so the Germans wouldn't hear us. Dantesque scenes took place there. One of the little children began to cry, so his mother covered his head with a pillow to silence him. The child suffocated. Some of the older people lost their minds. One of the old men died and remained with the living.

My papa, with several other men, took down the wall at the last moment before the liquidation of the ghetto. Transports of men to death camps had already begun. Papa met with the same fate—he was put on one of the last transports to Auschwitz and killed within a few months of arriving there, as part of a collective retribution for one man's escape. However, he had managed to free us!

Mama and I tried to escape to the Aryan side on our own, as did the other people who came out of the hideout with us. We ran more than a dozen meters under fire. In our presence, a mother who was running with her small child in her arms was shot to death (the child survived). We managed to hide in a wooden outhouse, where Mama and my sister held the latch, while I squatted—this went on for two days. We made believe the outhouse was empty.

When Mama finally saw through a crack a Wehrmacht soldier who wasn't shooting at people, we ran as fast as we could. Mama gave him a handful of gold (all her jewelry, gold tooth caps, and everything she had). He then let us cross over to the Aryan side. By a miracle, we were able to reach 11b Sebastian Street, my grandfather's house. The caretaker there was very involved in resistance work and in Żegota, an organization helping Jews led by Zofia Kossak-Szczucka, alias "Weronika," a well-known writer and historian.

Weronika was in charge of *Ochronka* [shelter], that is, a unit serving people in need of immediate help. She raised funds for those who escaped from behind the wall. She pestered the intelligentsia and landowning families for this cause. She had contacts among the prewar military. Priests whom she knew helped her in fabricating false documents and baptismal certificates, as well as in placing children in homes run by nuns. She saved several thousand Jewish children.

Weronika also helped provide us with false documents, with the name Kwiatkowska. Afterward, under the care of a liaison, Mrs. Aleksandra Mianowska, alias "Krysta" (who is now a physician), Mama and I were transported by train to Warsaw and placed—thanks to the personal intervention of Zofia Kossak—with an educated family, Mrs. Janina and Mr. Henryk Jętkiewicz. Mr. Henryk Jętkiewicz, a highway construction engineer, had completed his university studies in St. Petersburg and knew several languages well; before the war he had worked for the Polish Bureau of Standards. He was closely related to the well-known family of Józef Birkenmayer—a writer, whose son, Professor Krzysztof Birkenmayer, is currently well-known as a geophysicist, polar explorer, and lecturer at Jagiellonian University. The family was very friendly with Weronika and worked with her to meet the needs of the Polish underground, the representatives of the Polish government-in-exile, and the organization Żegota. They lived at 11 Twarda Street (within the bounds of the former ghetto).

My sister Ewa, because of a very serious, third-degree frostbite on her feet, acquired while hiding in the wooden outhouse for two days, had to remain in Kraków in a hospital. It is fortunate that the doctors were able to save Ewa's feet, as gangrene had already set in. They amputated only three toes and part of the underside of her foot. The frostbite on my feet was less severe, only second-degree.

Equipped with "good" documents, Mama and I reached Warsaw. Mr. Aleksander Kamiński from Kraków, who was helping Krysta, handed us over to Weronika at the train station in Warsaw. It turned out much later (I learned about it in January 1997) that Mr. Kamiński had also greatly helped my sister in Kraków. He had supplemented her food during her stay in the hospital, and after she left the hospital, he helped transport her in a hackney carriage prior to her trip to Warsaw with the liaison Krysta. He also helped arrange false documents for Ewa and provided her with money. Because of her very Semitic features, my sister Ewa was transported with her face bandaged, pretending to be a child sick with some infection. This is how she got safely to Warsaw. There, she was, of course, picked up at the train station by Weronika.

In 1997 I received a request from Yad Vashem Institute in Jerusalem to confirm the role of Mr. Aleksander Kamiński in saving our family, because the liaison, Krysta, had proposed that he be honored posthumously with the medal Righteous Among the Nations of the World. In my reply to Yad Vashem, I strongly stressed how much he had contributed and how deserving he was of receiving such a medal.

After coming to Warsaw, my sister Ewa was placed, at Zofia Kossak's initiative, at the home of Colonel Ignacy Lubicz-Sadowski and his wife, Anna, on their estate in the village of Góry on the Pilica River—post office Promna, Białobrzegi Radomskie *powiat* [county]. There she was in hiding with many other people (many people were saved by this splendid couple). My sister stayed there for a long time. Colonel Ignacy Lubicz-Sadowski had at one time been under the command of Zofia Kossak's husband, Colonel Zygmunt Szatkowski, hence their friendship and cooperation on behalf of those in danger. Ewa remained on their estate until liberation. Due to Colonel Sadowski's grave illness and the lack of a school in the village, Mrs. Anna Sadowska placed her in the Jewish Children's Home in Śródborów so that she might "return to her roots." However, Ewa missed Góry, and after the death of Colonel Sadowski, she returned to the estate.

Zofia Kossak made use of all her connections to save "those from behind the walls." This splendid woman was arrested by the Germans in 1943, imprisoned in Pawiak,[1] and then transported to Auschwitz. However, the underground organization managed to buy her out for a huge sum, collected especially for that purpose, before the Germans realized whom they had in their hands. She used various false names, and that is why she wasn't recognized by the Germans. If she had been, she would have been killed immediately.

It should be emphasized that it was indeed due to her initial decisive actions, arranging the most important and most difficult matters, that so many people are indebted to Zofia Kossak. It is to her that they owe their salvation in the first place, and next, to a whole chain of people of good will who offered assistance. Such people became involved, endangering themselves and their families, to save Jews—often entirely without compensation. The help received by my family is a good example of that.

My life from then on followed a similar path to that of other child survivors—I had an adopted family. Quite soon after Mama and I came to live with the Jętkiewicz family, it became apparent that Mama was very ill. After suffering pneumonia in both lungs, she had contracted tuberculosis due to exhaustion and starvation. It became necessary to place her in a better environment. Mama had fever and was growing weaker. Mrs. Jętkiewicz arranged to place her with Mrs. Ulanowska in Milanówek on Podleśna Street, where she could rest in the garden. My guardian and I took food to her there. However, Mama wanted me to come and look after her. She must have felt that she did not have long to live, and that indeed is what happened. Unfortunately, I caught tuberculosis from her.

As Mama's consumption was progressing rapidly and she was growing weaker, she was placed in the Ujazdowski Hospital in Warsaw. Mrs. Jętkiewicz used to visit her there. One day Mama asked her to bring me to the hospital. Mrs. Jętkiewicz dressed me nicely and took me to her. As it turned out, Mama's bed was empty—she had already died. I was in such great shock that I didn't even want to see her in the mortuary. I have regretted that all my life.

Before her death, Mama wrote a letter to her brother in America, begging him to save me and my sister and to take care of us. I took this letter to my uncle only in 1961 (having sent him a copy earlier). After Mama's death, it became evident that by having placed my fate in the hands of the Jętkiewiczes, she had assured my future life.

Despite their already very dangerous situation, because their home was a hotbed of underground activity—a place of secret training for AK [Home Army] soldiers (on a few occasions I saw a pistol fall out of a young person's pocket) and a contact point for the representatives of the government-in-exile[2]—the Jętkiewiczes decided to take me under their wings, for better or for worse. At that time I was still being pulled in different directions by various women from Żegota who wanted to be my "mamas." I defended myself against that and did not allow myself to be torn away from my adopted family. I believed that after all my tribulations, it was the safest harbor for me. I knew that these people had saved, fed, and protected me despite the terrific danger to themselves and that my mama had entrusted me into their welcoming hands and kind hearts.

I was not allowed to talk about myself when playing with other children in the courtyard. The neighbors only knew me as an orphan who had come from the countryside to stay with relatives. Other than that, because I had so-called "good looks," it was not dangerous to play with the neighbors' children.

In the meantime, Zofia Kossak's children, Witold and Anna Szatkowski, after first asking me and the Jętkiewicz family whether I wanted to become Catholic and, after getting a positive answer, began to teach me catechism. I very much wanted to be like all of them; I had even asked them several times for it myself. Besides, Mama had begun to teach me how to cross myself and recite some of the prayers during our stay together at the Jętkiewiczes. She thought, as I did, that it would be safer that way. To a large degree, the so-called "good looks" that Mama and I both apparently had, as well as a certain knowledge of the Catholic religion, made it much easier for us to survive and emerge unscathed from the turmoil of war.

I again went through many difficult experiences. From the balcony at 11 Twarda Street, we observed together many tragic events—roundups and executions; more than once someone lay in our street who'd been tortured to death. This, to a great degree, was responsible for aggravating my neurosis, which, caused by past experiences, was still enormously troubling to my whole being. I would immediately throw up any food I ate and was afraid to sleep in a dark room. On top of all this, as I mentioned, I caught tuberculosis from Mama. Thanks to the connections of Zofia Kossak and Janina Jętkiewicz, I spent two successive terms in a sanitarium in Otwock, where the active lesion was healed. The food there was very poor, mainly lentils, so Mrs. Jętkiewicz often brought me additional food, despite the constant shortages at the time (especially in cities).

The next difficult turn of fate was the Warsaw Uprising.

There was hunger and fear. Though it seemed most unlikely, fate ordained that I come out of it alive. Four times the entire Jętkiewicz family and I managed, by a miracle, to escape with our lives. Mrs. Jętkiewicz was the commander of a unit of nurses from the *Odwet* [revenge] battalion and was often in the very heart of the fighting.

The first time was at 11 Twarda Street when, during a bombardment, the half of the building which contained the cellar where I usually hid during bombings collapsed. That day, when I had dashed down there, all the places were already taken, so I went to another wing of the cellar. All the people in "my" wing of the cellar perished when a bomb dropped on it, and I survived only because there had been no room.

The second time was when we were crossing Jerozolimskie Avenue on all fours as the Germans were strafing the sandbag barricades next to where we were crawling. Many people were killed, but we survived.

The third time was at 4 Sienkiewicz Street, where we were staying in a cellar in which we and many other people had sought shelter. (Some of these people no longer appeared completely normal and were running around with bottles of water and wet rags, applying them to their mouths in case there was a large quantity of dust from bombardments.) Three bombs fell on that building—and none exploded. We managed to survive once again.

The fourth time was on Wspólna Street, where we had moved into the apartment of Professor Aleksander Janowski, a former president of the Polish Tourism Association. I went out into the courtyard to get in line for water to drink. About eighty people were standing there when a so-called Big Bertha bomb fell onto the courtyard, and most of the people standing with me for water were killed. This was a horrid sight—human body parts strewn all over! I do not know how I survived—but somehow, I ended up inside a crater, a big hole in the courtyard.

After the uprising, we left Warsaw. The entire Jętkiewicz

family and I, thanks to the help from some Germans who showed us the way, managed to avoid being taken to the internment camp in Pruszków.[3] After a long and exhausting trek on foot, we arrived in Głowno near Łowicz. From there we were directed (taking our turn with other refugees from burning Warsaw) to the nearby village of Antoniew, where we were quartered. We camped out there for quite a long time under very difficult conditions, sleeping on straw in an enclosure made of rough boards (like one used for pigs). It was cold, and we were short of clothing and food. I used to go to the woods to gather kindling, barefoot in the snow because I had no stockings. We all had ulcers from a lack of vitamins, and we were full of lice.

Finally, after long correspondence, Mrs. Jętkiewicz convinced her brother, Mieczysław Markiewicz, who lived in Płock, to agree to take the entire family, including me, into his apartment. Although he worked very closely with the Germans—he ran an industrial goods store for them—he agreed to our coming. And so we crossed the so-called green border,[4] I, with false papers and the letter from Mama to my uncle in America sewn into the lapel of my coat, and they, with a large amount of jewelry sewn into their clothing—which belonged to Janina Jętkiewicz's brother and had been left with them for safekeeping. It was a very dangerous expedition but, surprisingly, was a crowning success.

In Płock we all settled into the very small apartment of Mieczysław Markiewicz, which, already occupied by seven people, became overcrowded. Moreover, it was like walking straight into the lion's mouth, as there were lots of Germans around. That is where liberation found us. Afterward, we were assigned an apartment left by a German named Neyman, who must have murdered a lot of Jews, because we found a huge number of Jewish prayer shawls piled up there, one on top of the other.

I would like to add that during the entire period of the war, as well as after liberation, my uncle, David Zwanziger, tried to bring my entire family, and later, my sister and me, the two of us who survived, to the United States. I have all the documents. He spent a lot of money and experienced a lot of anguish trying to arrange it. Unfortunately, all these efforts failed to produce a positive result.

I was able to see my relatives for the first time only in 1961 when I applied and was accepted to study English in the United States in a course for foreigners (my uncle paid for the course). Before that, I had been refused a passport many times. It was only then that I was finally able to hand my uncle the letter written by Mama on a scrap of paper in the hospital, in which she implored him to take care of me and my sister (two orphans), as she was then about to leave us forever and Papa was no longer in this world. Amazingly, this letter survived through the entire turmoil of war.

It was a very moving experience for my uncle—a brother reading a letter from his sister who had been dead for many years, written just before her death. I have to admit that meeting my own flesh-and-blood relatives at the age of twenty-four was an unbelievable experience. I cried for several days. In my aunt and uncle's home I found many family mementos, photographs, letters, and knickknacks. It was only then that I learned many details about my own family. Thanks to this I was able to answer most of the questions during an interview for Steven Spielberg's *Survivors of the Shoah* archive.

After many meetings with members of the "Children of the Holocaust" and listening to their stories, I came to the conclusion that I am one of the lucky ones. I know my roots and family history, I received some information about the members of my family, and I was able to find and spend some time with a part of my family living in the United States.

I only wish such a fate for many other members of our association. I know that many of them are still troubled by the unanswered questions of where they came from, where they lived, what happened to them and their families, and what their real names were. It is certainly not easy to live with the realization that one will never find out any of this.

I also know people who are tormented by the fact that a horrible fate befell Polish families who saved them. It is a feeling of guilt troubling them their entire lives and difficult to get rid of.

---

1. Pawiak was a notorious prison in central Warsaw.

2. The Polish government-in-exile, operating from London, had representatives in occupied Poland who coordinated underground activities.

3. When the Warsaw Uprising collapsed, the Germans forced residents of Warsaw to vacate the city. People were taken to the nearby town of Pruszków and interned in camps.

4. The "green border" was the section of the border out in the countryside where it was easier to cross illegally, in this case, between the General Government, where Głowno was located, and the area of Poland incorporated directly into Germany (Warthegau), where Płock was located.

JANA PROT

Born in 1926

Fragments of Memories

A Remembrance of Stefan A. (1939–1944)

My friendship with Stefan A. began during a vacation we both spent in Pionki. Irrationally, it seems as if we had known each other for many years, but in reality we only spent the last summer before the war together, in 1939, and a few short Christmas and Easter breaks in 1937 and 1938. I don't remember what he looked like—I think he was broad-shouldered, stocky, his dark eyes set in a face with prominent cheekbones. Older than I by four years, he was already attending the Rejtan Lyceum in Warsaw. I was impressed by the friendship of a boy who wore a red, and not a blue, emblem on his jacket sleeve.[1] We spent the vacations riding bikes to ponds, to the Kozienice Forest, or sitting at home and reading everything that fell into our hands. I tried—unsuccessfully—to get through Conrad's *Lord Jim.* We read Carrel's *Man, the Unknown,* Huxley's *Eyeless in Gaza,* and I even got to Zegadłowicz's *Zmory* [*Nightmares.*] This last book was one of the few that my father had moved to another shelf and forbade me to read. It didn't help much.

My endless conversations with Stefan, our discussions and arguments, picked up even more after Stefan's cousin, Henryk, joined us for the last month of vacation. Both my summertime friends picked on me, supporting each other's efforts. They said I was inexperienced (and to this day I really don't know what experiences they were thinking about), that I attended a stupid school (which was the truth), and that I didn't know anything about politics (which was also true). So they explained to me what the right wing was, as well as the left, and what the ONR and the Falanga were.[2] Of course, not all our conversations were serious. They also told various jokes and anecdotes from school.

We already had plans for the future. Stefan, during some trip to the Kozienice Forest, told me, "Next year I'm going to graduate, then I'm going to university, and then I'm going to marry you." I had to refuse, as I had just decided to become a nun.

The end of August 1939 was approaching. Henryk was getting ready for his return home to Volhynia after being summoned by his father, because "the times were uncertain." (Henryk was deported by the Soviets to the east with his whole family in 1940. All trace of him disappeared.) My younger brother, Tomek, and I were supposed to return to Warsaw after August 20. One evening, right before the end of vacation, we sat on the terrace in the dark, looking upward, looking for shooting stars, everyone trying to be the first to make their wish. And then—was it because we were looking up at the sky, or maybe because we were surrounded by an atmosphere of uncertainty?—we started arguing about the existence of God. Stefan said that God didn't exist because his existence was impossible to prove scientifically. Henryk supported his argument but not very enthusiastically. I, in turn, opposed them vehemently: "God exists, he created us and the whole world. He sees everything and takes care of everything. . . ." None of us wanted to back down, and Stefan finally gave up and said, "Oh, why are we arguing with you? You're too young to understand. Wait until you're sixteen—by then you'll certainly not believe in God. Let's bet on it." And so we bet on the existence of God. And then the war broke out.

I turned sixteen on February 8, 1942. I lived near Wilson Square. Mrs. K., with whom I was living at that time, threw a little party. A few of Zofia's and Krysia's (Mrs. K's daughters) friends came, the gramophone was playing *"J'attendrai le jour et la nuit, j'attendrai toujours ton retour. . . .*" [I will await day and night, I will always await your return]. It was evening, past curfew, I think, when the phone rang. Zofia called, "Jana, I think it's for you." I got puzzled and worried—after all, nobody ever called me, and nobody should be calling me now. I lifted the receiver. A familiar voice said, "Jana, so do you still believe in God?"

I never learned how Stefan found me, just as I never learned how he had found me that terrible night on September 25, 1939, in a cellar of a bombed-out building at 9 Czacki Street, in darkness, lit up only by the burning houses on Świętokrzyska Street. We later lost touch, and I hadn't seen him since the end of 1939.

After that first telephone call in years (on my birthday), he called me every few days, always in the evening. Our conversations were careful and banal. His name was now Marian; he worked as a night watchman in some factory. Zofia and Krystyna pestered me with questions, "Why didn't you say you knew a boy? Why don't you invite him?" I avoided the subject as much as I could, and then the calls stopped, because Stefan had changed jobs. Over the next few years, we saw each other a few times, always only in the street, always in the evening, just before curfew. In the dark it was safer, the streets were full of people hurrying home; nobody paid any attention to us.

I don't remember how many of these meetings we had between the winter of 1942 and the summer of 1944. I don't remember exactly what was said or when, either. I successively found out about his father being shot in the street, his mother dying of typhus, and his girlfriend—his first girlfriend—being taken to *Umschlagplatz* and pushed into a railroad car. His sisters went over to the Aryan side; they had false papers. It didn't help much. The older one worked as a servant. There was a search of the apartment, nothing was found, but right before leaving, a Polish policeman took a good look at her and asked, "Are you a Jew?" Surprised and horrified, she admitted it. The younger one lived with people engaged in resistance work. Their illegal printing outfit was discovered by the Gestapo, and the residents were dragged to the courtyard and shot.

The conversations with Stefan filled me with horror and confusion. My own fate was hard to take; fear and uncertainty followed me throughout the occupation. I asked, but I couldn't decide whether I really wanted to know. I suspect that I was the only person with whom he could openly talk at that time, the one he could—or rather had to—tell things, the only one who "knew." I, too, knew that Stefan understood my fear, that with him I didn't have to pretend I was someone I really wasn't. The infrequent and short meetings were both a burden and a relief.

At the end of July 1944, the streets were filled with throngs of people. German military convoys were rolling in disorderly fashion through Jerozolimskie Avenue from the Poniatowski Bridge—cars, horse-drawn carts, Tatars on their little horses, hapless ranks of people who seemed more like refugees than soldiers. The atmosphere was of excitement and expectation. It was warm, there was a light drizzle. I was walking along Koszykowa Street in the direction of Trzech Krzyży Square. I was wearing my new black raincoat. I was not afraid—what a new and strange feeling that was! Suddenly, someone grabbed my arm—it was Stefan, whom I hadn't seen for several months, with a beaming expression on his face.

"Jana, look what's happening! I can't believe it; it seems we've both survived. Wait . . ." He ran to a stall selling flowers and came back with two bunches of fragrant pea flowers. We walked over to Jerozolimskie Avenue. "My love, I have to go," he hugged me and kissed me on the cheek. "See you later."

I never saw him again. Searches through the Red Cross yielded no result.

Father's Friend (Summer 1942)

It all probably happened at the beginning of the summer in 1942. I was with my mother; we boarded a suburban train. I don't know whether it was the one going across the Vistula toward Otwock, the EKD[3] going to Pruszków, or some other one. After a perhaps forty-five-minute ride, we got out at a little station and walked to a big white house surrounded by a large garden. I remember a meadow behind the house, a gate in the fence that surrounded the garden, and a tall, good-looking lady with blond hair pinned up in a large bun in the back of her head. After a short conversation, my mother left, while the lady turned her attention to me, kindly, and without asking any questions. She showed me the house—nobody lived there besides her, as her husband was in a prisoner-of-war camp. I was to take a room upstairs—yes, my own room! There were bookshelves everywhere, I could read anything I wanted, and if I felt like it, I could help in the kitchen and in the garden. I felt as if I had been transported into another time; suddenly everything was like before the war—the house, the garden, the books, the pleasant lady, unrestrained conversation. I became a regular sixteen-year-old girl, not an adult constantly forced to make independent decisions.

Evening came, and the lady of the house announced that there would be guests for dinner—three gentlemen. We set the table—a white tablecloth, pretty plates, and a vase with flowers. The guests arrived punctually. They were slim men, about forty years old. They carried themselves straight, and one of them wore military officer's boots. They clicked their heels while greeting us, after which they stood at their chairs, waiting for us to sit down. I had no doubt, I knew who these gentlemen were.

I brought the soup from the kitchen in a vase and was introduced to the guests. "This is my friends' daughter, Janeczka Prot, who will stay with me several months. I'm not going to be as lonely, and maybe she'll help me a little." A flash of interest ran through the oldest guest's face. "Prot? Was your father's name Jan?" "Yes." "Oh, I knew him back in the army. What a nice man," he said with enthusiasm. "Yes, we later used to meet in Warsaw, he would come on business. Where is he now?" "I don't know, he didn't come back from the war," I replied curtly. All those questions didn't foreshadow anything good. "Oh what a shame, we liked each other a lot . . ." Then he looked at me carefully. "So, you must have terrible troubles now, right? Because you're really Jews. . . ."

And thus fell that terrible word, the taboo word, the insult, the word that couldn't be used in normal human relations. Silence fell. My spontaneous reactions were then already extinguished. I didn't get mixed up, didn't blush, didn't answer. I looked dully into my plate. Our hostess interrupted the silence with some neutral remark, and a banal conversation ensued in which I did not take part. I took the dishes to the kitchen, said goodnight, and went upstairs with a book. I was awakened early in the morning, "My child, I am terribly sorry, but you'll have to leave today."

I don't remember any more. I don't know how I got back to Warsaw; I don't know where and to whom I went.

I can't place this event in time. I don't remember where I was immediately before and after, but I can see this short day clearly, like a crisp photograph. I don't know what the name of the lady of the house was, nor the town where I spent those twenty-four hours. I don't know the name of the man who used to know my father, either.

I wish to dedicate this short tale to human stupidity.

An Encounter (Spring 1942)

One Saturday after school I came home to get my backpack, put on my old ski boots and a shawl on my head, and took the streetcar to the last stop in Bielany. From there I walked along a path I knew, toward Wawrzyszew and Wólka Węglowa, diagonally across a gray muddy field or pasture, scattered with melting snow. I avoided the larger roads on which one ran into peasants' carts, drawn apathetically by skinny horses, or peasant women, wrapped in shawls, carrying milk canisters on their backs.

Finally, after a two-hour march, I came to the village of Laski—shabby cottages, fences, mud—and went out on to the road. That route from Laski to Izabelin was paved with large round cobblestones. In the holes in the road and along the pavement there were dirty puddles and remnants of melting snow. The sun was setting, the cold wind chased away the gray clouds. I was walking along briskly, hunched down, because I was cold. Just before the road took a right turn toward the Home for the Blind, I lifted my head. . . . In front of me, in the middle of the empty road, stood a tall, destitute woman. She seemed huge in front of the setting sun. Her black, matted hair fell down below her shoulders. She was barefoot. Her dark, tattered rags blew in the wind. She held two incredibly skinny children by the hands. One of them had long, tangled hair. The woman and the children looked straight ahead. Their black, expressionless eyes seemed huge in their shrunken faces. Not a word was uttered. After a moment the woman moved, jerked the children along, and disappeared among the trees of the wood that extended on the left side of the road.

Could I have imagined seeing them? Did they really exist?

This story was submitted by the author in English.

1. A red emblem was worn by students attending lyceum, the last two years of secondary school, while a blue emblem was worn by students in gymnasium, the first four years of secondary school.

2. The ONR *(Obóz Narodowo-Radykalny)* [Radical Nationalists] was a right-wing party. The Falanga party was an extreme right-wing spin-off of ONR.

3. The EKD *(Elektryczna Kolej Dojazdowa)* was an electric commuter train.

ESTERA ROSNER

Born in 1939

They Didn't Live to See It

In memory of Chana and Chune Rosner

I was born on April 11, 1939, in Tarnów, as the daughter of Chune Rosner and Chana, née Grüner, from Gorlice. Father and his parents, Wolf and Saala, were respected citizens of Tarnów, related to the family of Rabbi Unger. Unfortunately, they all perished, shot to death by the Nazis, and Father died of hunger at the end of the war in the concentration camp Gross-Rosen.[1] Only their memory remains.

What can I write about myself during the war that is interesting? As a little child, I can only remember staying in a cellar on mounds of uniforms and the fear, the constant fear. At the sound of a door opening, I, as a two- and later, three-year-old, was hidden under heavy overcoats and had to lie there silently.

After the war, when I was already a schoolgirl, I found out that the cellar had been in the ghetto, located on Goldhammer Street in Tarnów. My parents hid me in it because the women and some of the men were sewing German military uniforms there. Father, however, used to go out of the ghetto to work as forced labor, repairing railroad equipment. There he met a railroad worker who promised to look after his child. This is how I happened to leave the ghetto in 1942. I never saw my loved ones again.

I was taken out of the ghetto at night by my new guardian and his son. The next day, under a new name, I was taken to Dębica, to distant relatives of my rescuers. After three months in Dębica, probably as a result of neighbors informing on me, I returned to

Tarnów under the pretense of being a cousin from Lwów, and that's how I survived the war.

And after the war? Of course, waiting for the return of my parents—unfortunately, to no avail. My guardians, after a long search for my close and distant relatives, adopted me and became everything to me. It was in their name that my daughter and I, in 1987, planted a tree in Yad Vashem and received the Righteous Among the Nations of the World medal, which had been awarded to them in 1984. Unfortunately, they did not live to see it.

I finished elementary school and a general education high school in Tarnów, and then I studied medicine. I became a physician in 1963 and since 1974 have been a specialist in internal medicine—not in Tarnów, however, because people there pointed their finger at me and called me "the Jewess."

As the head of the department of internal medicine, I have trained more than forty physicians who have gone on to get their first and second degrees of specialization. Many of them are good people and great doctors. They never saw a Jew in their lives, yet they are proclaimed anti-Semites, not realizing who had been supervising them for twenty-five years. My husband is also a physician. We have one daughter, who is also a doctor, and a one-and-a-half-year-old grandson who has big, dark brown eyes like his mama, grandma—and perhaps his great-grandparents?

And this is the whole story of a small child, very badly crippled during the war. Fear and a feeling of inferiority have followed me all my life.

---

1. Gross-Rosen was a concentration camp in Lower Silesia set up in 1940, first as part of Sachsenhausen, later as an independent camp. Most of the 40,000 prisoners who died there were Jews.

JOANNA SOBOLEWSKA-PYZ

Born in 1939

Searching for Traces

My first memories go back to the moment when I met my new parents. It was in the apartment of Mrs. Wanda Niczowa.[1] When they entered, I was sitting on the floor, playing. "This is your mama and your papa," said Mrs. Niczowa. I was very pleased; my new mama was lovely, all made up and colorful. I liked Father, too, though not quite as much. Mrs. Niczowa dressed me in a large hat and an oversize jacket, and in this funny outfit, I got into a horse-drawn cart with them. Nineteen years later, my father, in a letter to my Israeli family, described these events as follows:

> It was 1943—the harshest period of the occupation. The Germans were liquidating the ghetto; there were roundups in the city, horrible reports about arrests and people being burned alive in the ghetto. Over the ghetto hung black smoke. All of Warsaw was tense and depressed. People suddenly became kind; they wanted to help the unfortunates who didn't know what the next day would bring. This is when a waterworks and sewer maintenance man showed up at my office and told me that while cleaning sewers in the ghetto, they had found a little girl, a few years old, and carried her out in a coal basket.
>
> A few days later, a typist from my office told my wife that there was a very pretty little girl at the home of her teacher, Mrs. Niczowa, who was available to be taken in by someone. We thought that it

might be the same child. My wife got excited about this, because we were a childless couple. Mrs. Niczowa lived on Krasiński Street. Public transportation was disrupted by the liquidation of the ghetto. It was restored a few days later, but only by horse-drawn carts that kept a certain distance from the ghetto. On May 2, my wife and I set out to visit friends in Żoliborz for Zygmunt's name day celebration,[2] and on the way, we stopped at Mrs. Niczowa's to have a look at Inka. She was a very pretty little girl with platinum blond hair and blue eyes. My wife liked her a lot, and we decided we would pick her up on our way back from the party.

Since the atmosphere at the name day celebration was rather gloomy, we left early and went to get Inka. We were worried that she would cry and raise suspicions, especially since she was dressed so horribly—in an old hat and an elderly woman's old jacket. When we sat on one of the five benches on the cart, the other people began looking at us suspiciously, because our clothes were so different from what Inka was wearing. Only if she had cried could it have been worse, but fortunately, she did not cry. For the sake of appearances in front of these people, my wife and I began talking and complaining about our cousins from the countryside who had sent Inka to the doctor in such awful clothes. Most likely this little scene didn't fool anyone, but fortunately, there were no mean-spirited people there.

Going around the ghetto through side streets, we sat on that cart as if on burning coals. A small group of people standing on one of the streets leading into the ghetto was pointing at something. A three-story house in the ghetto was burning, and people were throwing themselves from the balconies. We saw a woman jump from a window with a child. We could hear the shouting of the Germans and Ukrainians down below.

Finally, we got to Miodowa Street, where our nerve-racking trip ended and where there were already streetcars and [bicycle-powered] rickshaws. I caught one of them, and, taking side streets, we made our way to 8 Wilcza Street. Inka did not cry. We didn't encounter any Germans on the way. Getting into the elevator, we breathed easier. In the apartment were my two young nieces, who gave Inka a bath, and my wife, together with a friend, set about sewing a dress for her. In one of the photographs I am sending you, Inka is wearing precisely that dress.

After some time, we started worrying again. A neighbor from one floor below stared intently at Inka on the staircase. We were afraid that she might suspect something. Such a suspicion, in the absence of an alibi, could mean a death sentence for the whole family or, at best, costly blackmail. Thus, we had to think about getting proper documents. My wife went to see Mrs. Niczowa so that she could go through the formality of handing Inka over to the Father Baudouin Children's Home. We later picked her up from there, based on Declaration Number 331/43, dated June 28, 1943. This wasn't a document that would guarantee safety, but at least it gave us the possibility of explaining ourselves.

I have described for you, though in fragments, what we lived through then, and what Warsaw was experiencing, in order to show how often these matters are poorly understood today. . . . I would like to take this opportunity to invite you to visit us in Poland. We would welcome you as our guests during your stay here. Respectfully yours, Walerian Sobolewski. Warsaw, August 28, 1962.

So much for my father's letter. I myself remember little from those years, barely a few scenes. I remember the moment we entered my parents' apartment on Wilcza Street. My father's niece, Halka, welcomed us. "Oh, what a pretty little girl!" she said. These words pleased me greatly. Evidently, I was vain right from birth.

Recalling that time, I can't fathom how it is possible that I can't remember anything at all from my days in the ghetto. It is a complete blank. My life began on Wilcza Street, or perhaps a moment earlier, on the floor at Mrs. Niczowa's.

In the winter of 1943, Father was put in Pawiak prison as a hostage. Every day families of prisoners scanned the lists of those who had been executed, posted on the walls. On one of the lists appeared the name Stanisław Sobolewski. Upon learning this news, Mother fainted in the apartment and fell on a burning carbide lamp. I began screaming and ran out on the stairwell. I can't remember whether Mama came to by herself or whether one of the neighbors helped her. In any case, there was no fire, although it was a close call.

In her despair, Mama forgot that she was the only one who called Father "Stach"[Stanisław]. Even though he celebrated his name day on May 8,[3] Stanisław was his middle name. The tragic news referred to someone else. A few months later, Father returned.

As a child, I particularly liked it when the sirens wailed. We would then go down from the fifth floor to the caretaker's apartment in the basement. It was a great attraction for me and the other children in the building. Unaware of the danger, we were happy that, despite the late hour (air raids happened mostly at night), we could meet and play by the little stove with a fire burning in it.

Thus passed, as far as I can remember, the years associated with Pawiak prison, fear about Father's fate, and the wailing of sirens. At the end of July 1944, the entire family—including Lalka, our beloved spitz—moved to Milanówek. This is how Mama described the beginning of the trip: "We barely caught the last EKD train.[4] Stach was running, holding Inka under one arm and Lalka under the other. Halka and I ran after him, choking with laughter at the sight of the two bouncing balls under his arms." She meant my head and Lalka's tail—both equally shaggy. Meanwhile, the last car of the train was being shot at, because the Warsaw Uprising had started.

In Milanówek we were taken in by my parents' friends, the Michałowicz family. I felt good there and used to play in the garden. One summer day I decided to accomplish a great athletic feat, to jump down from as many as three steps leading up to the porch. I easily jumped down from one, then with some trepidation from two, and finally—with great fear, but also with a great feeling of achievement—all the way from the third. I was completely absorbed in play when I suddenly saw a German gendarme in front of me. I had heard so many horrible things about Germans that I was stricken with fear.

Crying loudly, I ran back inside the house. Not knowing where Mama was, I ran upstairs. Then I heard her voice. Instead of coming back downstairs, I stuck my head between the posts of the handrail and started screaming, "Mama! Germans!" My head got stuck between the posts, and the German tried to free me. Mama tried to calm me down, but I jerked around and tugged. Everyone ran out onto the stairs. Someone suggested getting an ax or a saw. I was afraid they meant for my head. Fortunately, my head was somehow freed without those tools. Then the gendarme picked me up and asked me to give him a kiss. He took a candy bar out of his pocket and gave it to me. I tried to break free, but Mama told me, "Give the gentleman a kiss. He says he left a little daughter like you at home." I pecked the air next to his cheek and ate the chocolate later. It tasted very good.

For a time we moved to a village near Mszczonów. I don't know why. Perhaps it was easier to get food there or perhaps my parents were afraid of a *Volksdeutsche* family who had just moved into "our" house. For a long time, I thought *Volksdeutsche* was a family name. Toward the end of the occupation we returned to Milanówek, and it turned out that this *Volksdeutsche* family was the most decent family under the sun. They obtained meat, marmalade, and coal for us. They shared everything they themselves had and invited me for meals; I played with their children. When, during a roundup, Father ended up in the town square with a group of people to be deported, the *Volksdeutsche* family we knew took him out of there. Many people in Milanówek benefited from their assistance.

I remember how Mother despaired when this family fled west to escape from the Bolsheviks. They ran away at the last moment, and Mother was afraid that they might not make it. Born in Ufa in the Ural Mountains, Mother had lived through the Russian Revolution, and she simply didn't know whom to fear more, the Germans or the Russians. I couldn't understand her strange behavior. When Russian soldiers showed up, she would treat them to *lepioszki*[5] and talk to them merrily in Russian, but after they left she would sob, shaking with fear. Perhaps she was afraid that they would discover that she was a "White Russian."[6]

From the final weeks of the war, I remember the rumbling of artillery, the sound of bombs, and the glow over the city. We could see Warsaw burning all the way from Milanówek. Father decided to check whether our house at 8 Wilcza Street still existed. It turned out that out of a seven-story building with four wings, only one apartment got burned—and that was ours. My parents talked about it a lot, because it didn't look as if it happened by chance. The apartment was located on the fifth floor of an inner section. They suspected that it had been set on fire deliberately. We were left without a roof over our heads. Father decided that we would take another apartment in the same building, also on the fifth floor, but in front. Before the war it had belonged to Dr. Gutner and his family. I don't know what happened to them. The apartment was ruined, full of rubble, with no glass in the windows. There were a few pieces of damaged furniture there, and our entire furnishings consisted of one singed piano stool.

The destroyed city made a great playground for children. In the surrounding rubble, one could find unbelievable treasures, such as a chair leg, a broken doll, a vase with a broken handle, a candle, a bead, a postcard, or a photograph. Afraid that we'd come across unexploded shells in the ruins, our parents would not allow us to play there—but nothing scared us away. The ruins were everywhere; even my way to school led through rubble.

Life was slowly getting back to normal. Father decided to reactivate his prewar business, a hydrotechnical installation firm. Mother, opposed to this idea, said, "Stach, you don't know the Bolsheviks. The worst job with the state is better than the best private business." And that's how it really was. The Stalinist era had a tragic impact on the fate of my family. Without going into details, I will just say that Father was accused of economic sabotage and at first sentenced to death and confiscation of property. Due to a reprieve, the sentence was changed to life in prison. Eventually, thanks to two amnesties, he was able to leave prison after six years. Before that happened, however, Mama and I would stand by the prison gate every Sunday—first on

Rakowiecka Street then at Gęsiówka[7] —waiting for a short visit with him.

Father was not idle in prison; he worked on technical projects and trained young people in his trade. Some then joked that studies in sanitary engineering had been moved to Gęsiówka. Many of those young people later finished regular studies and found employment in Warsaw's best architectural construction firms, one of which was started by my father.

Meanwhile, we were forced to share our apartment on Wilcza Street with other tenants. Father had bought a plot of land in Anin already before the war, and right after the war, he began building a house there. Now, the authorities gave Mother an ultimatum: She could either move out of Wilcza to Anin, or they would confiscate the land in Anin together with the unfinished building.

Father, who was still in prison at the time, insisted that she not give away the land in Anin. And so we moved into the unfinished house, which was very cold and damp. It cost Mother much effort and money to make it habitable.

Mama fell ill in Anin. Because she didn't speak Polish well, she had to do physical labor. She commuted to Warsaw, where she got a job in a laundry. Working conditions were a nightmare there—inside the temperature reached 50° C [122° F]—and Mother had a bad heart and high blood pressure.

Father came back in 1954. He was cleared of charges in 1956. Mother died in 1958. She did not survive the next heart attack, even though she was not yet sixty years old. I sat by her side in the hospital on Stępińska Street during her last night. She said to me then, "Don't count on anyone. You're my little daughter, and only mine." She died before my eyes, and for a long time afterward, I did not realize that these were her last words. I did not grasp their real meaning. I understood that I was Mama's illegitimate child, the fruit of a great and, most likely, forbidden love affair. This kind of piquant detail of our family history appealed to me.

When Father and I were left alone, we didn't get along very

well. He wanted me to take care of the house, but I was studying for my matriculation exams and preparing for university. Besides, I was a pretty unruly, socially active girl, talkative and restless. I very much liked doing things that were forbidden—for instance, smoking cigarettes (in fact, preferably the ones Father kept in his drawer). So, when during one of our arguments, he said, "You don't know what you owe me," I replied, "I know that I am not your daughter. I am my mama's illegitimate child." "You're neither my daughter nor Mama's daughter. You're a Jewish child rescued from the ghetto," Father said. It was an awful moment for both of us. I took a cigarette out of my school bag and lit up in his presence for the first time. He lit one, too. At first we were silent, and then he told me as much as he knew. Although Mrs. Niczowa's name was mentioned, the possibility of getting in touch with her did not enter my head. It was only while I was at university that Witold Jedlicki, a teaching assistant in sociology with whom I was friendly, gave me the idea.

I found Mrs. Niczowa in 1961. She described to me at length, quite vividly, how a Polish policeman had brought me to her, lice-infested, dirty, and in a terrible state. This was on April 18, 1943. Mrs. Niczowa knew me well, because even earlier, as she told me, my mother had brought me to her house, leaving the ghetto through the sewers. It was then that I learned that my parents were called Halina, née Zylberbart, and Tadeusz Grynszpan. Mrs. Niczowa knew only that they had gone to *Umschlagplatz* and that I was left behind. However, she didn't know what had happened to me from that time until the moment I was brought to her place.

But what still remains unclear to me is the connection between what my adopted father described in his aforementioned letter to my relatives in Israel and the Polish policeman who "delivered" me to Mrs. Niczowa, hiding me under his jacket like a kitten. Another unanswered question is how this policeman knew to whom he should take me.

Mrs. Niczowa had been friends with my mother's parents. My

grandparents—Marian Zylberbart and Rozalia Ewelina, née Gesundheit—were physicians who worked, among other places, in sanitariums in Otwock. Thanks to Mrs. Niczowa, I also found out that I am related to the wife of Adam Czerniaków[8] —Felicja, née Zwayer.

As a result of the conversation with Mrs. Niczowa, I began remembering events from the past that were related to what she had been talking about, but which until then I had not understood properly or at all.

And thus I remembered that when I was a little girl, I heard our neighbor say in Russian, "It seems to me that your Inotchka is *Yevreika.*" These words were said to my mama by Mrs. Tkachenko, mother-in-law of Professor Aleksander Gieysztor. My adopted mother came from an aristocratic Russian family, and both ladies loved to converse in Russian. Mother might have been a little taken aback by these words, and perhaps that's why I remembered them so well. Many years later, when I began learning Russian in school, I found the words "*Yevrei, Yevreika*—Jew, Jewess" in a dictionary, but that still didn't mean anything to me.

Almost every year I spent my vacations with my uncle who was a parish priest in a village near Białystok. Another girl my age also came to that same village to visit her grandparents, and we used to spend whole days together. We also used to play with the country children. There were times when the boys would yell after me, "Cross yourself!" "What's that all about?" I'd ask. They answered with silly expressions and pointed looks.

The priest's housekeeper once told me (I don't remember the context), "A mother is not the one who gives birth but the one who brings you up." I was a little girl and did not understand what she was talking about. My vacation friend, with whom I stay in close touch to this day, told me that everyone in the village knew that I was a Jewish child, adopted by the priest's family.

Did people know about this in my high school? I don't know, but in Anin, like in that village, everyone knew each other and a lot about each other. One of my friends once told me that her mother had said, "Inka looks very much like a Jew." Was that by chance? To me it meant only that I must be very ugly.

I found my Jewish family at the beginning of the 1960s. I turned to the Israeli Embassy with a request that they place my ad and my photo in some well-read newspaper in Israel. The ad, and especially the part about my being a relative of the wife of Adam Czerniaków, caught the attention of my cousin, Bolek Prusak. Here are some fragments of his letter to me: "I left for Israel already in 1935. In her last letter of August 25, 1939, my mother informed me, 'On July 31, Hala gave birth to a daughter; she is doing well and so is the child; her name is Joanna.' Here in Israel you also have your mother's cousin, Bronka Diamant, née Milner. Your grandmother and her mother were sisters. In Warsaw, we had a house at 57 Nowolipie Street, and that's where the whole family lived. . . . I hope that after these explanations, you will not have any doubt that, thanks to your ad, you have found your family. Dear Joasia, write back right away; after all, we don't know anything about you. How did you survive that period? What are you doing now? I hope you would like to come to Israel to join the family. Your mother and I lived like siblings for many years, and today I feel as if I have known you all your life."

Bolek and Bronka invited me to Israel right away, but time after time the Polish authorities refused to issue me a passport. I finally managed to get there illegally in 1974. I received a passport to go to Sweden, and from there, with an Israeli visa not stamped into my passport, I arrived to see my family. I was welcomed with exceptional warmth. To them, I was a child of their loved ones', with whom they had spent their childhood and youth. At first they seemed like strangers to me, but we quickly established warm and close ties.

I went to Israel again in 1994. That trip has special meaning, because unfortunately, both Bolek and Bronka died a short time later. To this day I keep in close touch with Bolek's wife and Bronka's daughter, Zosia, and her husband, Amiram. Zosia and I differ in age by the time span of the war—I was born at the beginning and Zosia at the end. After the war, Zosia and her mother, upon returning from the Soviet Union, lived in an apartment complex called MDM[9] in central Warsaw. I lived close by on Wilcza Street with my parents. We might have passed each other in the street without realizing we were family.

In Israel, thanks to the flourishing spread of news by word of mouth, I unexpectedly came across a trace of my father's half sister who now lives in England. I got in touch with her and then visited her in London, where my miraculously discovered Aunt Marysia welcomed me very warmly, together with her daughter and son-in-law. To her own amazement, my aunt, who considered herself a reticent person, just talked, talked, and talked; until that time, she had had no opportunity to talk about her family. Wartime trauma had caused her to hide her origins, even from her own daughter. The subject of our unending conversations was the daily life of the Grynszpans. It was a very large family, and a particularly interesting and colorful figure was my grandfather, Herman Grynszpan, a man exceptionally unconventional for those times—a freethinker, philosopher, and lover of women (not necessarily in a Platonic way). He perished in the Warsaw Ghetto in 1942.

It was only from Aunt Marysia that I learned that my father's mother and sister escaped from the ghetto, were in hiding in Warsaw, and died almost at the same time, in the mid-1960s. They were buried in Bródno Cemetery.[10] I live not far away and visit their graves quite often.

My adopted father died in 1965. His family—his second wife and three of his siblings—decided to deprive me of my inheritance. They petitioned the court to annul my birth certificate, in which I appeared as a child born to Anastazja and Walerian Sobolewski. The petitioners thought that if they proved that my identity was different than that entered into the documents and that I was neither the natural nor formally adopted daughter of my parents, then they would inherit the house in Anin. Their incompetent lawyer did not know that a petition for the annulment of a birth certificate can only be made by the person involved or the person's parents. They lost the case.

This whole matter affected my relationship with my father's family, which had been fairly decent until then. What bothered me the most was the fact that they sought to justify their petition to invalidate the birth certificate in a way that was dishonest and indecent. Among other things, they wrote that after my father explained to me my family history, "all emotional ties between the defendant of this case and her adoptive father were broken." They wrote further that "the defendant does not at all consider herself to be Polish. She openly acknowledges her Jewish origins and—through the Israeli Embassy—has been trying to find her close family in Israel. On every occasion she stresses her separate ethnicity."

In my article "Children of the Holocaust," written thirty-three years later,[11] I answered their accusations in this way: "The problem of identity deserves attention. It is especially important and painful to people who discovered their Jewish roots late in life. I am one of these people myself. I found out about my origins when I was eighteen years old. I was raised in a Polish family. When I say 'parents,' I mean my 'second' parents, because I didn't know any others. At the same time, I am investigating traces of that other world. I know a great deal about my Jewish family. I discovered my more distant, and probably the only surviving, relatives in Israel. I search for people who can tell me anything at all about my relatives. I explore archives. The fate of people who died in the Holocaust, as well as of those who survived, has been the subject of my interest for decades, and I can definitely say that there is little that matters to me as much. At the same time, I do not feel any connection with the Jewish religion or culture, with which I am not familiar, and have no desire to learn more about. I am rooted in Polish culture and tradition and feel connected to everything that relates to them. However, I believe it would be improper for me not to admit to my Jewish origins, especially in the face of anti-Semitic behavior, precisely because my relatives were murdered only because they were Jews. For me it is a matter of honor. In truth, my Jewish identity is mainly a tribute to those who died."

In another part of the article I wrote: "The Association (of 'Children of the Holocaust') tries to help its members find their families. Everyone searches—those who have already found out something about themselves, those who have already found someone from their family, as well as those who hope that a miracle will happen and they will find someone close to them."

My life story is filled with both miraculous discoveries and unexpected results of my searches. In the Otwock Archive there is a prewar registration book,[12] and in it, among other things, is my mother's year of birth. In the Central Medical Library,[13] I found a work by Witold Trybowicz entitled *History of Otwock as a Health Spa* that includes much information about my grandparents, Rozalia and Marian Zylberbart. In the Jewish Historical Institute, there is a *Register of Account Holders of the Postal Savings Bank.* My grandfather, Henryk Grynszpan, is listed under number 166. I finally saw how my last name was spelled. In the Institute I also found a "List of Non-Aryan Doctors," prepared by the Warsaw-Białystok Medical Society. It includes my grandmother's name. Just the existence of such a list, dated May 1, 1940, is of itself very interesting. In the 1925 guidebook, entitled *Otwock Spa,* the last name on the list of doctors practicing in Otwock is my grandfather's: "Dr. M. Zylberbart, 32A Warszawska Street. Diseases of the ear, nose, and throat. Office hours 5:00–7:00 P.M."

It would be impossible to name all the people or enumerate all the documents that have permitted me to at least partially recreate this lost world, but I can't leave out something that happened to me very recently. Quite by chance, I happened to be at a meeting of the Association of the Friends of Otwock and the Otwock Region. I asked one of the older men there about my family. It turned out that he remembered my grandfather but couldn't tell me anything about my grandmother or mother. However, he promised to help me, and he kept his word. He put me in touch with his acquaintance, Mrs. Anna P., who, in her personal collection, had a photo of her mother's class in gymnasium.

My mother and my father's sister are also in this photograph. On the back of the photo there are a few signatures and among them, Hala Zylberbart and Krysia Grynszpan. The photo was made in the second half of the 1920s. It shows a picturesque group of about thirty male and female students in front of the Municipal Coeducational Gymnasium in Otwock, and among them is a serious-looking teenager wearing glasses. This is what sets her apart. Nobody else is wearing glasses, even the teachers. It's difficult to describe how touched I was when I saw that photo.

Writing a biography is conducive to summing up. I can definitely say that I was born under a lucky star, and incomparably more good things than bad have happened to me in my life. Just the fact that I am alive is of itself good fortune. Along the way, from the beginning, I met nice people. First, someone saved my life and then surrounded me with care. Then, I got everything a child could get from her parents—love, care, and family warmth. I had warm ties with my father's siblings and their children for many years. I got much that was good from them in my childhood.

My present household consists of my husband, Julek, my son, Wojtek, and two cats—Mysia and Malusia. My husband is the person closest to me; I can depend on him in every situation. He supports me in my searches and knows more about Judaism than many experts in the field. I also have the warm support of my husband's family. My in-laws, regrettably no longer alive, always treated me with great fondness and warmhearted interest.

At the university and at work I was generally surrounded by friendly and interesting people. I have many devoted friends and the conviction that this, also, worked out well for me in every respect.

---

1. Wanda Bruno-Niczowa was a Polish language teacher who conducted secret classes during the occupation. She hid me and the child of her cousins (she used "impeccable" Aryan papers for herself). (Author's note)

2. Poles celebrate "name days" rather than birthdays. The name day is the feast day of the saint a person is named after.

3. May 8 is the feast day of Saint Stanisław.

4. The EKD *(Elektryczna Kolej Dojazdowa)* is an electric commuter train.

5. *Lepioszki* are Russian-style cheese blintzes.

6. "White Russians" were Russians who supported the czar rather than the "Reds" during the 1917 Bolshevik Revolution.

7. Gęsiówka was a prison on what was then Gęsia Street (now Mordechaj Anielewicz Street).

8. Adam Czerniaków was the head of the *Judenrat* [Jewish Council] in Warsaw. He committed suicide in July 1942 rather than carry out orders to liquidate the Warsaw Ghetto.

9. *Marszałkowska Dzielnica Mieszkaniowa* (MDM) consisted of several blocks of Soviet-style housing, built in the Stalinist years 1950–52 along Marszałkowska Street.

10. Bródno Cemetery is a Catholic cemetery in Warsaw.

11. In *Tematy żydowskie* [*Jewish Topics*], edited by Elżbieta and Robert Traba (Olsztyn: Wspólnota Kulturowa "Borussia," 1999); also in *Kronika Stowarzyszenia "Dzieci Holocaustu"* [*Chronicles of the "Children of the Holocaust"*], No. 7, 1999. (Author's footnote).

12. A *Księga Meldunkowa/Księga Ludności* is a municipal registration book containing census-like data about all members of a household.

13. The Central Medical Library [*Główna Biblioteka Lekarska*] is located in Warsaw.

SVEN SONNENBERG

Born in 1931

Journey to Hell: Under Fascism

I was born in 1931 in Grudziądz, Poland. My family home and business were located in Jabłonowo, about twenty-five kilometers east of Grudziądz. This was less than twenty kilometers from the border of East Prussia, where the Germans mounted their invasion of western Poland in September 1939. In 1939 my family consisted of my father, Martin, my mother, Louise, my sister, Sylvia, and myself, age seven at that time. On the same premises lived my grandmother, Laura, and three uncles, Alfred, Magnus, and Ari.

The family owned and operated a wholesale warehouse situated in the center of Jabłonowo. The property consisted of two multistory houses and several utility buildings, all situated on a large piece of land. The warehouse was a distribution center for the vicinity, and it prospered. Before the outbreak of the war, expansion was contemplated.

My family was a close-knit unit, all working in the business at their assigned duties. My father was the accountant and salesman. My parents were very dedicated to each other; the feeling of mutual love between them permeated every single day as far back as I can remember. They never argued. This feeling of being blessed, of having each other, made any issue that could have come between them small and insignificant. Although my mother was a strict disciplinarian, her love and care for us children was obvious and ever present. Her devotion to us made any punishment that she meted out for my misbehavior bearable and of lasting educational value. This is how I remember them. Unfortunately, only very few photographs survived the Holocaust years.

Prelude

My first year of school ended badly. I went into the recess of summer 1939 with turmoil in my seven-year-old head. Right from the start, the beautifully embroidered Tyrolese shorts my mother so insistently outfitted me with were trouble. The whole first grade and beyond had a field day. My first love, Zosia, a playful little blond, sneered at me mercilessly—but the end of my first-grade year was more serious and ominous.

One day the teacher asked the children, "Now, each of you tell me, what do you have on the wall over your bed?" The variety of things was not great, mostly crucifixes and the Virgin Mary. "Sven, what do you have?" I had the framed portrait of Marshal Śmigły-Rydz (the supreme commander of the Polish Forces). "Look children, a little Jew, and what a patriot!"

That has stayed with me to this day and will forever. I understood right there that I was different, and no matter what merit I might show, I was basically flawed, and there was no escape from that. From that point on, I tried to excel in whatever I was doing to diminish that flaw in the eyes of whomever I was with. Until, one day, I did not give a damn any more, and I experienced a reversal. I saw the entire gentile world with a healthy dose of skepticism and no longer did things because I was viewed as a Jew.

In August, during the school recess, exciting things were happening. The Polish army was conducting maneuvers and mock battles in the surrounding countryside. A contingent of soldiers camped in our yard, which was large, and slept in our utility buildings. To the utter dismay of my mother, I became uncontrollable. I would not eat her spinach, because I ate with the soldiers from their tins while sitting with them in a circle. The coarse dark bread was such a delight after the white fluffy rolls. The soldiers let me do little chores around their equipment. Great times!

At home the conversation was more and more about a possible war. My mother implored my father to leave Poland, to go to Switzerland, or anywhere out of the line of a possible German advance. Switzerland was most often discussed, because I think they had some connections there. I knew they had business associates and friends. I myself was not too concerned; the mighty Polish army would protect us. Certainly the parades through Main Street were impressive. The radio and the speeches were also very reassuring. "We will not let them have a single button" (from their uniforms, apparently). "If they attack us, we will be in Berlin in two weeks." And so, a busy summer passed, the soldiers were leaving, and I was sad again.

I remember vividly the early morning of September 1, 1939. We children had just crawled into our parents' bed, which was allowed on that day, and the weather was shaping up—it would be bright. That was clearly visible through the window opposite the bed. Suddenly, we heard rumblings as if a thunderstorm were approaching. My father said not to worry, as I was with them. I was always terrified by thunder and lightning. The rumbling got louder, and suddenly, a big explosion could be heard in our yard, and two fair-sized holes appeared in the window. A shrapnel fragment embedded itself in a piece of furniture. That is how World War II began for us.

My parents grabbed us, and we ran into the basement. The basement was somewhat prepared, with sandbags in its windows, water containers, and some towels to put over our mouths as a protection against a possible gas attack. Looking back now, it was all naive to the point of stupidity. I think it matched Poland's preparedness for war.

Once the shelling stopped, our family decided to pack a few things on our horse-drawn wagons and run deeper into Poland, since we lived only twenty kilometers from the border. So we ran—for three days. The smell of fresh hay in the barns where we slept in the countryside comes back now every time I mow the grass.

After we had meandered around for three days, we realized that the Germans were everywhere. The only logical thing to do was to head back home. At home the new instant owners—of what for generations had been ours—met us. These were the business tenants who rented store space in one of our buildings. They declared themselves to be of German ancestry and became what was called *Volksdeutsche,* which means ethnic Germans. Not *Reichsdeutsche*—which were real Germans. Still, *Volksdeutsche* were vastly superior to anyone other than *Reichsdeutsche.* These "ethnics" wore distinguishing armbands and were "holier than thou." We were "put up" in one room in what was once our house. All our belongings and business assets were under the control of this ethnic German family until further disposition by the new German military administration. In two weeks we learned that the territory would be made *Judenfrei*—free of Jews, and we were packed into a special train with one suitcase per person on our journey to—nobody knew where.

The Journey

This was an ordinary train ride, you might say. The compartments were full, since all the Jewish families were crammed into a special car attached to a normally scheduled train. This car was shunted around a lot at several junction stations in order to be attached to other trains heading toward a destination only the Germans knew. I think there was only one car initially, because there were only a few Jewish families in Jabłonowo, judging from the attendance at the synagogue where Father took me on Saturdays.

We finally arrived at a station called Działdowo. To say that we stepped out would not be correct. When the train stopped, we saw soldiers alongside it holding sticks and waiting for the train to make a full stop. They then opened the doors and shouted, *"Raus, schnell, raus, raus, Jüdishe Schweine!"* (Out, quick, out, out, Jewish pigs!) They handled their sticks so as to hit selected people and made everybody hurry to form what turned out to be a long column, four in a row.

When that column was ready, the march began. Apparently, many rail cars like ours were assembled into a purely Jewish train. We marched through what appeared to be a small, dingy town and arrived at what looked like military barracks. The column stopped at an entrance, which turned into a fairly broad alley with a tall chain-link fence on both sides. Alongside each fence there were soldiers stationed every few yards, each with a horsewhip in his hand. Then their fun began.

The commanding officer shouted, "Run to the barracks, on the double!" We started running, my parents on each side trying to shield my sister and me from the blows of the whip, which fell on us as frequently as the soldiers managed to bring their whips around. The commotion was huge. The sound of whips, the screams of people, and the shouting of the Germans, *"Schneller, schneller!"* (Faster, faster!)

At first I was so terrified that I could not think of anything—the fear drowned all other emotions. The alley was between fifty and a hundred yards long. No lashes reached me as we proceeded, because my father, by my right side, blocked them. I started to be concerned about Grandma, who was one row behind us; she was eighty years old then. I turned to see that my uncles were half carrying her, dragging her feet on the ground, terror on her face. The lashes fell on my three uncles, who managed to shield her perfectly.

Finally, we reached a building and ran inside. It was getting dark; we could barely make out the interior. It was a large interior, certainly not a barracks, rather like a huge storehouse or maybe an empty stable for horses. On both sides along the walls were areas with a layer of straw on the ground, framed by planks so as to form passageways in the middle along the vast interior. The space was filling up rapidly; families were grouping on the straw areas, lying down, making the best arrangement with the few meager belongings not lost during the running of the gauntlet.

I can't remember how long we were kept there, camping on the straw the whole time. This is where family clusters organized their everyday lives, including all functions except going to the open latrine behind the building. Only two vivid memories remain from this long, terrifying sequence of events. The next day a small group of Germans (at that time I was unable to distinguish uniforms or services; they were all military of some sort) came in, with one of them obviously being the boss, for what looked like an inspection. He stopped at a place where he could be heard by most people and loudly announced, "These quarters were carefully prepared for your comfort. I want them kept clean. The passageways must be swept and free of even one stalk of straw. I do not want my soldiers to stumble and get hurt. Therefore severe punishment will follow any noncompliance."

We saw the punishment the next day. One bastard, having found a straw, selected a young man from the group near where he found it and whipped him unconscious.

Close to our family group camped another large family. There was a baby who started crying at some point and would not stop; we could not sleep because of it. The baby carried on most of the next day. Toward evening the mother spoke out loudly, "My baby is sick; something is wrong. Please pass this down the line. Is there a doctor somewhere? The baby has not peed for two days."

Sure enough, there was a doctor; I was very curious and tried not to miss any detail. The doctor said that the little guy needed an operation on his penis because of a blockage. The doctor obviously did not have what was necessary for that, but he performed the operation anyway, with a pocketknife, and improvised with whatever the neighboring clusters of people were able to find for him. The little guy peed very soon, and we could sleep again. Happiness reigned among our neighbors.

Somehow my parents protected me from the entire nasty goings-on until our departure, which was, again, terrifying. I remember getting on the train under the blows of sticks wielded by the Germans. They obviously enjoyed herding us from place to place. From the safety of the compartment, I saw a scene to be repeated many times in the future. The train platform from which people were driven into the wagons, German soldiers milling around, some closing the doors, and everywhere there was debris left on the ground—some purses, hats, pieces of garments, and a body here or there. And so we set out for an unknown destination.

They unloaded us in Płock, a historic Polish town. The ghetto was installed in the midtown area along Szeroka (Wide) Street, ringed by monuments of this town's splendid past. Cathedrals and churches and other places of historical significance sat all along the high banks of the Vistula River.

With the onset of the extremely cold winter of 1940, life became harsh right away. The biggest problem was hunger. My father went out day after day trying to find some food for us. Little by little he sold the few pieces of jewelry my parents still had. Amazingly, there were buyers. The problem was—where to get food for the money. The ghetto was a holding area for thousands of people without any normal economic activity. There were no jobs, no flow of supplies, and no stores.

This semblance of an isolated minisociety was in a state of suspension and lingered from day to day, waiting for various ominous developments. The only civic organization existing and allowed to function was the *Gmina Żydowska*—the Jewish Community Council—which passed German orders to the populace and attempted to distribute what meager supplies reached the ghetto from outside. It also organized the work contingents requested by the Germans and tried to implement all kinds of foul ordinances.

One day, in utter exasperation, my parents asked me to go outside the ghetto and buy some food. They agonized about it because it was very dangerous. Eventually, they decided that I did not look all that Jewish and had a chance to pass as Polish. Any Jew, if caught outside the ghetto, with or without the Star of David armband, could be shot. So, I went out of the ghetto.

The store was only a block away, I got into line and soon arrived at the counter. "Two loaves of bread, please, and a quarter kilo of butter." "Sure, but are you not a little Jew, by any chance?" "No." "Well then, cross yourself."

To do that meant to take two fingers of the right hand and touch the forehead, left and right shoulders and belly in the right sequence. I did not know how to do that! This was a moment of terror I have never forgotten. I did not know what to do. Run? Not possible. The store was too crowded. So I stood there befuddled for a while.

"What is the holdup?" shouted from behind. "I think a little Jew has wiggled his way into the line here." "Somebody get a policeman; I will hold him."

I was numb with terror. Suddenly an older woman pushed her way from behind until she was close to the counter and me. She spoke to the clerk. "What is going on here? What do you want from this little boy? Don't you see that he has been scared stiff by you and the crowd here?" "What do you need, boy?" "I . . . I wanted bread and a piece of butter." "To me he speaks perfect Polish. Give him the bread and don't waste our time. I don't want to have to complain to my son about the inefficiency in this store." "Yes, Ma'am."

I would never know who that lady was. With my purchase, I tried not to run home but to walk casually on my shaky legs, my face paper white from the slowly subsiding numbing terror.

The pervasive everyday hunger—that is what I remember most from the Płock ghetto. My father would come home in the evening with everything he had managed to get that day. Hunched over with sunken eyes, he would set it out on the table and wait for mother to figure out what to do with it. That usually was our only meal for the day. We would go to bed with the pangs of hunger only slightly dulled. There was another worry my parents had that seems silly in retrospect. It was my education. They found a teacher to prevent me from losing time. I wonder now if this was denial on their part, or did they genuinely not comprehend what was happening?

I received one lasting lesson and that was not from my teacher. One day, late in the afternoon, there was a commotion in our enclosed little yard, a yard surrounded by high walls on all sides with one entrance from the street. I was playing with some kids when the gate opened and a young man of about eighteen was thrown facedown on the cobblestones. In the door stood two German soldiers. "Find yourself a place here, Jew." "I am not a Jew, I was born a German, I am from Hanover. My name is Adler; please, I do not belong with these stinking Jews." "You stink enough, and don't make more trouble. Settle in."

Adler got up and tried to move toward the gate. When he did so, one of the soldiers took the rifle slung over his shoulder and struck him in the stomach with the butt. Adler doubled over. The gate slammed shut, and we got a new inhabitant in our little world. From that moment on I saw Adler coming and going, always with his head high and contempt on his face for whoever was around. Only once did I hear him speak. Passing through the yard someone shouted to him, "Hello man, where are you from?" "You will address me as Mister Adler, and I have nothing to say to you except that I am from Hanover, and I do not belong here. I was born a German, and I will die as a German."

People gossiped a little but not much. They said that he was from a mixed marriage. The Germans had strict rules of heritage by which they determined if one was Jewish or not. That incident taught me a lesson never to forget. Never try to claim that you are anything but a Jew. I would learn this later to an even greater degree when I found myself among the Poles. They were usually such pure Poles! Although born in Poland, I was very impure. I had gotten a hint of that already in my first school year before the war.

Mister Adler had barely settled in when the Płock ghetto ended. One day there was an announcement by a German soldier with a loudspeaker from the middle of the yard: "All Jews must pack and be ready to assemble in the street tomorrow at daybreak. Only hand-carried luggage is allowed."

That message was repeated three or four times as the soldier turned to face each of the four sides of the yard. After the soldier left, we had all afternoon and night to "pack." The streets were suddenly alive with people rushing in all directions in bewilderment, trying to find out more information or trying to place some prized possession with someone with a lesser burden. One woman on our floor, who was always elegantly dressed, brought over a pair of beautiful cherry-colored leather boots. The only trouble was, these ladies' boots, with medium heels, did not fit my mother. She said to my mother, "Let your son put these on, and you pack his small shoes. If we get separated and I cannot retrieve them, they are yours. I can't bring myself to leave them behind. They are brand-new and a present." Out of all the terrifying hours of that time, I still remember the lady's face and my distress at being forced to put on those boots.

In the morning we were ready with our hand luggage and dressed in multiple layers of clothing. We put on everything we possibly could. My parents were sitting on their beds, my mother holding my sister in her lap. I was sitting by the side of my father, all of us in total silence, our anxiety mounting by the minute. Finally, we heard the troops entering the yard. The noise was unmistakable. We jumped up, ready for whatever might be coming.

"Raus, schnell, raus!" [Out, quick, out!] As we entered the yard I saw Mister Adler fly out the opposite stairway entrance, shouting, "I am a German, I am a German." One of the soldiers dispatching people at the door reached over and gave him a good whack over his shoulders. Then he was swept away by the stream of people, and I never saw him again.

We assembled on the street in rows by families, so that the whole long street (it was called Wide Street and had a median of grass and two cobblestone lanes on each side) was filled with people as far as one could see—everyone with a heap of clothes on and small suitcases in their hands. On the side lanes, German soldiers of all kinds of service units were busying themselves with maintaining order in the column. We were standing there waiting for who knows what.

Here and there, toward late afternoon, older people and the sick started fainting. We heard calls for water, but no water or food was delivered. The soldiers, oblivious to the cries, kept patrolling alongside the column. Later, the word was passed that the Germans would forgo the transfer of the ghetto to a new location for a price. People should give up their valuables, and if they did, the whole thing would be called off. The representatives of the ghetto council went along the column to collect whatever people threw into their baskets. When this was finished, I saw a group of soldiers appear from a side street. They all carried sticks. On command they fell upon the column, hitting left and right, and shouted, "Go home! Go home!"

Evidently, there were a number of groups of Germans whose job this was, to run people off the street fast. In panic, our family ran to the nearest door. We went into a building, and from the safety of a room that appeared to be an empty onetime store, I looked out onto the street and saw the by now all-too-familiar landscape. The area was strewn with all kinds of possessions—garments in pieces, packages, and here and there, a body lying motionless. One could see two or three silhouettes sitting up and rocking slowly back and forth under the darkening sky and the Germans walking over the area, casually poking with their sticks at this or that item on the ground.

The next day was quiet. Nothing happened, and we camped in that storeroom as best we could. The following day at dawn, the whole assembly in the street was repeated. No one was surprised at the ruse the Germans had played on us with the collection of valuables. In midmorning, trucks came, stopping at intervals along one side of the column. The Germans then separated out sections of the column and directed each section toward a truck. Usually a chair or stool was placed at the back of the truck so that people could climb up on that unstable support. Leading up to each truck was the familiar deployment of two rows of German soldiers with sticks. Then, there was more "fun."

In front of us was a family with an obese man who could not get onto the truck. We waited as he kept falling off the chair under the blows of sticks. Finally, the Germans ordered him to stop trying and step aside. The two rows of soldiers closed around the fat man, and the real beating began. The heavy man fell to the ground and tried to protect his face and head with his arms. The Germans kept hitting him as if competing to see who could deliver more blows. After a short while they stepped away to resume the driving of people onto the truck. On the ground, I saw what looked like a big bundle of rags, motionless. A big balding head was stuck to it, with a bloody, messed-up face turned toward me, as we ran to the chair behind the truck, that now frightening piece of furniture. My father shielded me from the blows of the sticks.

After the truck was packed tight, it moved out. I do not remember a guard in the back with us. During this drive of a few hours, we passed small villages where people had lined up at the roadside and threw food into the truck. Apparently, they were from ghettos that were still in existence along our route.

Eventually, we ended up in Końskie, a dingy little place. From our stopping point we marched through the middle of town, and there was total indifference on the faces of the Polish townspeople, as if our march was the commonest everyday occurrence. We passed through town uneventfully and settled into the march to our destination about twelve miles away. That is how we arrived in the Drzewica ghetto, the last stop before Jews were taken to the extermination camps, one of which was Treblinka.

We stayed in Drzewica for a while. My father took care of our immediate family, whereas my three uncles and Grandma formed another group. We got a single room, and my uncles, a corner of a now empty synagogue. About two thousand people were crammed into a small area in this tiny village with no fences or guards. The perimeter of the ghetto was not even marked except later when typhoid fever kept breaking out. At the first Jewish house on each street, a poster would be placed—DANGER! TYPHOID FEVER BEYOND THIS POINT.

The ghetto formed a minisociety, with "rich" people, "middle-class" people, and the destitute. The rich were somehow trading their possessions for food, and that trade moved across the magic invisible ghetto boundary line. Middle-class people—artisans and service people—were somehow surviving. The poor and most newcomers to the place, like us, were starving. This group grew larger by the day. Soon, there was a routine horse-drawn wagon full of bodies of those who had died of starvation, departing every day from the village to the cemetery on the outskirts.

The Hasidim formed a distinct group. They ran a cheder (religious school) and prayed incessantly. They tried to maintain a corner of the synagogue and were constantly moving books in brown leather covers from one place to another, wherever they thought it more secure. Their behavior antagonized the rest of the community, and we became especially angry with them during the outbreak of typhoid fever. They would not let a doctor near them and, most dangerous, would not follow the basic rules of hygiene and quarantine. "If God wants me to die, I will die, no matter what is done." They opposed any action aimed at containing the disease. They were also magnets for the German raiders who came to town periodically. The Germans would seek out a few Hasidim and line them up to amuse themselves by testing the sharpness of their bayonets on the beards of those poor devotees of God. When finished, the Germans would argue among themselves whose was the better shave.

The Drzewica ghetto was slowly starving. Amazingly, people were still preoccupied with trifles, and holy rituals were adhered to as much as possible. I remember an older man sitting on the stone steps at the entrance adjacent to our building. He was cutting his fingernails and very methodically collecting the cuttings on a white cloth. Asked why, he said, "Don't you know that there is a commandment that requires hair and any other bodily clippings to be properly disposed of?" After that, I always wondered what I should properly do with my nail clippings.

Apart from the everyday mundane death scenes, there were some more dramatic ones. There was a man who lived in an abandoned railway freight car not far from our one-room dwelling. I saw him going about alone; evidently he had no family. His loneliness and the fact that he had a railcar all to himself piqued my interest. One day I saw him sitting with his feet dangling, having a feast of goodies neatly placed on the floor at the car's entrance. He ostentatiously drank and ate for everybody to see. Two days later, I saw the death wagon come by and some men carry the body of the loner out, to dump him on top of the already high heap of bodies. I was told that he had traded everything he had for food, ate it all, and hung himself.

I witnessed the slow starvation of my grandmother and uncles. Uncle Ari died of typhoid fever and was carried out by the daily death wagon. Uncle Alfred and Uncle Magnus starved to death and were, one day, also taken out to the cemetery on the outskirts. I saw them first get thin, skeleton-like, and then become bloated and grotesquely swollen. That is the last image I have retained of both of them. I do not know exactly how Grandma died. One day I was told that she was not with us anymore.

The time came when rumors started that something big was going to happen, though nobody knew what. It was said, among other things, that the entire ghetto was to be sent somewhere. My life in the ghetto up to this point had been a strange mixture of feeling secure within my family and experiencing jolts of terror from all the goings-on around me. Whenever there was something terrible happening in the streets, I was always able to run to the relative safety of my family. Mom and Dad so far had managed to keep the most horrible things that were happening to others away from me. I felt somewhat alienated from other children because of my mixed parentage—my mother was German. No strong rejection, but the kids would call me a *yeke.*[1]

Since they saw me sometimes sitting on the steps in front of the house and sipping a cup of fake coffee, it became *yeke mit a tepl kave.* So, I was a *yeke,* and that stuck with me ever after. It reminds me of the famous orphan character from Sholem Aleichem who said, *"Mir is git, ich bin a yusem"* (I have it good, I am an orphan). I can say, *"Mir is git, ich bin a yeke."*

Moritz of Opoczno

Opoczno was a drab little town in the middle of rural Poland, about fifteen kilometers from Drzewica. In 1942 it was the seat of a German garrison for the district and had a few buildings fit for the occupying military and civilian authorities. The surrounding little towns and villages had no German forces stationed there and were controlled from Opoczno by frequent forays. In between, the Germans entrusted the administration to the blue-clad police recruited from Polish collaborators. Drzewica, as mentioned before, had no Germans stationed there, even during the existence of a Jewish ghetto in the years 1940 to 1942. There was no barbed wire outlining this ghetto's boundaries. Everyone knew which was the last Jewish house on the central and side streets, and a Jew was not supposed to cross that unmarked line. If he did, the consequences were dire. Inside the ghetto, starvation was the order of the day, with no goods or human traffic crossing the "magic line."

I once witnessed the following scene. My family's dwelling in the ghetto was the last one on the "main" street before the boundary line, and looking out the window, I saw a girl about fifteen coming from the "Aryan side" toward the ghetto line. She had a bowl in front of her, which she held with outstretched arms, since it was large, like one used for kneading bread dough. She hurried to get across the line—and almost made it. A group of four young Polish men caught up with her, grabbed the bowl, and overturned it. Out poured a heap of potato peels. One of the men grabbed the girl by her long hair, and kneeing her in the back, pushed her over the line. The others laughed and made rude remarks, shouting, "That should teach you not to leave your Jewish place again!"

Undoubtedly, there were Poles who had given the girl the potato peels (cooked, they were a delicacy in those days). However, there were always those who willingly and voluntarily maintained a watch over Jews to keep them where the Germans intended. The locals who smuggled food into the ghetto ran the risk of denunciation by their own—and death. Many took that risk, and some, only some, are memorialized at Yad Vashem in the Avenue of the Righteous.

By and large the ghetto was isolated, with about two thousand sick and starving inhabitants crammed into a small area. Sporadic outbreaks of typhoid fever added to the terrible toll from starvation, and the isolation was made even more complete by the German scare propaganda.

The head of the commando unit stationed in Opoczno was named Moritz. He raided the district villages with German precision and regularity. Often, because of that German predictability, our ghetto was forewarned of his arrival. To be in the know often made the difference between life and death, since there was a nasty ordinance in place that the streets should be clear when he arrived. One day, a sunny summer day, he came unexpectedly. His three military vehicles, each holding a few of his cohorts, stopped in the middle of the town square. I was looking out the window and saw people running to get off the street into the nearest buildings and away from the town center where the Germans were jumping out of their cars.

The Germans hurried, with guns leveled at whoever was still in their line of vision. The shooting that began immediately left several bodies on the ground. I was mesmerized by one man who ran toward a fence in a zigzag pattern, one German shooting at him, loading his gun repeatedly, missing every time. Then, when the man got to the top of the fence and balanced there for a moment, the German aimed carefully. I did not hear the shot I expected. The man got over the fence, while the German swore loudly and started to pull at his gun breech. Unable to open it, he took his bayonet and with its handle tried to knock the gun open. He held the gun upright against the ground with his left hand, bent over, and swung at the breech with the bayonet, swearing all the time.

Before long all the shooting stopped, and from a corner of the half-open window, I saw what must have been Moritz, standing in the middle of the circle of his helmeted troops. He was slender, not tall, but carried himself very upright. He did not have a rifle or machine gun but a pistol holster and brown gloves. He swung energetically around as if surveying the scene and then barked some order that I did not hear. The helmets started moving out in a widening circle.

At that point fear started seeping into me; I slid onto the floor in the corner of the room so as to be totally out of sight. I did not know what to do next, so I sat there motionless. My mother, after going to the door and locking it, took my little sister and sat down under the window in the opposite corner with her in her lap. She signaled for silence with a finger at her lips. Soon we heard a commotion in the adjacent room. There was a locked door opposite the entrance of our single room that led to another dwelling that we knew was some kind of an administrative office with a telephone. I heard voices; among them was the loud commanding bark of what had to be Moritz.

Then there was silence. Shortly after, another set of noises became apparent under the window—sounds of footsteps, as if a number of people had gathered. Then the wailing and crying started. This was interrupted by a loud guttural shout *"Ruhe!"* (Silence!) After a moment a male voice, "Sir, please, the ropes are so tight; it hurts terribly." I heard the crunching footsteps of a soldier's nailed boots. "Yes, it is too tight." Some muffled sounds, and after that, the man's voice, "Thank you, sir, thank you."

The wailing started again but very subdued. I could not make out the words mixed with the faint moaning. Shortly after that, there was the clatter typical of soldiers when they assemble. All the equipment they carried made a distinct noise of canteens dangling, boots grinding against the ground, et cetera. The sound of guns being loaded was unmistakable. The wailing became louder. Then, we heard "Fire!" and shots rang out.

After a short while, the commotion in the adjacent room started again. Moritz was at the telephone calling Opoczno, and his voice this time was sweet and gentle. He gave an account of the day's work: "Darling, it was really great fun." After this, he must have started eating his lunch, because whenever he spoke, it was as if with a full mouth.

We did not dare move until we heard the German cars departing. I stood up and looked out the window, trembling. Horse-drawn carts came close to the wall and assembled in a line. Men carried the bodies and piled them up in the wagons. After this was done and the carts departed, two men with rakes came and raked dirt beside the wall below the window. Only when everybody had left did I venture out to look. The soil under the window was freshly raked, but I could clearly see darker spots, and here and there was what looked like a shiny ligament or a piece of flesh torn away by a bullet. That sight has never left me and is as fresh in my vision as if it had happened yesterday.

As mentioned before, the ghetto was not guarded. One autumn day we woke to noises in the street, a big commotion, and an announcement that we were all being sent to a larger ghetto. Consolidation. This time the ghetto was surrounded by a motley group of Germans and blue-uniformed police with some other troops said to be Ukrainians. We were trapped. We were told to pack, one suitcase per person, and be ready for transport in the morning. This time, in the evening, my parents held a soul-searching and dramatic meeting to decide whether to go along. It had finally dawned on them that something was very fishy and that we should not go. I remember some of the conversation.

Mother: "If we must die, I want us to be together." Father: "You cannot make such a decision for the children. We must save them. I will come out and join you when I can. We might raise suspicion if I disappear now, too. They might start looking for all of us. We cannot risk that."

They decided that my mother would sneak out with both of us children, and Father would join us the following night, since he had learned of two groups being formed for transport. For this to succeed, he had to find a "blue" policemen and bribe him to let us through. So, in the morning before dawn, we sneaked past an "unseeing" blue-uniformed policeman and then hid in the forest for two or three days.

Finally, we ventured out of the forest. With my mother holding us both by the hand, we walked toward the village. There came a peasant with his horse and carriage. "What are you doing here, Jews? All the rest have gone to the gas. You can dig yourself a grave here. Do you want a shovel?" He drove off laughing. As we got closer to the village, we saw a cloud of feathers. That was the result of looting by the hordes of locals—ripping the feather bedding is a necessary step in the search for valuables.

We waited outside for one night, and the next day we entered the desolate area that had been the ghetto. Devastation was everywhere—a hurricane would have created a scene like this. Belongings and broken furniture lay in the streets, and many windows were smashed. My mother selected a half-caved-in house—hopefully, no one would claim this one for a while. We went in to hide there from the elements, since the autumn weather was growing worse. It was now November 1942.

Drzewica

Until the fall of 1942 we had been confined to the smaller of the two market squares in the village of Drzewica. The larger square was adjacent to it, beyond a row of houses. These houses divided Drzewica and made a barrier through the middle of the village. Opposite these houses was a large church complex. The ghetto territory was enclosed around the smaller square. To one side, right by the dividing row of houses that allowed a narrow passage between the two squares, was the synagogue. Drzewica served as a center for the surrounding countryside. The *odpusty* (church fairs) were held on the church grounds, and I would guess that before the war, the synagogue also served the needs of some nearby Jewish families from the smaller settlements.

The house that Mother selected for our dwelling was tucked in the corner of the smaller square with its back to the larger square and facing the synagogue. This house, partially caved in, looked like a heap of rubble from the outside. Beyond the debris inside, we found a room intact with a window looking out toward the now empty and looted synagogue. The view was partially obstructed by beams and other parts of the house. It looked as if one corner had collapsed and wrapped itself around the front of what remained standing.

We settled into this room. From the possessions strewn around the ruins, we were able to arrange relatively comfortable living quarters. For a stranger looking at the heap of rubble, with the small portion still standing but partially obstructed by debris, it would seem improbable that someone could live there. Of course, our settling there was largely by chance, but once there, we felt that its appearance was perhaps what was needed for a reasonable "hiding" place. The problem now was how to sustain ourselves.

The greatest danger came from the locals. Would they leave us alone or would they denounce us to the Germans—especially to the gendarmes or the SS outfits that passed sporadically through the village to make forays into suspected partisan strongholds? Drzewica now, as before the liquidation of the ghetto, was free of any German military presence. The Nowe Miasto gendarme outpost was twenty kilometers away, and Moritz, with his outfit, was in Opoczno, about fifteen kilometers away. Drzewica was free of Germans except for "actions" that were carried out after being precipitated by a variety of factors.

These actions or forays struck terror in us. Most of the time we had some warning, because the Germans came into the village by two access roads, both of which led into the big square. There the Germans would make their base, and the commotion gave us time to hurry into the adjacent woods before they fanned out into the village. We would spend the day, or whatever time was necessary, waiting until they left. We could tell what was happening by approaching the edge of the woods close to the village. The actions mounted by the Germans usually lasted a few hours until their goals had been achieved, whatever they were. The danger to us was that some of the locals might point our ruin out, and that would doom us.

The next worry was food. Hunger was our ever-present torment. I went out to forage into the fields for leftovers from the harvest. I dug out and collected everything I could find, frozen or not. Carrots and potatoes were sometimes buried deep enough to be edible. One day I hit a bonanza. I found an abandoned flour mill, and the flour and grain I collected from crevices sustained us for a short while. Times became better when the crops began to ripen. I went out and collected (stole) much of what was needed to keep us from outright starvation.

Our everyday hope was that Father would come back as was planned. That hope sustained Mother; she was so sure that we would see him any day. That was not to be, but Mother never lost hope, although chances that we would see him again at all diminished with every passing month. The three of us marked the days in fear and desperation, hoping for some change for the better. By this time we were approaching the winter of 1943, almost a year from the time of our escape from the ghetto.

What saved us was an event that occurred before the winter set in, quite some time after the ghetto liquidation. On the other side of the river, a huge commotion started one day. Construction equipment arrived, along with a lot of black-uniformed Todt Organization units. This organization, named after General Todt, had the mission of supporting troops by constructing roads, fortifications, and whatever was necessary. This was their mission and concern, not chasing Jews or any other military/political pursuit. With typical German single-minded dedication to their narrow mission, they went about their task to build barracks for young Polish conscripts in a work organization called *Junacy*—Young Men's Labor Brigade. These young Polish men did all kinds of auxiliary work for the German war machine.

They were rounded up and given a choice: to be sent to Germany for slave labor or to "volunteer" for the *Junacy* organization and stay closer to home, doing work for the Germans out of their "free will." I think the Germans considered that arrangement more efficient.

When that camp started functioning, and we continued to be pressed for food (my digger-gatherer activity barely allowed us to stay ahead of starvation), my mother said one day, "Children, I have to go there and see if I can get some work. Maybe they need some kitchen help." "But Mother . . ." "Sven, I have no choice; we will starve otherwise. These are Todt people; maybe I will find some human soul there. I will tell them some story about how we are temporarily here, waiting for our paperwork to be processed to restore my rights as a pure German (a *Reichsdeutsche*)."

So, my mother got a job as kitchen help in the *Junacy* work camp. This had an immediate and huge benefit; it gave us food, and it also confused the locals utterly as to our status. Now they saw my mother go to work every day in the German compound. I was a little bit more relaxed and did not scurry around like a hunted animal anymore. I ventured out to go and watch the kids play a game called *palant*—something akin to baseball. I stood there on the side, a picture of shyness and poised to run at any sign of hostility. One boy much older than I—a lot of them were sixteen or older—moved in my direction and said, "Hey, little Jew, catch that ball."

He threw the makeshift baseball in my direction, and I caught it nonchalantly with my left hand. His face went from a derisive smile to very serious. "Do you want to try a game with us? I will put you on my team." No doubt that I would try a game! I became a prized player. The team captains would draw lots to decide which team I would be on. I was proficient catching with my left hand, and that was a premium. I gained confidence and felt safe as long as I was in the company of these familiar boys. Being now more on the Aryan side, I had a chance for a bit of insight into the life of Polish society during the years of the German occupation. The days now passed in an effort to avoid dangerous situations and, most important, dangerous people.

The village and the surrounding countryside were teeming with partisan activity. There were many factions constantly feuding with each other. On the average there were two funerals a day in Drzewica as a result of assassinations carried out by rival units against each other. All I knew was to keep from crossing the path of any of those units. I was unable to distinguish between the Communists (AL), the Home Army (AK), and the Nationalists (NSZ).[2] At times some of them would behave so brazenly as to parade in prewar Polish military uniforms through the village. While none of them ever bothered us, danger nonetheless loomed everywhere.

There was a large farm/estate run for the Germans by its Polish tenants. This is where I went, when crops were ripening, to dig out some new potatoes and look for anything else that was edible. One day a farmer who had no interest in protecting German property (or so it seemed) caught me. His fields were not even adjacent, but here he had caught a Jew obviously stealing German property, and my uncertain status notwithstanding, this should do me in. He tied me to his cart with a rope and started dragging me to the nearest German authority. Where would he find one close enough so that I would still be alive after being dragged like this? I did not know. The farmer was driving his horse, and I ran behind the cart in terror, stumbling and wiggling, trying to free myself. Eventually I was able to scrape the rope against the rough wood of the farm cart and break it. I ran into the nearby bushes and escaped. The bastard gave up looking for me after a while—the head start I had before he could stop the horse and get off the cart made the difference.

There was a brief period of heightened fear, and it was not directly from the Germans; in 1944 the Warsaw Uprising took place. We watched the glowing sky over Warsaw in the distance, and after a while, refugees from Warsaw started arriving in Drzewica. A number of people escaped the burning capital city, which was being systematically dynamited, house by house, by German troops. People scattered in all directions, and a number ended up in Drzewica.

Some turned out to be nasty. City slickers—they tried to show off. Inevitably, some got interested in my family, trying to show how tough one ought to be with Jews. They started harassing me at every turn. What saved us, and particularly me, from harm were the tough local farm boys whose respect I had gained through games. Besides, they had their own animosity toward the so annoyingly arrogant city slickers.

The importance of judging people by subtle or not-so-subtle clues was hammered into me by another memorable incident. One day I went to meet Mom at the *Junacy* compound. Usually I waited near the main gate, out of sight, though, at an abandoned shack. The windows of the shack were missing, and the part of the wall away from the compound was missing, too. I would join Mom when she came out after she finished her shift. On that day I saw a girl, about eighteen years old, dressed in a lightweight black dress. The dress was short, showing her legs, and it was snug around her breasts, which being nicely outlined appeared very firm. Her face was handsome but bore a strange expression of bewilderment and absence of mind. Her movements toward the gate were erratic, as if she was not sure of her purpose. She had a bag slung over her shoulder, the kind beggars sometimes have to hold things. One of the *Junacy* was standing at the gate, and the girl asked if she could get some leftover food. The man said, "Wait here, I will check."

He walked back into the compound, and I saw him collecting some other young men, and four of them came out of the gate. Seeing this, the girl started drifting toward the shack, and I was able to pick up the conversation among them. The leader said, "We need a rope or something to tie her dress above her head. One of you, go get it." One of the other men added, "Yeah, I saw her before. I am sure she is a mental case; she won't know what happened."

The girl was moving around aimlessly. The men came toward

the shack and corralled her there. One of the men pulled her dress up over her head; the other quickly tied it up with the rope. They pulled her panties down. The girl was moaning and thrashing around trying to free herself, and it was now that for the first time I saw a naked girl. She was beautifully shaped. Her dress pulled up high over her breasts, conical shaped breasts, firm and tipped up. The men forced her down in a corner. At that moment, there was a shout from the gate, "Hey guys, what are you doing there outside the compound?" "Nothing, Sarge, just having a smoke." "Back inside, on the double!"

Obviously he could not see the girl inside the shack. The four men moved in a hurry toward the gate and the sergeant. Shaking, I went over and untied the rope; I saw her face close—it was sheer terror. She was moaning and sobbing softly. I picked up her bag, she slung it over her shoulder, and still sobbing, she moved away without a word. I sat down with my face covered, devastated. Among all the horrors of that war, this one episode has etched itself into my memory, so that, whenever I think back to the war, that scene floats up every time. I resolved then and there to redouble my caution around people, be they German or not.

Nonetheless, my curiosity about all kinds of trades brought me into contact with a local Polish cabinetmaker named Ramus, living with his family and working in his shop near our hiding place—the abandoned ruin. I would spend a lot of time in his shop, helping with whatever he allowed me to do. He also gave us shelter if there was an unexpected raid, especially in winter, when it would be difficult to hide in the forest. He did so matter-of-factly, with a calm demeanor, as if it were the most routine thing. He risked the destruction of his family, if not worse, by doing this, and he knew it.

Soon the Russians were approaching, and the situation changed dramatically. We heard the rumble of artillery in the distance. There was anticipation, anxiety about impending events. The German occupation was drawing to an end. In addition, there was the assassination attempt on Hitler, which temporarily threw the Germans into some confusion. I remember frontline soldiers marching westward through the village, bedraggled, foraging for food, and ingratiatingly saying, *"Hitler kaputt."*

Suddenly, the area was flooded with Wehrmacht troops from all kinds of units, preparing to take a stand. We huddled in the deepest crevices of the building we had found, not daring to breathe loudly. One morning we saw two German soldiers searching, and eventually they came upon us. A tall sergeant yanked me out of a corner. "People here tell us that you are Jews. Are you?" "Ehhh . . ." "You, boy, come with us to the major." The major asked a few questions, but his main interest was to see if I spoke fluent German, which I did. "You will be assigned to the sergeant, boy. We will give you some provisions now, and you report tomorrow at dawn to him. We have trenches to dig, and you will translate instructions to the locals who are already organized in work groups."

Some more bastards tried again. One day, while going busily about the trenches, I saw a vehicle stop in the distance. Out came four or five black-clad *Totenkopf* SS[3] (the skull insignia was their mark, placed on their caps). One of the trench diggers stopped and went over to the SS men, and I saw him pointing in our direction. I could feel the blood draining out of my face. All one had to do was to point a finger and say *Jude* (Jew) to these guys. The sergeant, as if alerted by something, looked at my face. "What is the matter?" I barely came out with a whisper, "SS." He took one look and barked, "Get behind me." We inched toward the nearest structure. "Crawl into a hole and stay there until I come for you." I heard his boots crunching away in the direction of the SS men.

The end of the German presence came swiftly. One day, in the morning, we heard all hell break loose. Heavy guns were thundering and small firearms crackling. We ran into the cellar and stayed there until all was quiet. After we left the cellar, I went exploring with the throng of people that also came out of their hiding places. The first dead German soldier I saw was lying facedown in the middle of the street; his boots, belt, and coat were gone.

We moved beyond the river where the fiercest fighting had

taken place. Bodies lay everywhere on top of the trenches as if killed in the process of trying to get out and run. Most of them were stripped naked. The ones still partially in uniform were being stripped before my eyes. Looters with armfuls of all kinds of German clothing were running toward home in fear that someone would stop them. I saw an elderly man pick up a handkerchief and put it on the exposed genitals of a soldier who lay on his back—an exception. Some wounds were terrible. One German had his skull partially blown off—little blood, just the exposed brain.

The throng of people was moving like a swarm of bees from one place of excitement to another. The Russian soldiers moved in groups, rounding up hiding Germans. I went back to the town square and saw a lone German soldier wandering around in a daze. He kept muttering, *"Mein lieber Gott, meine Frau, meine Kinder"* (My dear God, my wife, my children). He repeated the phrase over and over. One of the Russian commanding officers pointed to a group of other Germans and told him to go there.

In a little while, two Russian soldiers marched the group toward the other side of the river. The spectators followed. The Germans were lined up at the edge of a trench, and the executions started. One of the Germans, apparently only painfully wounded, fell to his knees and made a movement with his right hand as if asking for more shots, to be finished. The Russians turned around and left. The people fell upon the dead to strip them naked. Some were left in their long johns.

Mother decided to wait in Drzewica long enough for Father to return and find us. The next day Russian soldiers came to the ruin where we lived and took me to their officer. My mother did not speak Polish. "Who are you people?" "We are Jews who escaped from the ghetto and have been hiding here in this ruin since then." "You were pointed out to us by the locals here as having aided the Germans." "When the Germans came to town, we were pointed out to them as fugitive Jews and our hiding place disclosed. The Germans forced me to interpret for them. We were trying to survive."

That was the end of that. I established good relations with some of the Russian soldiers and stayed around them as much as I could, fascinated with their equipment.

After the war, we waited for my father in that cursed place, Drzewica. Out of two thousand people, only twenty-five showed up to look for their relatives. Many more had taken the initiative to run and hide, but like my father, they never came back. Two weeks passed, and Father did not show up, so Mother decided to go to Łódź, a big city. The Jewish Committee placed my sister and me in a children's home in Helenówek, a suburb of Łódź, and gave Mother a job in the kitchen as a cook.

One day we traveled to our home in Jabłonowo, where we found both our houses were a heap of burned-out bricks. All the rest of our business establishment was gone. Not an item from that extensive property remained, and all that was left to us was a few acres of wasteland. The war was over. All that was left of our family was the three of us, Mother, my sister, and me, with the shabby rags on our backs as our only possessions. Mother kept hoping that Father was alive and would find us. She kept that hope to the end of her life. She died in 1949.

From here on I embarked on a new journey through another bewildering period, of the Stalinist regime in Poland.[4] My drifting alone through space continued, a stranger in any group of people no matter what its makeup. The feeling of not belonging anywhere deepened as I moved along the path of my new journey. In 1968, during the anti-Zionist campaign in Poland,[5] I emigrated to the United States and began a new life.[6]

Epilogue

After reading this remembrance, some people have asked me how the experience has changed me. And further, what were my emotions during these years of calamity? The first question is a very valid one, and I will address it in detail below. The answer to the second question lies within the text, and any reasonably sensitive and imaginative person can figure this one out. I will, however, describe one other episode from those hellish years that has been evoked by this question.

THE PERSONAL CHANGES

I have often tried to imagine what and who I might have been if I had not experienced all of these horrors and sustained the losses. I can see what I might have become by simply observing people who have been blessed with a normal sheltered life, affluence at home, a carefree youth, no war, no army service, college, and then a smooth transition to a job, marriage after that, et cetera, et cetera—so smug and confident, believing themselves to be virtually invincible. It is tempting to wish for that innocence, and yet I would no longer have within me the knowledge of human nature, the understanding of the level of evil to which a human can descend, and the height of sacrifice and goodness of which man is capable. I have seen and experienced and learned the mechanics of human behavior in a laboratory that is impossible to duplicate in normal life. In short, I feel as if I have a kind of wisdom that is so much a part of me, it defines me and makes it impossible for me to imagine anything so remote as a life without horror.

What is the price of that wisdom in the makeup of my character? Did I acquire a hatred for Germans, Poles, and Russians? Did I become permanently depressed or otherwise strange? The answer is complicated. I did not fall into a permanent state of bitterness or hate, although I'd be less than truthful if I did not admit to having those moments of hatred, especially against the Germans, and powerless fury with an intensity that is much too well earned. More often I am reminded of Don Corleone in *The Godfather,* who verbalized a principle which I practiced by instinct all along: "Never hate your enemies; it will cloud your judgment."

This understanding came to me with great ease. To avoid the bastards one meets in life and to fight them down, if necessary, is just business. That spared me an all-consuming desire for revenge or the constant torment of remembering how profoundly I had been wronged. Indeed, I sometimes felt guilty that I did not join the magnificent Simon Wiesenthal in his pursuit of the Nazi perpetrators but instead went on to build a "normal" life. The justifying rationalization is clearly that I was a mere youngster after the war and unfit to do any such thing at the time.

In a sense I have been walking through life as if in an altered state of being, wherein I am able to see a level of complexity that few around me can perceive or even imagine. I would argue that it has indeed made me "strange," and perhaps more so over the years. I am generally in a state of anxiety, always expecting or at least prepared for doom, with a predominantly pessimistic outlook. I am trusting and friendly but with a healthy dose of suspicion and caution. President Reagan had the right idea but butchered the pronunciation of the famous Russian saying: *Doveryai no proveryai* (Trust, but verify).

I seem to have been born with, or have somehow developed, the perceptive ability to determine an individual's trustworthiness, and this ability has spared me many disappointments. My experiences have also made me brooding and introverted yet very proactive in life situations. A well-known statesman once said, "When I close my eyes, I see the map of the earth and the tumult of battle, the cries of suffering, and death rising above it." I do not have to close my eyes; this image is with me all the time. It does not leave me, even in moments of exhilaration and joy, which are always muted and tinged with a dark underpinning. Indeed, I have become essentially a sad person, and that sadness became a scar that was impossible to conceal and made me appear strange to other people.

Having said all that, one might wonder whether I would exchange this emotional burden for the innocence of an unscathed life. Perhaps the fact that I cannot imagine such a life speaks volumes in itself. If I met my more fortunate clone or some parallel-universe version of myself, I would no doubt consider him immature, naïve to a fault, and view him with a tinge of contempt and affection, like an old soldier views a greenhorn recruit. I would wish to warn him, "Wake up, man, to the real world that surrounds you. Wake up to the beauty and the evil that are only a fraction of an inch away from each other."

I cannot emphasize more strongly that the price of my sad wisdom is both horrible and unacceptable, and yet it is not possible to wish it away. Under no circumstances would I knowingly set someone on a course of life like mine to gain the sad wisdom I have acquired. It truly would be akin to condemning a human being to hell, and hence the title of this narrative. The fantasy I often thought of would be to have some of the experiences I had—but with a happy ending. Nobody gets killed, the family reunites, the previous conditions of life are restored. That would be an ideal lasting education, albeit still unspeakably harsh, to appreciate life and its complexities. Yet sadly that is not possible, and I am left to grieve for my lost family and my parents mostly, who were such magnificent human beings, and yet God allowed them to perish in suffering. Who could be idiotic enough to believe "what does not kill us, makes us stronger"? Such fools "know not what they say."

THE EMOTIONS

Finding the words to convey an emotional experience seems almost impossible. Reading the greatest literary works describing emotional states still leaves even the sensitive and imaginative person without a true feeling of what the subject experienced. It was my intention in writing this to communicate the events rather than attempting a futile analysis and conveyance of my emotional turbulence. There is, however, one emotionally charged experience that floated to the forefront of my memory as a result of this discussion.

We were playing the cherished *palant* game in Drzewica during the somewhat "looser" times of our hiding on the Aryan side, when a boy came running and shouting, "The Germans, the Germans, they are fanning out and surrounding the village!" Panic set in immediately. Some of the boys were teenagers and were always afraid of being caught up in a roundup and sent for slave labor to the Reich. I, of course, was in danger for my very life. We abandoned all implements, and, in a herd, without a moment's hesitation, started running toward the forest. Without much thinking, I followed the leader and the throng. We scattered a bit and ran at top speed toward the trees about a hundred yards or so away. Suddenly, we heard the ominously characteristic crackling of submachine fire. Looking back, we saw a line of German soldiers advancing toward us. They were not catching up, because they had stopped to aim and fire; their advance was thus not as fast, and bit by bit, we were leaving them behind.

Nevertheless, the bullets were whistling around us, although I did not see anybody hit. That was one rare instant when I turned to God, and I remember putting my hands together for a brief moment of prayer, begging to be spared. That never happened again, not for myself anyway. I prayed for others, but to no avail. My chest was heaving, and my head flashing fragmentary horrible scenes of being doomed. In all this there was an instinctive retainment of reason that often makes the difference between death and life. Once I heard the machine gun fire, I started weaving to thwart the aim. Utterly exhausted and out of breath, we reached the tree line. Once inside the forest, we just looked back for a brief moment to see that the Germans were giving up the chase. The shooting stopped once the last of us reached the trees.

The terror slowly subsided, but we all proceeded deeper into the forest as fast as we could, regaining our composure. The moment I felt safe, the worry and the feeling of helplessness about my mother and sister set in, and the overwhelming guilt of leaving them behind became unbearable. I tried to rationalize and console myself, reasoning that I would not have been of any help and also that it was all so sudden, that it was an instinctive reaction. Nevertheless, the hollowness in my stomach and fear for their safety would not leave me until I returned—and found them shaken, but alive. It was just a flash raid again, and they had stayed in the ruin until the Germans left.

I wandered with some of the boys deep into the forest and came upon a small settlement where people spoke a strange dialect and never saw a German. They heard that there was a war somewhere but did not know what it was all about. We lingered there for a day before heading back to our village. That experience, seeing those people as if from another world, utterly amazed me, and I cannot forget their strangely different faces and the way they moved around their primitive huts doing their daily chores.

Years later, reading *The Painted Bird* by Jerzy Kosiński and seeing the reaction of people to it—"Fantasy, it could not be true"—I answer their skepticism, "Do not tell me, I was there!" It is now with thorough understanding that I view films like *Deliverance.* I often wonder what people feel and think when they see war stories like *Schindler's List* or other true depictions from the Holocaust or other wars. I could not watch *Schindler's List.* When I saw an excerpt and the little boy in the transport, I was saying, "That was me there." I lived through it once, and I am not going to live through it again.

It is at moments like that when my fury of helplessness and hatred flares up. Indeed, I must admit that what propels me in life is a well of spitefulness; I feel it in my chest. I want to thumb my nose at the human or heavenly (if there are any) generated forces that are trying to stomp me down and strike blows—as if to see if they can knock me down for good. Even in retirement, after a lifetime of combat, these forces do not give me rest. Instead they struck one of the cruelest blows by taking my only joy in life, my beloved wife. We always expect the good outcome of human stories, the "Hollywood ending," where the lovers walk on the seashore, hand in hand, as the credits roll. It gives us a smidgen of hope that things can be right and maybe we, too, will have our share of happiness in the final reels of our own lives. The best I can offer in terms of hope is that I have survived to write this, and I have won some battles. I am preparing myself for the ones yet to come; maybe I will win some of those as I managed to do in the past.

My ghetto experiences come out of the recesses of my memory at the slightest stimulation. Even a seemingly remote association is enough. Reading Bruno Bettelheim's essay "Freedom from Ghetto Thinking"[7] easily brought it out and made me go back in time in an attempt to examine my state of mind and that of my parents and fellow ghetto dwellers. The central point of Mr. Bettelheim's thesis is that Jews in the ghettos, by a long tradition maintained in the Diaspora, acquired an attitude of total submission and meekness, making the job of their extermination astonishingly easy for the Germans.

What was my state of mind at that time, at age eleven? I had no broad historic knowledge of the Nazi movement or its stated goals, of course. Fear, hunger, and preoccupation with the day's survival are the only things I remember. Mr. Bettelheim considers it a given that even minimally educated Jews must have known the truth about the Nazis. My parents certainly were very well educated. Had they seriously considered or talked about the ultimate consequences of what the Germans were doing? Not that I remember. There was disbelief about the possibility of mass extermination even when someone hinted at it. "This is the twentieth century, things like this are unthinkable," was the usual consensus. What about events like the ones described? These were thought to be the excesses of a few devilish types like Moritz. If only the higher German authorities might learn about them!

To add confusion to Mr. Bettelheim's argument that the eastern ghettos were bereft of those who had had the initiative to leave the ghettos for the "past three generations," I must point out that the ghettos established by the Germans collected all those who were outside in the gentile world, like my parents. So there were plenty of bright, modern, educated people in each of the ghettos, people who had freed themselves from ghetto culture. What perhaps might be a plausible explanation is that these people hadn't had the time, willingness, or opportunity to bond with the "masses" from the ghetto and become their leaders and turn them away from "ghetto thinking."

The so-called masses of Jewish shopkeepers, shoe repairmen, and tailors had no inkling of the world outside their narrow confines, much less about Hitler's writings and the global political goals of the Germans. The elite were naïve, trusting, and "innocent." Sometimes people develop an instinct without too much theorizing or verbalizing; they "feel" that something is out of kilter and then act. Even for this to happen, there needs to be leadership. Advocates of a certain course of action have to come forward.

In Poland instinct and leadership were lacking. I grant this to Mr. Bettelheim. Suppose they were present—this instinct and leadership—what then, given the hostile surroundings where even the Poles were murdering each other across the political spectrum without any German encouragement? When I later lived outside the ghetto, I saw at least two funerals a day resulting from fights between different Polish partisan factions. Should a Jewish leadership (if there had been one) have attempted to organize armed resistance with that kind of outside conditions, plus the aversion of the ghetto Jew to even looking at a gun? Theoretically, it was possible. It did happen in a few places—with suicidal results. Should this have been the norm rather than the exception? Yes! I would, however, refrain from pinning blame on those poor, lost, bewildered, disoriented, and leaderless souls who, dazed, went to the slaughter.

The ghetto people felt trapped on all sides. The murderous Germans! The hostility outside! For many who ventured to leave the ghetto, it meant instant death if caught and delivered to the Germans. Mr. Bettelheim cites the fact that once the Jews took up resistance there was help from the outside, as in the Warsaw Ghetto Uprising. That was far from even a hope in Drzewica. So, Mr. Bettelheim, I would not be so ready to attach blame to the poor masses of downtrodden ghetto dwellers. Besides, to organize resistance, one needed not only leaders but also some rudimentary vestiges of the defiant and combative attitudes that were totally lacking in those unhappy souls beaten down for generations. So the notion that something could have been done is purely theoretical and unrealistic given the circumstances of that period. Do I wish we had fought, run, hidden, done anything but go on the transports? Definitely! What permeates me is not shame but regret that we did not fight.

To suggest, as Mr. Bettelheim does, that escape through the Pripet Marshes was possible is sheer fantasy. To ask a shopkeeper with a flock of small kids to pack up his family and head over the marshes into the Soviet Empire is completely unrealistic. Under Stalin, traditional, murderous Russian anti-Semitism was simmering, and Jewish leadership and culture were being destroyed. That much knowledge seeped through to the ghettos. The people who went to the Soviet Union were mostly Communist political activists acutely aware that they would be shot by their competitors, the Nazis, Jew or not. Their Soviet political comrades shot many on arrival anyway.

I accept Mr. Bettelheim's concept of ghetto thinking. For it is within me to a large degree. I have to watch myself and be careful not to fall too easily into that mold, even now. My first instinct is always appeasement, even if it is obvious that it would have a very temporary effect. I act on my second impulse and fight only if I am cornered without an escape route. Not fighting, even in extreme circumstances, was the survival method for the Jews in the Diaspora for ages. This conditioned them to ghetto thinking. However, the circumstances during World War II in the German occupied territories included the additional element of total entrapment; it would have been difficult for any national group even with the best attributes for resistance and fighting.

So, let's leave the total undiminished blame on the murderous Germans and the *szmalcownicy* (those Poles who hunted down Jews for profit)! It is also difficult to accept Mr. Bettelheim's assertion that "German Jews (and those of Poland, too) permitted themselves to remain innocent, avoided eating from the tree of knowledge and remained ignorant of the nature of the enemy."

To lump the other Jewish communities with those of Germany is not right. The Jews of other European countries had a right to expect protection, as had their gentile population. I clearly remember the Polish propaganda slogan just before the war's outbreak—"We will not let them have one button." Poland was smashed in six weeks, hardly much longer than the Warsaw

Ghetto Uprising lasted. When almost every neighbor of Germany crumbled in short order, there was shock and disbelief. How about those governments and elites, including the Polish? Were they stupid and incompetent? Were they "innocent"? If not, what were they? To expect from the Jews a superior foresight as to the outcome of the German onslaught is a bit much. I think one cannot escape the thought that things were much more complex than just the psychological makeup of the ghetto Jew.

So, we survived. I have to give this to Mr. Bettelheim; passivity was a sure death sentence. Many also perished by being betrayed, as I was—outside the ghetto.

This account was submitted to the Association of "Children of the Holocaust" in English.

1. *Yeke* is a pejorative expression for a German Jew, even though the author's mother was a German gentile.

2. AL was the acronym for *Armia Ludowa* [People's Army], AK for *Armia Krajowa* [Home Army], and NSZ for the right-wing group *Narodowe Siły Zbrojne* [National Armed Forces]—all underground fighting organizations.

3. The *Totenkopf* [death's head] group of the SS was a particularly vicious group.

4. The author's experiences under Communism can be found in his book *A Two-Step Journey to Hell* (Montreal: Polish-Jewish Heritage Foundation of Canada, 2001).

5. See Events of 1968 in glossary.

6. The following sections do not appear in the Polish version of this book.

7. Bruno Bettelheim, *Freud's Vienna & Other Essays* (New York: Vintage Books, 1991).

LILIANA STERLING

Born in 1935

I Still Have the Hope That Someone Will Find Me

I have put off writing my childhood memoirs for a long time. I have often wondered why I remember so little. I remember almost nothing from the time before the war, and I remember only very incidentally the brutal wartime period up until 1943. However, I have remembered much better the events that occurred after I left the Warsaw Ghetto in February 1943.

I was born in Warsaw. My mother's name was Stefania Sterling, née Blumsztein, and Father was Mieczysław Sterling. Although I managed to locate documents from the camp in Trawniki[1] near Lublin where my parents were most likely shot, I did not find their names on the list of prisoners. Perhaps this was because the first two pages of this list were missing. My own identity was confirmed by archival data at the Jewish Historical Institute, in the file CK2P645—Education Department, Care for Children, Search for Children, Children living with Poles—entries 69 and 105. I found this information in 1994. The woman who was my guardian had submitted it in March 1945.

In the summer of 1943 I learned that my parents had been imprisoned in the camp in Trawniki. A woman came to my guardians' apartment on Towarowa Street and said that because of my father's poor health, my parents could not both escape from the camp and Mama would not leave her husband alone. She stayed with him so that they might die together. My parents must have loved each other very much, but why did they have to die at such a young age? They were then both about thirty years old.

My parents and grandparents lived in Warsaw. In the 1930s my maternal grandfather, Mendel Blumsztein, lived at 17 Krucza Street. He was a *felczer* [medical practitioner][2] (there is still someone alive who knew him personally). My grandfather and grandmother (whose name I do not remember) lived with their two younger children, my uncle and my Aunt Mirka. At that time, I probably lived with my parents at 48 Krucza Street. My paternal grandfather, whose name I believe was Aleksander Sterling, most likely worked in an office. I think he lived at 18 Wronia Street and later, at 55 Wilcza Street—an address I do remember. As I have already mentioned, my mother had a brother and a sister. I don't know what happened to them during the war. Nor do I know what happened to my grandparents, the Blumszteins and the Sterlings. My father most likely did not have any siblings, although the name Róża keeps coming to my mind. I don't know, however, who she might have been in my family. I thought she was my mama's sister, but according to someone who worked with Mama and her sister before the war, that was not my aunt's name.

As I have already mentioned, I remember almost nothing from the prewar period. I must have had a happy childhood. I was surrounded by the love of my parents, my grandparents, and my whole family. From the time of war I remember a gas mask someone put on me, and then I remember hiding places, cellars, and camouflaged hideouts. I can't describe individual events; everything is somehow intertwined with fear and separation from my loved ones. In some manner I was being coached for leaving the ghetto. Unfortunately, I don't know when I was being taught this or who taught me. I memorized large fragments of *Pan Tadeusz*[3] and poems by Tuwim[4] and other writers of children's books. Of course, I could recite Catholic prayers and sing many Catholic religious songs.

I recall that I spent the beginning of the war with Grandma

Tunia Sterling. Later, I bid her farewell from a distance when she was deported from *Umschlagplatz* to Treblinka. I don't know, however, how she ended up in the transport, or when this took place. Grandma Tunia was my beloved granny, but I barely remember her face or figure. I do remember well, however, that she spent a lot of time with me, took care of me, and took me for walks.

I remember little of my parents. Mama was a beautiful woman—shapely, slender, and elegant. Papa was blond and in poor health.

I remember almost perfectly my leaving the ghetto. Mama took me out of my hiding place. A few hundred meters from the gate, without saying good-bye, Mama told me to keep on walking and instructed me to profess the Catholic faith for the rest of my life. A guard stood by the gate. He said something to me, but I can't remember what. When I went through the gate, I saw the woman who was to become my guardian standing a few dozen meters straight ahead. I didn't know her. When I approached her, she took me by the hand, and we walked to her home on Towarowa Street. I had no bundles with me. Most likely I had no idea what it was all about. Nobody had forewarned me.

The woman who took me in was Mama's friend from work. Before the war, they both worked for Schiller-Szkolnik, palmists (?). She and her husband lived in one room on Towarowa Street. I had there my own daybed on which I slept. Most of the time I stayed home. I read books that were there. The love of books has remained with me to this day. Books are my best friends. I helped my guardian with her household chores. I tried to be quiet, calm, and grown-up, because already in the ghetto I had ceased to be a child. All the time I was waiting for my mother to come and take me away. However, nothing like this came to pass.

I did not cry during the German air raids and didn't go down to hide in the cellar. A phobia remains with me to this day—I feel as if I am suffocating when I am in closed spaces without windows or with windows closed. As far as the neighbors were concerned, I was the illegitimate child of my guardian's husband. I don't recall anyone making any remarks about my stay with this family. However, one of my guardian's sisters threatened that if my guardian didn't meet her demands, she would denounce her to the Germans. I don't know what these demands were. Luckily, nothing like this happened. During prayers in the courtyard, I prayed fervently and also sang quite well because I remembered Mama's instructions.

I lived in the apartment on Towarowa until the Warsaw Uprising. In August 1944 the Germans threw us out. They separated the men from the women and children. I ended up in a camp in Pruszków together with my guardian. We were then transferred by cattle car to a camp near Wrocław [then Breslau, Germany]. In the camp, the Germans ordered us to go naked into one of the buildings. My guardian didn't say anything, but she thought this would be our end. In this building was located a bath. I remember the shower—cold water from a rubber hose held by some woman. During our shower, our clothes were sent to a steam room for delousing. After the shower, the *Arbeitsamt*[5] sent us to work for a German farmer. This was beyond our strength, however, so we went again to the *Arbeitsamt.* There we were yelled at and called names. I can't remember whether they beat us. But in any case, we succeeded. We were sent to work in a munitions plant in Brzeg on the Oder River.

My guardian was an energetic person, and I think she knew some German. In the factory she worked as a metalworker's assistant for twelve hours a day. As one who performed hard labor, she received a food ration card. We had our own room in the home for workers. Most likely it was she who managed to secure it for us. During that time, I did the shopping, cooking, cleaning, and laundry. To do the shopping, I had to learn German.

While out on my shopping rounds, I got to know some Polish prisoners who came in once a week to buy bread in the same store where I also shopped. When my guardian heard from me about the Polish prisoners, she quickly organized a collection of ration cards for them among the workers in the factory. She gave me the cards so I could take them to the prisoners. The prisoners were very moved by our gesture but did not accept these cards. Moreover, they gave me some food. However, I don't remember what. They also gave me as a souvenir a ring that opened up, with a heart in the center, and on the sides, hands supporting the heart. However, the ring was too large for me, and I lost it. What a shame! We agreed on another meeting, but I never saw them again. My acquaintance with the prisoners was short but wonderful. We met several times in some nook near the bakery. These were joyful moments for me.

Until the time when the factory was evacuated, we had lived with the hope for a quick end to the war. Winter was approaching, and we had no warm clothing. After all, we had left our home in August, without any luggage. It was already cold. I went around in just my socks. Some people on the street gave me a pair of stockings, but I couldn't wear them because all the elastics were broken. I also got a coat from someone.

During the evacuation of the factory, probably in January 1945, we deliberately got lost, and in this way, we were not deported deeper into Germany. Fortunately, in the general confusion, this was possible. We headed for Warsaw with a group of Poles. We saw corpses everywhere during this migration. We also encountered various soldiers, who happened not to be fighting at the front just then and wanted to have a good time. My adopted mother had to pay ransom to save herself and me from their "merrymaking." Somehow she managed to do it. We had some alcohol from somewhere, and that helped a lot in these situations but not always. If there was a young and beautiful girl in the group, then even alcohol didn't work. I don't remember how long we continued like this.

When we finally reached Warsaw, my guardian came down with erysipelas.[6] She couldn't walk and had no medication. Thus she was applying some kind of home remedies. We stopped for a time with her family in Praga. This was a part of Warsaw that had not been destroyed. However, the family could not keep us for very long. The building on Towarowa Street was destroyed.

We were without any means of livelihood, hungry, and without clothing. However, neither my adopted mother nor I went begging.

Soon someone appeared who offered a helping hand. There was a place where people posted notes with information about who was alive and where they could be found. In this way a neighbor from Towarowa Street found us and took us in. We lived with her, her husband, and daughter in one room on Nieborowska Street. The woman was a seamstress. She had a little work, so we helped her with sewing and housekeeping. We lived with these people for several months. We ate what they ate—very modestly. We also had a place to sleep.

This is how we lived until the fall of 1945. Then, my adopted father, who after the Warsaw Uprising had been deported for forced labor to Głogów,[7] returned from his wanderings in Germany. Together we moved to a burned-out apartment on Częstochowska Street and settled there. There were no windows or floors, no kitchen, no doors, not even an entrance. We did not have any pots, furniture, or food. But we did have a will to live. I wanted to see my parents, my dear ones, my real family. To this day I have the hope that I still might meet someone. . . .

After the death of my adopted mother, I no longer maintained contact with her family. I did not know anyone from my adopted father's family.

I know that I owe my life to my adopted family, my guardians. For their selflessness, struggle, sacrifice, and courage, they were awarded posthumously, through my efforts, the medal of the Righteous Among the Nations of the World.

In the difficult moments of my life—and there were, and still are, many of them—I turn to my mother for help. I know she is watching over me.

Today my greatest problem is difficulties with my health. In retrospect I can see that I did not manage my life very well. The difficult financial circumstances under which I lived after the war caused me to go out to work too soon. I finished my university education by working and studying at the same time. I always tried to be strong psychologically. However, lacking support from my natural family, I was not always able to make the right decisions. The cruelties of war wounded me very severely. Although fifty years have already passed, I feel the effects of the war to this day. I do not understand people who fail to realize what an enormous influence childhood, a child's world, has on a person's adult life. When I was a child, I didn't have dolls or toys. I also didn't play with my age mates. Later, there was only work and study. I was employed in an office, which did not fulfill my professional ambitions. Satisfaction from studies and good marks did not bring me happiness, either.

After I received my baptism certificate (I don't remember when this happened), I became the daughter of my adopted parents. I addressed them officially as my parents, but all the time I hoped that someone from my real family would find me. I turned to the Polish Red Cross for assistance—unfortunately, without any results.

---

1. Trawniki was a forced labor camp for Jews and Soviet prisoners of war located twenty-five miles east of Lublin. Approximately 10,000 Jews were killed there.

2. A *felczer* was a medical practitioner or surgeon's assistant, someone with medical training but not a physician.

3. *Pan Tadeusz* [*Mr. Tadeusz*] is a very famous epic poem by Adam Mickiewicz.

4. Julian Tuwim was a well-known Polish poet of Jewish origin.

5. The *Arbeitsamt* was the employment office, where work assignments were given. (Author's note)

6. Erysipilas is an acute streptococcus infection of the skin, similar to cellulitis; also called Saint Anthony's fire.

7. Głogów is a large town in Silesia, ninety kilometers northwest of Wrocław on the Oder River.

BRONISŁAWA SZWAJCA, NÉE EISNER

Born in 1932

Among the Silesians

The story that I am about to present here is, to me, unique, just as I know that each of us "children of the Holocaust" regards his or her survival as such, because all of us survived only thanks to some incredible decree of fate. I owe my life to luck, chance, my mother's courage, and above all, to the selfless assistance of many noble people. My mother and I were saved by Silesians, Germans, and Poles, a Catholic priest, and Jehovah's Witnesses, by both very poor and fairly affluent people, some fully aware of our origins and situation, others who knew only part of the truth. I survived, as if in spite of the great course of history, in my native Katowice, a city in Germany at that time—which was supposed to be already *Judenfrei* [free of Jews] from the very beginning of the occupation—whereas my little brother was denounced and killed in the Polish city of Sosnowiec.[1] It is for me particularly important that through these recollections I can commemorate and pay tribute to those people of generous spirit to whom I owe my survival. I am no longer able to reconstruct many of the facts, but fortunately, I have remembered the names of our most significant rescuers.

The war dramatically shattered my life. It took away my family, my childhood, my lightheartedness. I was seven years old on September 1, 1939. I was preparing for school. I remember my school uniform—a navy-blue pleated skirt and a blouse with a white sailor's collar. I was excited. I already knew some little poems, which my dear brother, Pawełek, two years older than I, had learned in school. However, it was not until five and a half years later that I actually attended school.

I remember my childhood as a happy and idyllic one. We were an assimilated family, reasonably well off. We spoke Polish at home. Our parents spoke Yiddish only when they did not want us to understand what they were saying. They were not originally from Silesia. Father came from Galicia (his parents apparently owned a tar paper factory in a village called Osiek). Mother was from Congress Poland,[2] from Zawiercie. Their marriage was a misalliance, which Father's wealthy, educated family did not want to accept. Papa was a lawyer, as was his brother, and his sister was a pharmacist. Mama was a manicurist at a hair salon on Królowa Jadwiga [Queen Jadwiga] Street. She stopped working there after they married but continued to call on a group of her former clients.

We lived in a two-room apartment in the center of town on Lubecki Street, which intersects Warszawska Street. We had a housekeeper, Lotka, a young Silesian girl from a large, poor family. She was a half orphan who had been abused by her stepmother, so my parents took care of her and later arranged her engagement reception and wedding. She loved me very much, and when the war broke out and we were expelled from Katowice, she offered to take me in as her own child. Mama was offended by this. She still didn't know how tragic the next few years were going to be for us.

My brother was the only child in our building who had a bicycle, which all the other children always wanted to borrow. He attended a private school; when the war broke out, he was about to enter third grade. Father was a tall, dark-haired man. When he would go for walks with his much shorter brother (who lived nearby) and his family, they would switch partners. His brother would accompany Mama, and Papa, his brother's tall wife.

My parents were not religious; nonetheless, my brother was circumcised. I remember that father's name was Józef, but I don't even know his Jewish name. He was a Communist and for that reason had problems, perhaps even a court case. He was supposed to spend several months in prison or under arrest, but I don't remember much about it. He later worked in the office of the Biskupski Company on Gliwicka Street. I don't know what kind of firm this was; I just remember the name. As someone politically suspect, he could not reside in the border zone, so he had to fictitiously register in Sosnowiec.[3] But in reality he continued to live with us. We did not expect then that soon we would all have to leave our home and, in addition, not at all fictitiously.

The Germans marched into Katowice on September 3, 1939. We were evicted from our apartment already at the beginning of 1940. We had to leave our furniture there and move to Sosnowiec. Katowice, the administrative capital of the German Upper Silesia, was to be first in line to become free of Jews. We moved to a basement, to a one-room apartment.

From that time on, Father would travel every day to some factory in Tarnowskie Góry. He did physical labor there, probably for the first time in his life. Mama worked in the Schoen factory. After the invasion of Russia,[4] she made thick straw covers there for soldiers' boots. Food rations for Jews were at starvation level, so she smuggled food from the surrounding villages. I myself remember little from that period.

Father received a summons, probably in the summer of 1942. He was to take with him just one suitcase with a few personal belongings. Mama insisted that he not obey the summons, which he most likely received from the Jewish Community Council.[5] He, however, bid us farewell and left. I never saw him again. He was one of the first ones to be "resettled" from Sosnowiec to Auschwitz. In the 1960s my husband noticed a suitcase with our family name on it among the displays in the Auschwitz Museum. It was his suitcase. Now, I don't see it there anymore. I remember Papa as a very good man, an ideal father. Always calm and collected, he didn't allow my much more impulsive mother to reprimand me. He pampered and protected me. I used to miss him very much and miss him still today.

Father did not live to see the creation of the Sosnowiec ghetto.

It was established in Sosnowiec-Środula,[6] very late in October 1942. The three of us moved there; we lived there from its beginning. Father's family was also there—his brother and family, as well as his sister, by herself, as her husband and sons had escaped to the Soviet Union at the beginning of the war. They were quite well-to-do. She had stayed behind to watch over their property. Everywhere she went she carried a small case stuffed to the brim with gold. After Father's death, Mama wanted to get some of those valuables, but she refused. She believed that this treasure was going to assure her survival. When the time came for the final liquidation of the ghetto, she went to Auschwitz, undoubtedly with her little case.

Two or three years after the war, her husband and sons found us. They had survived in Russia. He then wanted to marry Mama, but she already had someone else. Offended that she had so quickly forgotten her husband, they left for Palestine. We never had any contact with them again. They were the only members of our family who survived the war. I am not even sure of their family name. I think it was Grinberg (but possibly Brinberg or Grinstein). Perhaps at least the sons are still alive in Israel.

Overcrowding, great poverty, and hunger reigned in the ghetto. We were not allowed to go out of it, although at the beginning, it was not closed off. People employed in the "shops"[7] would leave it in organized groups. Mama, who worked in the Schoen plant, managed several times not to return at night to the ghetto. Poles also worked in the factory, in addition to Jews. Thus, by taking off her armband, she could get out to the Aryan side. She brought us some food then and tried to keep in touch with the outside world.

I don't remember too many details of our existence in Środula. I don't know if this is due only to my being then barely ten or eleven years old. Perhaps I wanted very much to forget the whole nightmare. There are things I can't forget, however—for instance, the huge roundups, allegedly to get people for work. I don't know how, but the three of us found ourselves in a long column of Jews being led from Środula to Sosnowiec. We walked in fours, Mama and I in one row, and Pawełek several rows back. Mama called my brother over, and he moved close to us. She told him that a few intersections farther there was a street, and we should all turn into it. He returned to his row. The two of us escaped into this side street, which was very short, and we could almost immediately turn into the next side street. I was very frightened, and Mama had to hold me firmly by the hand, but nobody shot at us, and we hid in a doorway. There we waited for Pawełek, who was supposed to join us soon.

However, he did not show up. In the evening we returned to the ghetto with a group of workers returning from the shops. He was not in our room, either. Desperate, we cried the whole time, sure that he had not been able to escape—but he returned several hours after us. He was not able to sneak out into the street where Mama and I had escaped and had to wait for another opportunity. He couldn't find "our" doorway. This time we were lucky. We were together once again.

The liquidation of the ghetto took us by surprise, even though everyone knew it was coming. Mama believed she would know when it was about to happen. A friend of hers, a native German—ironically named Deutsch [German]—often came illegally to visit her Jewish husband who was in the ghetto. She was supposed to inform us if she heard any disturbing signals from her acquaintances at the police station or some other office—but she did not find out anything. On that ill-fated day she herself was in the ghetto. Her authentic German papers apparently did not help her, because she never returned to her apartment in Katowice, where Mama later sent someone to get in touch with her. Our plan was to leave the ghetto at the last possible moment. This was because hiding three people on the Aryan side without a lot of money was not easy. The Germans managed to get ahead of us, however.

The liquidation "action" began at night, I believe it was a Friday or Saturday, at the very beginning of August 1943. When the shooting started, everyone who could, ran for cover to hiding places prepared earlier. Luckily, one of those places belonged to a neighbor and friend of Mama's, a very beautiful, dark-skinned, black-haired Hungarian-Jewish woman. She offered to have us hide with her, her husband, and their two sons. One of them was about my age, the other, younger.

The hiding place was a relatively primitive one. In the courtyard of our house stood small sheds in which coal or some household odds and ends had once been kept, and in them, people dug out cellars with camouflaged entrances. We too found ourselves in such a small cellar, measuring maybe two by two meters. We climbed down there by a ladder; I don't know if anyone covered up the entrance behind us. There was only a large solid round table in it, some food assembled earlier, and clothes which we had hurriedly brought with us. We sat in darkness and absolute silence on the table, with our backs to each other.

Starting in the morning we could hear wailing, crying, and screaming. Later everything got quiet for a short time. We could not come down from the table because water was slowly seeping in from somewhere above, perhaps from a broken pipe. The water level was steadily rising. After a while, it reached the height of about one meter. It was troublesome, but it possibly saved our lives.

The Germans searched the area of the ghetto intensively for about a week. We could hear the howling of dogs and sporadic shots. Not far from us they uncovered a hideout. The Jews pulled out from there screamed, wailed, and pleaded for their lives. I think they were shot on the spot. The dogs did not track us down, however. It seemed to us that we alone were left in the ghetto, which just a short time before had been so crowded. But we could still hear shots, though much less frequently.

We soon ran out of food, so at night my brother, Pawełek, would slip out, barefoot, from our hiding place and search for food for all of us in the empty apartments. At that time one could already hear Polish being spoken. Poles worked there during the day, cleaning up the area of the ghetto, carrying out furniture and clothing. As time went by, it was harder and harder for Pawełek to find any food, and the water was rising ever higher.

There were fewer and fewer workers about, but we started to hear female voices. It was the wives of the workers bringing them their midday meal.

Then Mama decided, "We must come out." I don't know how long we had been hiding, six weeks perhaps, maybe a little longer. But the Hungarians decided to stay. They were determined. They said they preferred to die there of hunger rather than come out and fall into the hands of the Germans. We said good-bye to each other. Mama put a scarf over my brother's head, dressing him like a girl. We washed up a bit in the water, which was in plentiful supply in the cellar, and left. Mama had some acquaintances on the Aryan side; we had a chance.

I remember that day; I'll never forget it. It was fairly warm and very sunny, although it was probably already October. Accustomed to life in darkness, I could barely see anything. I moved with difficulty, because all the time we had been hiding I had never left our table. Mama took us by the hand. We walked. Time dragged on mercilessly. We finally passed near a guard post. Two policemen sat on the ground on either side. They had nodded off, with their heads slumped, leaning on their rifles. When we were passing by, one of them raised his head and yelled, "*Wohin?*" [Where to?] Mother responded in Polish that she had brought food for her husband. The policeman waved his hand that we could go. Our legs almost folded under us as we passed right by them.

We immediately went to a friend in Sosnowiec. I don't remember on what street she lived, but I know her last name was Twardzik. When she saw us, she was taken aback and scared. After being assured that no one had seen us coming in, she let us bathe and gave us some food. I don't know whether we slept at her home or whether we went right away to Katowice. Mama was afraid to travel with two children, because there were frequent checks between Katowice and Sosnowiec, especially after the liquidation of the ghetto. Therefore, she asked who wanted to go first. I got up and started yelling, "Me, me, me!" And so we went.

Once in Katowice, we immediately went to Mrs. Syndutka's. I stayed there while Mother immediately went back to get Pawełek. She didn't find him. Mrs. Twardzik told Mama to run away at once. She told her that my brother had insisted on going out in the courtyard where some children were playing. Someone had called the police. Pawełek supposedly almost escaped over a wooden fence to the adjoining courtyard. When he was caught, he apparently already had one leg on the other side of the fence. Supposedly he knelt in front of the policeman and begged him to let him go. Whether this is really what happened, I don't know, and I will never find out.

During the whole occupation Mama lived with the hope that Pawełek was alive somewhere in a camp or at forced labor and would one day return. For a long time still after the war she waited for him. We don't know where he died, how, or when. All that is left of him is one little photograph. In it, he is sitting, at perhaps age four, a plump little blond boy in short pants on a big rock on the bank of a river. I don't recognize him anymore in this picture, but sometimes I think about what would have happened if it had been I who had waited for Mama in Sosnowiec. After all, I was not circumcised, had "good looks," and I would not have gone out to play in the courtyard. Perhaps we would both be alive.

After returning to Katowice in despair, Mama found there not only a hiding place but a warm, sympathetic atmosphere with Mrs. Syndutka. She was the caretaker of a multistory apartment building owned by Mama's prewar acquaintance, a Silesian named Mrs. Dębińska, on what is today Wojewódzka Street. She lived with her husband in a one-story annex, in just one room. In the corner, at an angle, stood a big, three-door wardrobe, behind which we found refuge. We slept there and stayed there also when our hosts were home. As caretakers, they were constantly at risk of having tenants of the building call on them.

They were incredibly decent, honest, and heroic people. A childless older couple, over fifty, they were Jehovah's Witnesses. They did all they could, completely selflessly, to make us feel comfortable with them. In the evenings they read us their religious pamphlets. They were sure that after the war we would convert to their faith. They encouraged us to come out of our hiding place behind the wardrobe, not only in the evening, but also when they were out cleaning the courtyard. At those times they could easily alert us if anyone was approaching. They shared their food with us. Mama still had some jewelry at that time. Mrs. Syndutka didn't know how to sell it, so she would take it to Mrs. Dębińska, who would take care of it and give us the money. She knew that we were hiding in her building. We were there several months, but I don't know exactly how long. In this way we endured what was probably for us the most difficult period psychologically.

In time, the jewelry ran out. Not wanting to be such a big burden for our none-too-wealthy benefactors, Mama began to leave our hideout to earn some money. From that time on, she used to go to the homes of Silesians and Germans she knew to give them manicures. Usually, she did not get money for them but rather ration cards or some food. She knew these people from before the war, from the time when she worked at the beauty salon, and later, as a married woman, she used to visit them in their homes to make some extra money.

Mama, who did not have Semitic features, did not disclose her origins, although the ethnicity of Father must have been known to them. Did they not suspect then? I don't know—on the one hand, there were only a few Jews in Katowice before the war, and they were more assimilated than in other places. Also, marriages between people of different religions were theoretically feasible, because in Silesia, it was possible to have a civil wedding. Perhaps, indeed, Mama was for them simply a Pole from former Congress Poland who had migrated to Silesia in the 1920s in search of a better life. Or, perhaps they knew, but for them it was not important. Maybe they wanted to help or just wanted to take advantage of her well-performed low-cost services.

In any case, we never experienced anything bad from the Silesians, and I feel good in my native Katowice, where I live to this day. I associate the whole nightmare of the war with Sosnowiec, the place of our greatest tragedies, where I have not really been since the end of the occupation, despite the fact that it is located only a few kilometers from Katowice.

From one of her German-Silesian acquaintances Mama found out about the great decency of a certain family, Mr. and Mrs. Czapla. He was a police officer and on the number two *Volksliste,*[8] but at home, everybody spoke only Polish. They had two daughters, Zuza, who was my age, and little Ingrid. The parents of Mrs. Czapla lived with them. The mother, suffering from a mental disorder, caused them a lot of trouble by running away from home or uncovering windows during air raids. The daughter had to struggle to keep her out of a mental institution. Despite these problems, the Czaplas welcomed me under their roof. They treated me almost like their own daughter. I lived in their three-room apartment on what is today Korfanty Avenue. I became friends with Zuza and looked after two-year-old Ingrid, who loved me so much that when she was lying in the hospital with diphtheria and we visited her, she cried through the window and repeated only my name. She never returned from the hospital; she died—from what at that time was a dangerous disease.

These good people, who had been so harshly treated by fate, provided me with the semblance of a normal life in the very midst of that cruel war. Mrs. Czapla even took me with her to Vienna instead of Zuza, who had just then come down with some infectious disease. She took me to an amusement park there. I remember as if today my emotions when I was hurtling down at head-spinning speed on a huge Ferris wheel, the largest one I had ever seen.

Nor will I forget another situation in which my benefactors were involved. Once Mr. and Mrs. Czapla, Zuza, and I were walking down what today is Korfanty Avenue. Mr. Czapla was in uniform. We were approaching the theater, when suddenly a woman whom I recognized as our prewar building caretaker called out to him, half in German, half in Polish. He walked up to her, and she asked him whether he knew who the girl was who was with him and immediately added, "She's a Jew; I know her." Mr. Czapla grabbed his pistol, called her a Polish pig, and threatened to personally shoot her if she let out so much as a word. She ran away terrified, apologizing.

But that was not the end of it. She appeared in our lives once again in a similar situation. Namely, some time later, she ran into Mama and then started shouting in broken German, "What's that Jewess doing here?" Some military officer stopped, but Mama kept her cool. She spoke German fluently and acted outraged. She called the woman crazy and made the officer intercede on her behalf.

So Katowice was not a safe city for us, and danger could come from the least expected direction. Before the war, this malicious caretaker was very poor and had several children. Mama used to send her a piece of cake every week and got repaid only with hatred. At that time, the woman still did not yet know she would fall victim to her own aggression. When after the war Mama told a Russian officer with whom she was friendly about our experiences, he found the woman and shot her with his pistol.

I lived with Mr. and Mrs. Czapla until liberation, probably almost a year. I lived in a German apartment building, where the other residents greeted me on the stairs with "*Heil Hitler, kleine* [little girl]." I always responded with "*Guten Tag*" [Good day] or "*Guten Abend*" [Good evening]. I knew that every one of them would have denounced me if they had figured out my origins, and I remembered that there were plenty of people walking the streets of Katowice who knew about us.

I couldn't free myself from fear even for a moment, despite having "good looks"—Aryan features, blond hair—and despite the fact that Polish was my native language and that I had learned German. I tried to leave the house as seldom as possible, especially after the incident with the caretaker. Even going out to the store might occasion a dramatic episode. I remember once when a tall, middle-aged civilian stepped out of line and slapped an older woman in the face because she had asked the saleslady for something in Polish.

After the war everything got turned around. Mr. and Mrs. Czapla did not want to run away from the Russians; they felt they were Poles. Mr. Czapla, as a German policeman, however, was quickly arrested. He was supposedly beaten. When mother found out about this, she went at once to the militia, and, invoking her Jewish origins and her husband's Communist activities, told them about everything the Czaplas had done for us and secured his release. This is the only way we repaid our unselfish benefactors. Nevertheless, they had to emigrate and left for East Germany. We corresponded with each other for some time but later lost contact. Mr. Czapla died there a few years later.

During this last year of the war, I did not see Mama very often, because we were hiding in different places. Mama was staying with Mrs. Szwestkowa on what today is Żwirko i Wigura Street. She was a woman of modest means who lived on the sixth floor in the garret of an apartment building. She was the building caretaker, just like our previous benefactor. I remember that apartment, the tall staircase, the long, L-shaped corridor, and the one small room. Mrs. Szwestkowa lived there, crowded in with Mama, for many months. Her husband, like all Silesians, was in the German army at that time, and her son had been killed, although I don't remember under what circumstances. She was a simple, honest woman. I also stayed the night at her place several times, in total, certainly more than a month.

The Czaplas knew that Papa was a Jew, but Mama usually did not disclose her own origins. She maintained that she had a room in Katowice and wanted people to think that we lived there at least part of the time. From time to time, she would visit me and say, "I have to take Bronia [Bronisława] now; she can't spend all of her time with you. She has to live with me in her own house a little, too." Instead of taking me to her nonexistent room in Katowice, she would take me to spend the night at Mrs. Szwestkowa's place. Mrs. Szwestkowa, of course, was helping us out of the goodness of her heart, because Mama had no money by then. Nor was she able to repay her after the war, either.

We were also helped by Dr. Schubert, the parish priest of St.

Mary's Church, the second oldest and most important Catholic church in Katowice after the Cathedral. Mama knew him already from before the war, although I don't know how. He assisted us financially. We used to go to the parish where Mama would give his two sisters manicures. They clipped out food ration cards for us, which we ourselves, of course, didn't receive at all. Following all the holidays, they would give us cakes to take home. The priest's sisters bought me shoes and tights, as I remember.

They knew that Father was a Jew. Father Schubert did not insist on baptizing me; he declared it could wait until after the war, and then he did indeed try to convince me. Anyway, he continued to visit us many times. But one time he asked, "Bronia, would you like to learn the prayers?" I answered that I already knew them. I recited "Our Father," "Hail Mary," and "Angel of God." I knew how to pray because Mrs. Czapla had taken me to church several times, and even before then, Zuza had taught me prayers—in Polish, of course. Dr. Schubert was very pleased and taught me several other things, gave me a little prayer book, and told me it would be good if I always carried it with me. He also presented me with a religious medallion, which I always wore from then on.

As fate would have it, Mama was quite soon able to repay the priest. Namely, he was arrested by the Germans and sent to Dachau.[9] His terrified sisters pleaded with her to go there and give him a blanket into which they had sewn the names of some Germans who were willing to attest to his pro-German sympathies before the war. He was one of the few priests who had been willing to offer confessions to non-Polish-speaking Germans in their native language.

The sisters gave Mama cigarettes and vodka to bribe the guard, and Mama went there and delivered the blanket. After a few days, the witnesses from the list he received were interrogated, and Father Schubert was allowed to return to his parish. He was very grateful to Mama. Where did she, being a Jew, muster enough courage to go deep into Germany and mill around a concentration camp to bribe a guard? She was always very brave. Before the ghetto was set up, she traded in food products between Sosnowiec and Katowice. She could always keep a cool head in difficult situations. I assume she must have had some Aryan papers, but I don't know anything about it.

The priest, having been released from a German prison, after liberation, ended up in a Polish one. Someone reported that he had returned from Dachau suspiciously quickly, considering that so very few returned at all. Unable to help in any way at the local level, Mama this time set out for Warsaw to the Ministry of Religions. She told them everything about herself and about what Father Schubert had done for us and explained the circumstances of his release from Dachau. He was soon released from this second prison but was not allowed to return to his parish. He took over the parish in Godula, a district of Ruda Śląska. Grateful to us, he visited us nearly every month for many years. He passed away already a dozen years or so ago.

We were also helped by Mrs. Kaźmierczak, who would invite us over for a meal from time to time and also send us home with something. Mr. Sitek, the owner of a bakery, used to give Mama bread. I also remember the names of Mrs. Świtałowa and also of Mrs. Ronczoszkowa, who, when Mama came to give her manicures, always asked Mama to tell her about what the Germans were doing to the Jews. The result was that after Mama's visit, she would quarrel with her husband, who I believe was an SA official.[10] The crazy fanatic threatened that he would shoot the manicurist himself, whereupon his wife assured him that she would then poison him. Consequently, Mama went to visit Mrs. Ronczoszkowa only when her husband had gone away somewhere for a fairly long time.

Benefiting from the help of all these people, we survived the war. The long-awaited liberation came on January 27, 1945. I think that not many Jews in Poland experienced such a long period of suffering, from the beginning of September 1939 to the end of January 1945. Nonetheless, we survived.

After the war we went to our old apartment. The caretaker had the keys, which she handed over to us with some resistance.

The apartment was completely empty. The German occupying it had vacated it probably some two months earlier. The empty interior reminded us too much of our former life, of our murdered family. We did not want to live there. An acquaintance told Mama about empty apartments in the center of Katowice. Mama managed to get one allocated to us.

When we showed up in our new place, there were three former Auschwitz prisoners living there. They were trying to regain strength before returning to their homes. In exchange for bread and something to eat, they had given the neighbors all the more valuable furniture in the apartment. Now they very much regretted having done it to the wife of a fellow inmate. After they were rested, Mama arranged with some Russians who were quartered nearby to have them taken home by automobile. For a long time afterward we battled with the big Auschwitz bedbugs they left behind. Later, a Russian officer was quartered in one of the rooms, and it was he who shot our prewar caretaker. I live in that apartment to this day.

During the occupation I experienced jaundice and suffered from painful lesions on my scalp. Just after the war, I came down with whooping cough. My lungs were weakened, and I spent three months recovering in a Jewish sanitarium. I remember the big bars of chocolate we received there every day, but which, not being used to such rich food, I couldn't eat. I was short for my age and very skinny. Not surprising, since I had suffered from constant hunger. The delicacy I used to dream about was a slice of bread, toasted in an oven and spread with margarine.

I was supposed to go to school September 1, 1939. As fate would have it, I ended up attending only more than five years later. During the occupation, an acquaintance, a former teacher, taught me just reading, writing, and a little arithmetic. After the war, I started my education in the third grade. I was older than my classmates. Perhaps, so that I would not feel inferior, Mama declared that I was born in December 1934, nearly three years later than in reality. Since then, I have been living with various dates of birth.

Mama and I were the only ones left. Some aunt on my father's side of the family, who had been living in Canada for years, corresponded with us for a time. She was childless, wealthy, and single and wanted very much for me to come live with her. Mama, afraid of being left alone, obsessively broke off correspondence and burned her address.

I did not pursue higher education. We were poor; I had to take evening courses to finish lyceum and beauty school. I often think that if Papa had lived, things would have been much easier for me, both materially and emotionally. In 1960 I started my own family, in which I am very happy. I have a loving husband and two sons. I am a member of the Jewish Community, of TSKŻ [Social and Cultural Association of Jews in Poland], and recently, of the Association of "Children of the Holocaust."

The war released energy and determination in Mama, which she had never shown before or since. To the end of her life, however, she kept an amazing clarity of mind. She lived still for forty-eight years. She tried to forget. She soon formed a relationship with a man who was not Jewish. We didn't talk about our wartime experiences with each other. Sometimes, however, especially later in life, she would mention our murdered Pawełek. She almost never spoke about her family. She lost them all—Lusia, her beloved sister, the youngest of her five siblings, who had been single; her sister, Frania Perces, with her husband and daughter; her brothers, Aron and Józek, the latter a Communist who left for Russia even before the war (where all traces of him were lost); and her parents, my grandparents, who lived in Zawiercie.

I remember my grandparents. I loved my grandmother, Laja Kerner, very much. Not far from their house was a carousel. Grandma used to give me small change for it, keeping it a secret from Grandfather, who was quite stingy, warning me not to let him see me there. On the carousel, my heart pounding madly, I would look all around to see if he was watching.

Grandma was lucky. She had a bad heart and died of natural causes at the beginning of the occupation and was buried in the Jewish cemetery. Her parents—named Altman, I think—were still alive then. I remember them, too, but of course, only faintly (they were my great-grandparents). They lived in a village called Żarki, on the edge of a forest. They were already quite elderly. They had a goat. Grandma, after milking it, would come looking for me with a jug of milk, but I would run away and hide because I didn't like goat's milk at all.

Mama also mentioned something, it seems to me, about a sister of my grandmother, an aunt of hers, by the name of Bergner. Grandfather had a sister, apparently named Szwarzbaum, who had a house in a suburb of Częstochowa, in Raków-Błeszno. All these names, however, no longer mean anything to me; I can recall them now only because I once wrote them down on a piece of paper that I just rediscovered. I know nothing about my grandparents on my father's side. I think perhaps they lived near Olkusz or Oświęcim.

Everything I have written about here belongs now to the distant past. Not for me, however, since for me it is constantly alive and painful. I am grateful that someone will be able to read about how I survived in Katowice among people who did not even know whether they were Poles, Silesians, or Germans but helped us instinctively from the heart. Only in this way can I repay them. I am happy that I could write about my murdered family, who now live only in my memory. I am not even sure whether my memory has not failed me at some points in this account. I had no notes, Mama died five years ago, and I was only a child during those nightmarish years. I believe, however, that despite these limitations, the description of my history makes some sense.

1. Upper Silesia, the southwestern part of Poland, which included Katowice, was incorporated into Germany at the beginning of the war. Sosnowiec, though nearby, remained part of the General Government, occupied by the Germans but not annexed to Germany proper. See General Government in glossary.

2. After Poland was partitioned in the eighteenth century, the part controlled by Austria-Hungary became known as the province of Galicia, and the part controlled by Russia as the Congress Kingdom of Poland. See 1772 in "Historical Notes."

3. Before the war Katowice, then in Poland, was close to the German border; Sosnowiec was situated somewhat farther away from the border.

4. Germany attacked the Soviet Union in June 1941. See "Historical Notes."

5. The Jewish Community Council [*Judenrat*] was required by the Germans, at various times, to supply a certain number of people for deportation.

6. Środula was the district of Sosnowiec where the ghetto was established.

7. A "shop" was a workshop of Jewish slave labor organized to produce goods for the German war effort.

8. See *Volksliste* in glossary.

9. Dachau, one of the first German concentration camps to be established (1933), was located near Munich. Its first prisoners were political prisoners, but the number of Jews rose to about thirty per cent. Tens of thousands died there through starvation, disease, torture, or from cruel medical experiments.

10. SA, *Sturmabteilungen,* were Nazi storm troopers; also called "Brown Shirts."

REGINA SZYMAŃSKA

Born in 1932

Fear and Dread

For my sister

My maiden name was Regina Wirszubska. I was born in 1932 in Wilno.[1] My mama, Eugenia Dworec-Barysewicz, was a native of Wilno, and Papa, Arnold Wirszubski, was from Grodno. Our family, both on Mama's and Papa's sides, was very large. During the war they were all murdered in Wilno and its vicinity.

My paternal grandfather was a rabbi in Grodno, while my grandmother was the proprietor of a sawmill and a large public bathhouse. My mama completed studies in Polish language and literature, and Papa received degrees in law and philosophy in Wilno; he was a judge and later an attorney.

Before the war, my parents, assimilated Jews, lived with me and my three-years-younger sister, Ada, in Wysokie Litewskie. My papa had his law office there. Mama did not work professionally. After the war broke out, we moved to Brześć on the River Bug, to our own house. We were thrown out of there by the Russians,[2] who took everything we possessed. We ended up in Hajnówka. My father worked as an accountant at that time. In 1942, after the German-Soviet war broke out, the Germans marched into Hajnówka and threw us out of there. They rounded up all the Jews from Hajnówka and the surrounding area onto the town square. Women and children were loaded onto trucks. Men had to run behind them. My father, who worked with his mind, was not very fit physically. He was shot.

All the men who could not run because of poor physical condition, illness, or old age met the same fate.

The Germans took us from Hajnówka to Próżana, where they created a ghetto. We spent nearly a year there. It is difficult for me to describe our time in the ghetto. My sister and I were little girls then. Mama took care of everything. However, I can remember very well when Mama came to us and said, "Listen, your papa is dead." We then burst into tears, crying terribly. I can also remember that after a few hours we were already playing with other children in the courtyard.

In the Próżana ghetto we lived in a tiny room with some other family. I was ten years old then, and I thus ought to remember these events, but I don't. They have been erased from my memory. I looked after my sister; Mama managed to get food for us. I don't know how, but in any case we did not go hungry.

During this time, Mama tried to establish contact with some of Papa's clients. Two friends of ours, Mrs. Lidia Lichnowska, who is unfortunately no longer alive, and Mrs. Anna Paszkiewicz, were helping us. When rumors reached us that the Próżana ghetto was about to be liquidated, Mama started fighting to get us out of there. We got Karaite[3] documents. We left the ghetto virtually at the last moment before its liquidation. I don't know how many people survived of those who were there with us.

I also don't know how we managed to get out of the ghetto in Próżana. It seems to me that Mama bribed the guards. We then traveled two or three nights to Wysokie Litewskie. On the way there we stayed with some peasants recommended to us by Mrs. Lichnowska and Mrs. Paszkiewicz. Both these women had been friends of our family already before the war.

Father had been the only attorney in Wysokie Litewskie. He had his office near the town square, and we also had a large apartment there. In 1939 I had begun to attend the first grade of elementary school in Wysokie. Because my father handled many real estate cases and often won them, he was on friendly terms with many landowners. Mrs. Lidia Lichnowska was the daughter of the mayor of Wysokie. Her family often gave receptions for local notables, which my parents attended. My parents also hosted parties, attended mostly by Poles and only a few Jews. One of these Jews was a doctor at whose home we stayed after our escape from the Próżana ghetto. We lived with him for several weeks until the time when proper papers were prepared for us. He was an internist, his wife, a dentist. They had two children—Jola and eighteen-year-old Zenek, on whom I had a bit of a crush.

Just before the establishment of a ghetto in Wysokie Litewskie (one was created there as well), thanks to the intensified effort by Lidka Lichnowska, we obtained Aryan papers. We could then leave for Narew. It was Lidka Lichnowska, I believe, who brought us the news that a ghetto would be created. Her father, who was the prewar mayor, continued to carry out his duties during the war. His attitude toward us remained very friendly.

None of our acquaintances survived the ghetto in Wysokie Litewskie. The doctors at whose home we hid were murdered, along with their children, about a month after our departure, most probably in the town square.

Mrs. Paszkiewicz, the other lady who was helping us, now lives in Switzerland. She is of Jewish origin. She was then a widow or a divorcée. She had two daughters. One of them, Jaśka, is a doctor in Warsaw; the other, Anka, also lives in Switzerland.

I think that people did not treat us any differently as Jews in Wysokie Litewskie, because of our assimilation and the type of life my parents led.

During the war, on two occasions, we managed to escape virtually "from under the knife," once, from the ghetto in Próżana, the day before its liquidation, and afterward, from Wysokie just before a ghetto was established there. From Wysokie we found our way first to Bielsko. We stayed with friends of Lidka Lichnowska, physicians. We were there for two or three nights. From there, equipped with letters of recommendation, we went to Narew, where we spent the rest of the occupation. We were helped by a Catholic priest to whom we were referred by Mrs. Lichnowska. It is difficult to say whether the townspeople knew we were Jews.

My mama was very likable, pleasant, hardworking, and very

obliging. We did not go to school. We played practically the whole time with the local children. My sister, in spite of having very dark brown hair, has a snub nose and never looked Jewish. Therefore, she could move around freely. With me, it was different; I have a long nose and chestnut-colored hair. During the entire occupation, Mama kept me hidden and bleached my hair with peroxide. My hair was so damaged by these treatments that I had to wear a white crocheted beret the whole time. Mama told everyone that I had bad sinuses, and that is why I had to be shielded from the sun. I think that people might have suspected the truth; however, they were tolerant.

We lived through the rest of the occupation relatively peacefully. We lived in terrible hovels, at first in a store infested by rats. Mama worked as a scrubwoman in a butcher shop. When she went to work, we stayed by ourselves. We sat on our beds with our legs folded. Mice and rats ran around the store. We were terribly frightened. It was a nightmare.

Later, Mama was offered a tiny room in exchange for her cleaning. We lived there until the end of the occupation. To get that room Mama had to give up a very beautiful wardrobe. I don't know how we happened to have that wardrobe. She gave the woman who rented us the room all her jewelry and her fur coat, which she had managed to save until then. The landlady was the mother of a priest. She was a very decent old woman, who embraced us warmly. She later arranged for a better job for Mama, cooking dinners for the clerks in the community office. Such a job made it possible to always get something to eat. Around that time, I learned to knit. I made stockings, skirts, berets, and shawls for people. The results were pretty disastrous, but the passion for knitting has stayed with me until this day.

When the war ended, we left Narew for Brześć. Mama hoped that in Brześć we would be able to live in our own house. It was a large, beautiful house, which she had received as a gift from my father on a wedding anniversary. Of course, it turned out that there was no such possibility. Instead, we met our prewar maid in Brześć and moved in with her. I began attending a Russian school. Mama traded in vodka and bread. After a period of time, she applied for repatriation.[4] We came to Łódź, where I finished high school. I began studies in medicine. My sister finished law and left for the [United] States. She now lives in Glasgow with her Scottish husband. I fell in love with my husband, so Mama and I did not go to Israel, despite the fact that she wanted to do so very much.

Today I am a pediatrician. I have a son, Piotr, who is also a doctor. Piotr feels very strongly about being a Jew. He visited Israel. He liked it there very much, but he married a Polish girl—our amiable and dear Dorotka.

My mother was a very brave woman. She saved her two daughters, thanks to her self-sacrifice and the help of good people. She brought them up and educated them. After the war, in Łódź, Mama met Mrs. Helena Nowacka. They went into business together. At first they traveled to Wrocław to trade in abandoned goods; later, when they earned some money, they opened a store in Łódź on Piotrkowska Street. They worked together for several years, until Mrs. Nowacka emigrated to Israel. Afterward, Mama ran the store by herself. When she reached fifty, she became ill. She developed high blood pressure and then had a heart attack. For a while she lived with me, and then she went to my sister's, to Scotland, where she died and was buried.

As you can see, my account of the war is not particularly long. What else can I say? That there was fear and dread . . .

The three of us survived the occupation. After the war we tried to find anyone else from our family, but no one else survived. We were the only ones from the entire family who made it, thanks to our mama, who had fought like a lion for survival.

I never visited Narew after the war, despite the fact that my husband quite frequently encouraged me to go and see the place where I survived the occupation. Somehow I could never pull myself together to do it. I think I experienced too much fear there. That whole period, until the arrival of the Soviets, was a continuous time of fear. There was not a day that we could go through without feeling fear.

Even during the occupation, Mama tried to find Father. It was impossible to find the place where he was shot, together with other Jews. It is certain that he was killed. The Commission to Investigate Nazi Crimes has confirmed this. The Germans killed all the Jews on the way from Hajnówka to Próżana. It was then that my father, the rabbi, the doctor, and more than a dozen other men perished. After the war, Mama tried to arrange a burial for my father. According to the local peasants' stories, the bodies of the murdered men were taken deep into the Białowieża Forest.[5] She never found out where he was buried. The man who buried my father said that he was still alive at the time. Still alive . . . I don't know whether he was buried alive or whether he died in the man's arms. In any case, he asked the man to say Kaddish for him.[6] These were the last words of Father, which reached us.

I want to dedicate my story to my sister, whom I love very much. May it serve her and her daughters. I think that beside this, it will be useful for my granddaughter, Adusia. Someday, when she grows up, she will learn something about her grandmother.

---

1. Wilno, part of Poland between the world wars, is now Vilnius, Lithuania.

2. The Soviet Union occupied eastern Poland from September 17, 1939, until June 22, 1941. See "Historical Notes."

3. The Karaites [People of the Scripture] were a Jewish sect emerging in the eighth century in Babylon, which believed in strict adherence to the literal text of the scriptures without any rabbinical interpretation. They later settled in Russia, where they gained equal rights—by claiming that because their origins preceded the rabbinical period, they could not be held responsible for the death of Jesus. The Nazis did not persecute them, accepting the notion that although the Karaites practiced the Jewish religion, their origins were not considered Jewish.

4. After the war, the eastern border of Poland was moved, and Brześć became part of the Soviet Union. Poles living there were given the opportu-

nity to remain and become Soviet citizens or relocate to Poland and be "repatriated."

5. The Białowieża Forest is a famous forest preserve in eastern Poland, the only place in Europe where bison still roam.

6. Kaddish is the Jewish prayer for the dead.

DZIUNIA ESTERA TATTELBAUM (VEL TAJTELBAUM)

Born in 1935

Writing about Myself for the First Time

As a preface to my recollections, I must emphasize that I am writing them for the first time, that for many years I was unable to speak about any of my wartime experiences, even to those closest to me. I simply could not do it. I first began to talk about my experiences in 1979, in Paris, when I met my aunt (my mother's sister), who survived Auschwitz. To this day I cannot understand how such a small child, which I was at the time, could remember so many facts and names. Of course, the events and dates have not been entirely preserved in my memory.

I was born in Czortków, in the Tarnopol province, as an only child. My father, Salomon, had two siblings—a brother, Jakub, who just before the outbreak of war had finished medical studies in Vienna, and an older sister, living in nearby Skałat, who had two sons. My mother, Chana-Sura, née Frydman, came from Radom, where before the war lived her two brothers and a sister with their families, as well as her parents.

I lived with my parents and grandparents (Father's parents) in Czortków at 3 Szewska Street in our own house. Father, together with my grandparents, ran a large shoe store. My mother died a year before the war broke out.

After the Soviet army marched in, in September 1939, my whole family left for Kołomyja, where we were not known, because we were in danger of being deported to Siberia.[1] Father remarried there. It was in Kołomyja that the German invasion and occupation found us.

In February 1942 we were enclosed in a ghetto. In Kołomyja the ghetto was set up relatively late, according to my guardians, because in the beginning, the town was under the jurisdiction of the Hungarian army.[2] I remember that we changed apartments several times during this period, probably because of the shrinking of the ghetto area. Initially, the living conditions in the ghetto were bearable. Later, they gradually got worse; we were tormented by hunger, lice, and diseases, especially typhus. My grandmother perished in the Kołomyja ghetto during one of the first "actions." My father had a good job, which protected him. His work involved the so-called rags.[3] All the members of my family carried poison with them in case the Germans captured us. Father had poison for me as well. I knew about it, even though no one had told me. I was afraid of it because I very much wanted to live.

One day a Jewish policeman who was taking away elderly people came to our house. My grandfather, quick as lightning, swallowed poison and collapsed. He died before my eyes. I shall never forget that sight.

There were more and more actions, and more and more people were being killed or deported to death camps. One day, the Germans ordered all the ghetto residents to report to the town square. My stepmother and I were concealed in a hiding place in the attic. Father went by himself. The Germans searched the houses. To this day I can hear their shouting and stomping of boots. Nonetheless, they did not find us. Father came back as well. After all these ordeals and the fear I lived through, or perhaps also due to malnutrition, all my hair fell out.

Father attempted to get me out of the ghetto. I remember that once we waited outside the ghetto for someone who was to hide me, but nobody came, and we returned to the ghetto. In the early spring of 1943, the liquidation of the Kołomyja ghetto was imminent. My father was killed during one of the actions. My stepmother turned me over for safekeeping to the Śledziński family. I was led out through the basement of a pharmacy in which my stepmother worked, which bordered on the Aryan side. My stepmother and her sister were planning to escape through Romania. I don't know what happened to them.

I was hidden by Helena Śledzińska (Grandma), her son Leopold, and her daughter-in-law, Maria. I had false documents; I was supposed to be Leopold Śledziński's illegitimate daughter, Jadwiga Śledzińska. My guardians were good to me. They taught me to read and write, as well as prayers and catechism. Several times they received anonymous letters that they were hiding a Jewish boy—in as much as I had no hair and wore a beret. Mrs. Śledzińska suspected one of her neighbors; she went to him and made a scene. She was a very energetic and forceful person. Moreover, the Śledzińskis deliberately did not change my way of life; I continued to play in the garden and go out in the street. I remember that both in the ghetto and also at the home of my guardians, I profoundly believed that it was impossible that I would perish. I believed I would live.

In 1945, after the war ended, my guardians and I moved to Warsaw as part of the repatriation program. I was turned over to the Central Jewish Committee in Poland and from there went to the children's home in Zatrzebie, near Falenica. The Śledzińskis were no longer in contact with me, which pained me very much, but I did not know their address.

After Zatrzebie, I stayed in the children's home "Śródborowianka" in Śródborów, then in Otwock, and finally, in Kraków. This wandering through various children's homes was related to the successive liquidation of Jewish children's homes as children found their parents or families, were adopted, or went abroad—even entire groups of children left illegally for Israel. It was very painful for me to go through one transfer after another. While in the children's home in Kraków, I passed my *matura.* Later, I lived in a student dormitory and, supported by a scholarship, completed studies in economics.

After I completed my studies, I got married and left for Silesia, where I worked the entire time as an economist in an industrial plant. I have two wonderful daughters, both of whom have completed higher education, and four grandchildren. In 1995 my husband and I were divorced. Since 1992 I have been retired.

At the end of the 1960s I managed to locate my wartime guardians. In 1990 Yad Vashem Institute awarded Leopold Śledziński and his late mother the medal of the Righteous Among the Nations of the World. In 1994 while on a visit to Israel, I found in Yad Vashem Institute the plaque with their name.

From my mother's family in Radom, the only one who was saved was her sister, who survived Auschwitz and now lives in Israel. I know nothing about my father's family, with the exception of my grandparents, who were killed. The likelihood of finding me after the war was made more difficult perhaps by a slight distortion of my name, either by my guardians or by the Central Jewish Committee in Poland. I learned about this only six years ago, thanks to data from the archive containing records from the lands formerly in eastern Poland.[4]

---

1. When the Soviets took over the eastern half of Poland, they deported to Siberia those considered "enemies of the people," which included many owners and operators of businesses.

2. Hungary was allied with Germany, and Hungarian military units were part of the German army.

3. Working with "rags" often meant the job of gathering up and sorting clothing and belongings left by Jews who had been deported.

4. This archive, called *Archiwum Zabużańskie* [Archive of Lands Beyond the River Bug], is located in Warsaw-Mokotów and contains birth, marriage, and death records from cities and towns formerly in eastern Poland and now in Ukraine.

JULIUSZ JERZY TOBER

Born in 1942

The Nightmare Continues

My parents, whom I did not know, because they perished in the Warsaw Ghetto when I was six months old, were of the Jewish faith. At the last moment, sensing their approaching death at the hands of the Nazis, they handed me over to the Tober family. Mrs. Tober was from then on my guardian angel and protector and treated me like a son. As she told me later, she managed, with the help of the underground resistance, to get my birth registered in the municipal office in Sochaczew with the birth date of January 15, 1942, the same as that of her son, Piotr, who had died as an infant. This helped her to pass me off as her own child. Because I had been circumcised, Mrs. Tober baptized me at the Evangelical-Augsburg [Protestant] church in Żyrardów in 1942.

The name Doński weaves in and out of my life story. Mr. Doński, who was also of the Jewish faith, was the intermediary between my parents and my adopted mother. He also was the only person who ever described to me what my father looked like. It was he, as well, who in later years told Mrs. Tober that my parents had perished in the Warsaw Ghetto. Mr. Doński must have received a significant amount of money from my parents with which he was to pay for my upkeep. This supposition was confirmed in correspondence in the 1950s with my guardian-teacher, Mr. Michał Cubert, who was also my sole support and help during the most difficult period of my early youth.

Mr. Tober was, without question, a German. He died in 1942 in unexplained circumstances. My adopted siblings (two brothers and a sister) made it painfully clear to me that I was a foundling of unknown parentage and of Jewish origins. Mrs. Tober, because of her husband's ancestry, had been on the *Volksliste,* which made it easier for her to provide assistance—though at the risk of her life—to other Jews and AK [Home Army] activists. Toward the end of the war, because of the ancestry and activities of her husband, as well as those of her sons and daughter (Nazi supporters), she had to escape to Germany. Seeking shelter there, she took me with her.

In Germany we settled in Bavaria in the Donauwörth district. I remember this period quite well; I was six years old at the time. But even there, I was beaten and harassed by my older stepbrother. My guardian, a woman with higher education, a person with a tender heart, gave help to everyone who needed it. But she herself, because of the extreme poverty that prevailed in Germany right after the war, had to beg in the streets to get us a piece of bread. Despite these difficult conditions, she made it possible for me to attend school there, and I finished the first grade. Due to her critical situation, she established contact by letter with Mr. Doński and her friend and former classmate, Mrs. Barbara Święcicka. They both insisted that she send me back to Poland, promising to take care of me and to educate me. My guardian placed her trust in these people, and believing that my fortune would change for the better, agreed to send me back to Poland.

In 1949 I returned with a transport to Warsaw. I remember the moment when the train station emptied out and I stood there like a living, abandoned parcel. Finally, after a few hours, Mr. Doński, my alleged guardian, appeared, and he handed me over to the children's home in Chylice. At that time I was a boy whose mental and physical health had already been affected by painful experiences. Mr. Doński's care was limited to making minimal payments to the children's home. There I completed five grades. Frequent illnesses and the rebelliousness of my young heart, thirsting for kindness and warmth, in place of which I encountered physical blows and threats, caused me to fall deeper and deeper into apathy, enclosing me in the pain of the "orphan's syndrome."

In 1955 the children's home was closed, and the children were transferred to the home in Ząbkowice. The friend and patron of the children's home in Ząbkowice was the aforementioned Mr. Cubert. He was also a frequent visitor there. The administration of this home urged Mr. Cubert, who was of the Jewish faith, to confirm their suspicions that I was circumcised. When he verified this, he spoke with me cordially and at length about my wartime and postwar experiences. He promised to do everything possible to get in touch with my guardian, Mrs. Tober, and to fill in the gaps of my history by finding Mr. Doński, who had so miserably betrayed the trust of my parents (whose names I do not know to this day). Mr. Cubert, with great warmth, which I had so lacked, always emphasized that Jews were one large family of whom we should be proud and that the complexes which I had acquired in various places of refuge were the product of stupid and malicious tongues.

Nonetheless, I was burdened by the stigma that I was a child from nowhere. Mr. Cubert, seeing my advanced stage of orphan's syndrome (as he told me), fulfilled his promise. He tried, with great effort, to find documents that I was not a person from nowhere. In 1956 he established contact by mail with my guardian angel, Mrs. Tober. She was overjoyed at receiving some news about me, because she herself had for a long time searched for me without success. She informed him that although Mr. Doński had possessed information about my parents, he had never revealed it.

Despite Mrs. Tober's and Mr. Cubert's valiant efforts to have me return to her, the administration of the children's home categorically opposed my leaving. At that time Mrs. Tober used to send me packages, which didn't always reach me. This bitter disappointment, that the prospect of a better life at the side of my guardian—whose circumstances had improved and who very much wanted to have me with her—had come to naught, caused a deterioration of my performance in school and changes in my behavior. The way I expressed my pain was to distance myself from the positive role models I saw around me—my schoolmates, who were fortunate to be by the side of their parents.

I was sent to a vocational school to train as a bricklayer, contrary to my interests and abilities. After the closing of the home in Ząbkowice, which was during the freezing winter of 1962, there was nowhere and no one to whom I could go. The beginning of my independent life was very difficult. I began building my "pseudolife" on my own. I regret many decisions from that time. To escape from this emptiness, I joined the army. There, after a thorough medical examination, it was found that I had balance problems, distortions of the spine (the result of carrying heavy sacks of soil at the children's home), stomach ulcers, and manic-depressive disorder.

After leaving the army, seeking a roof over my head, I married a person who could not understand me, and her family treated me, from the beginning, like a foundling stripped of his own identity. In 1981, due to the deteriorating atmosphere of our marriage, my wife left for the United States, and my mother-in-law took our sons. Divorce followed, and I was again left alone.

I tried to get work, but in a period of depression I sought to forget my problems in bad company. I shook off a nervous breakdown and an inclination toward alcohol by myself. During the depths of depression, there were once again casual, short relationships with women. There was also vodka and everything that comes with it.

I began to lose hope. I lost the roof over my head. At this critical time, when I was often cold and hungry, I met a friend from the children's home who advised me to go to Dzięgielów to the Diakonis Sisters' Home. This was in the fall of 1983, and I stayed there until December. But I could not adjust to it, and at that time I found warm hearts at the home of Mr. and Mrs. Breull, relatives of the Wojnars and the Grosses.

Then, searching for work that included the possibility of housing, I left Cieszyn and moved to Ustroń. However, my illness and frequent stays in hospitals made it necessary for me to obtain a permanent disability pension from the Social Welfare Office. The Welfare Office also allocated me a room—ten square meters.

Every day is like another; I don't believe that the sun will ever shine for me again. I don't expect much, just a semblance of family and a little heart, and perhaps the good Lord will let me find out who I really am. To this day, I am still searching for family—to no avail. It has become my obsession.

At the age of fifty-seven, I discovered that I belong to the large family of the "Children of the Holocaust," and this fact has become a bright ray on the dark horizon of my life.

Perhaps things really will get better?

HENRYKA TRZCIŃSKA-STRZELECKA

Born in 1937

Hidden by My Grandfather

I was born on April 11, 1937, in Warsaw. My place of birth, however, was changed in my birth record. My mother was a Jew and father a Pole. Mother's maiden name was Zylbersztajn, and Father's name was Stanisław Konopczyński.

Just before the outbreak of war, mainly because of my mother, my parents decided to escape the Germans by fleeing east to the Soviet Union and wanted to take me with them. I was then two years old and staying temporarily with my Polish paternal grandparents, who lived in Włocławek—which is where my parents were also from. Thus my parents came from Warsaw to Włocławek with the intention of taking me along. My [paternal] grandparents told them that if they were to take me with them on such a nomadic and perilous journey, I, as a small child, would surely perish or starve to death. My parents thus left me with my grandparents and continued on their way. They were not alone; they were fleeing with a large group of people, mostly Jews. They escaped east because they assumed the Germans would not get that far—beyond our eastern border.

My grandparents, Maria and Stanisław Konopczyński, baptized me, changing at the same time some of the data in my birth record—place of birth, from Warsaw to Włocławek, and name of my mother, from Perla to Apolonia. I know about all this from my grandparents.

After the Germans marched into Włocławek, there were people who reported to the Germans that my grandparents had a Jewish child in their home. We lived in a large apartment building on the second floor. On the ground floor lived a couple named Krygier, who had been there a long time. It was a mixed marriage; she was Polish, and he was German. Mrs. Krygier was a noble woman. She used to warn my grandparents when the Gestapo was about to come. She would say to my grandmother, "Mrs. Konopczyńska, you should go out with Henia [Henryka] today, because they are coming." During the entire occupation, day or night, I would be taken out of the house to the woods or to the fields, where I would be hidden in the wheat or in ditches overgrown with bushes. It was the worst in winter. Then we would hide in stables in order to be warmer. My grandfather always accompanied me. He hid me from the Germans at the risk of his life.

I don't know where Mrs. Krygier was getting this crucial information but probably from her daughter, who wore a German uniform. I know that my grandparents, for hiding a Jewish child, and Mrs. Krygier, for warning my grandparents of the impending danger, could all have been shot. We lived through all the years of the war like this.

We also hid in the countryside. My grandma was with me for weeks away from home. She knitted sweaters and socks from old wool unraveled from our garments. She would give them to peasants for a bowl of soup and a piece of bread. I remember that we walked everywhere on foot and that my feet were very sore. Because of all that knitting, Grandma almost went blind; she could barely see anything at night. We were both so thin that we looked like human shadows.

I also remember, although I don't recall exactly when it was, that Nazis once rode into our courtyard. There was no time for anyone to hide me. I climbed by myself into a huge barrel used to store marmalade. The Krygiers had a grocery shop in this building and had set out the empty containers in the courtyard. I sat in this barrel till evening came, scraping out the leftover marmalade from the sides of the barrel. I knew instinctively that I had to hide myself, because there was no one at that moment who could help me. To this day I can't even look at marmalade.

In the first days of the occupation, someone made it known to my grandma that my mother's father, my grandfather, a Jew, wanted to see me. Grandfather was a rabbi in Włocławek. I knew that he was a Jewish spiritual leader and that he "wrote letters to God." My grandma dressed me in my prettiest dress and took me to see Grandfather. I do not remember the place exactly, but perhaps it was a synagogue. We walked into a dimly lit space, and I saw from afar, seated behind a desk full of books, an old man with a long beard who gestured for me to come a bit closer to him. He stared at me for a long time and then signaled me to leave.

A few days later all the Jews in Włocławek, with my grandfather in the lead, were tied up by the Nazis with ropes and chains. Beating them cruelly, they set their beards on fire. Then they herded them somewhere beyond Włocławek and murdered them there. I learned the details only after the war. After all these years, I can still remember the way my grandfather looked—the elderly, emaciated figure, with a completely gray beard and long sidelocks. Before that, Grandfather had not kept in touch with me, because his daughter—my mother—had married a Pole against his wishes. For him, an Orthodox rabbi, she had simply died. He had "buried" her and grieved for her.

Throughout the whole war, my grandparents and I led a marginal existence because of me. We lived under enormous tension and were almost excessively vigilant. My grandparents didn't sleep nights, always straining to listen. I, on the other hand, was mature beyond my years and always ready to escape at a moment's notice. In those years that was our everyday life. Today the memories bring forth pain and tears. An irrational fear of lawlessness, humiliation, and danger has been with me from my earliest years and has remained.

As for my parents, I had no news of them for more than five years. My elderly grandparents were everything to me—parents, my whole family. To them alone I owe my survival during that nightmare.

After the war ended, my grandparents turned me over to the convent of the Ursuline Sisters in Włocławek. They claimed that it was for my safety. I was seven years old then and was thoroughly conditioned to keep silent about my Jewish origins. I think only the convent sisters knew the truth about me. My schoolmates always looked at me somewhat strangely—why was I so dark and why did I have no parents, only grandparents? I had such a fertile imagination that I had no difficulty inventing tales about myself. I remember that I always wanted to play an angel in the children's pageants and nativity scenes organized in the convent. I was told that there were no dark angels. I was very unhappy that I always played the devil; it was the tragedy of my childhood. I felt unhappy, but I already knew that even my saintly grandfather could not intervene with God on my behalf.

I don't know when I found out that Mama was a Jew and Father a Pole. For me, they were simply my beloved parents. I just told myself that since they were not with me, that meant I did not belong to anybody, and that is why I had to hide. I was consoled only by the enormous care I received from my grandfather and grandmother, their stories about my parents, and their assurances that they would return after the war ended. For many years I dreamed of my parents day and night. I awaited their return to the home created for me by my grandparents.

I do not know how my parents met. My grandparents told me it was a beautiful and intense love affair. My parents were dedicated to each other and very happy together, although their marriage lasted such a short time. Their escape to the east, as I understand it now, was a noble gesture by Father for Mother's sake. They both wanted to survive for me, for their little daughter left behind in Włocławek. Their escape was a nightmare. They traveled mostly on foot, at night, hungry and cold. When they finally reached the Soviet Union, my father was immediately arrested. That is how my parents became separated. Father was shipped off to Vorkuta,[1] where deportees like him were building a railroad in an arctic climate. The living conditions in the *łagier* [Soviet forced labor camp] were macabre. People were dying of exhaustion and hunger. My father was starving and suffered from scurvy, which they called *tsinga* there. He was so exhausted, emaciated, and starved that he couldn't stand up straight and walked in a squat. At times he could not remember my name or Mother's. His brain function was beginning to be affected by hunger.

The prisoners in that camp slept on raw logs (that is, unprocessed logs). One night, Father was huddled against another prisoner with whom he slept on the log. The man kept getting colder and colder. It soon became apparent that he was no longer alive. This is when Father removed the man's documents from his ragged clothing and put his own in their place.[2] From that time on my father went by the name of Stanisław Zaganiacz, while Stanisław Konopczyński was buried in the camp. Shortly thereafter Father escaped from the labor camp and joined the Anders Army.[3] He went through the entire route of combat and was wounded at the Battle of Monte Cassino. General Anders did not accept every Pole into his army; it was thus a distinction.

While my father was in Vorkuta, Mother went through hell in Russia. She suffered from hunger and typhus. She was cared for by another Jew, who was also from Włocławek. He lived in the same house as she and had a job. He saved Mother's life. His name was Mosze Knister.

Once a man came to see Mother and informed her that my father was dead. He said that he had seen him buried in the labor camp in Vorkuta.

After the war ended, Mother came to Włocławek to take me with her. She was going to Palestine with Mosze Knister. My grandparents did not believe the stories about the death of their son and tried to convince Mother to stay with them and wait for Father's return. Mother, at this time, was pregnant by Knister. She was sure that her husband, my father, was dead. She did not accept my grandparents' proposition. She left me with them and set out on a trip to Palestine by way of Austria.

Shortly after Mother's departure, a letter arrived from England with Father's photograph, signed Stanisław Zaganiacz. Father wrote in the letter that he was alive and about to leave for the United States and asked about me and Mother. I can't describe the joy this letter brought me. I understood that I was no longer an orphan and that once again I had someone to wait for. I was barely nine years old at that time.

After a certain time, Father and I established correspondence. Father tried to help us by sending parcels of food and clothing for me. Things had already gotten a little better by then, but my grandparents were growing old and did not earn much money. I don't know what we lived on, but in any case, I did not go hungry.

I didn't have any news from Mother for a long time. I finished high school in Włocławek and was accepted for studies at the Medical Academy in Białystok. Once again I could not admit my Jewish origins and presented myself as a total orphan. At that time I received a letter from Mother, which fortunately arrived at my grandparents' address. I wrote her back, telling her about everything, and the correspondence once again broke off. Perhaps this was not my mother's fault; it was simply because contact between Poland and Israel had been severed.

After finishing my medical studies I started work in Grudziądz (in accordance with my assignment, which was then obligatory). I got married and settled in nearby Łasin.

When I turned twenty-eight, my father invited me to visit him in the United States. In spite of the difficulties, I went—with his photograph in hand. I was terribly scared, but I could not deny myself the fulfillment of the dream that had been with me since early childhood—to meet my father and be with him. I don't know by what miracle we immediately recognized each other in an enormous crowd of travelers at the huge Kennedy Airport. I did not even look at the photo. This was perhaps the happiest day of my life. Father fulfilled all my dreams and the converse was also true.

At the end of my five-month stay, Father declared that since meeting me he could not go on living without me any more and that regardless of the consequences, he would return to Poland, for better or worse.[4] Shortly after that, he returned to Poland for good, "making up," with his fatherly love, solicitude, and wise counsel, the affection I had missed during my childhood and youth. We were together seven years, and these were the most beautiful years for me. The hunger, poverty, and adversity that he experienced in the Soviet Union and during the whole war took their toll. He died prematurely, at the age of sixty-four. He was a splendid father and human being. He loved my mother to the end of his life. He remains in my memory as a noble man, worthy of being emulated.

Unfortunately, my grandparents did not live to see my father's return. They died while I was completing my studies and earning my medical degree.

After my return from the United States, I gave birth to a son, Maciek. My father adored him and gave him everything he couldn't give me as a child. After a time I was divorced from my husband and left Łasin for Warsaw. At first I worked in the hospital on Kasprzaka Street, and then, because there was a shortage of positions, I was sent to work at the Sanitary-Epidemiological Station. I ran the Department of Work Hygiene. I completed my specialization in this field, and a few years ago I was named as the state regional sanitary inspector and director of the Regional Sanitary-Epidemiological Station.

While I was with Father in the United States, we both wrote letters to Mother in Israel. However, there was no response. Mother claimed later that she wrote to me the whole time and sent letters to Poland. I never received any of them. She, however, had all my letters. She read them over and over and knew them by heart. Soon after my return to Warsaw, there was a "thaw." Mother and I began communicating with each other, but I still couldn't go see her. That became possible only after Father's death.

We arranged a meeting in Romania. I flew there with my son, Maciek. He was nine years old then. A great tragedy for me and for him happened there—as I left the plane, it became apparent that my child had become irreversibly deaf. Beforehand, he had been a musical child (he was taking music lessons and had already given concerts in kindergarten). We had flown to Romania on a rickety old Russian plane. There was a terrible storm. My son screamed on the airplane that he was in pain. Nothing helped—not candy, not swallowing saliva, nor plugging the ears. This was the price we paid for the visit with my mother.

When I first saw Father after many years, I was twenty-eight years old. When I first saw Mother, I was thirty-eight. Mother wanted us to go to Israel with her. That was her goal in meeting me in Romania. But I couldn't drop everything all at once and run off with her. Thus I returned to Poland. We continued to correspond.

During the 1980s I married again. Mother invited my husband and me to Israel, where, in addition to Mother, her brother, my Uncle Izrael, was living. Mother at that time was very sick. She had diabetes. In our conversations she kept returning to the time when she was with my father. She knew by heart the letters he had sent her. She constantly wanted to talk about him, even though she was still living with Mosze Knister, with whom she had two grown sons. In Israel I met one of my brothers, Abram. The other one was living in the States at that time. I have not met him to this day.

We spent only two weeks in Israel. After our return, Mother and I were often in touch, mostly by telephone. There were moments went she tried to escape into the past. In 1992 I was informed that something had happened to her, that she had fallen down and was lying unconscious in the hospital. She soon died. I could not afford to fly to Israel for the funeral. Earlier (this was after my husband's and my return from Israel) my son, Maciek, had gone there at the invitation of Uncle Izrael. The purpose of his trip was a medical consultation related to possible ear surgery. Because such a possibility was ruled out, my son began working as a waiter and earned enough money to purchase a modern hearing aid. Three years ago, in 1992, my son married a splendid girl from Kalisz and settled there. He is a computer specialist.

Childhood and youth impact a person's entire life. I still haven't come out of hiding. I am stuck there, and it is stronger than I am. I have many friends and acquaintances, but no one besides my husband knows about my past, my origins, my experiences, or thoughts. Even my son does not understand them fully, and I can't really explain them to him.

Today I am a member of the Association of "Children of the Holocaust," and here I feel as among family. I don't have to hide from anyone. I feel safe and can be myself.

---

1. Vorkuta is a coal-mining town in the Komi Republic, fifty kilometers north of the Arctic Circle.

2. Author believes that her father switched identity papers because the dead soldier's imprisonment term was shorter than that of her father.

3. See Anders Army in glossary.

4. Anyone who had been in the Anders Army, which had been under British command, was considered suspect during the cold war and was not welcomed in Poland.

BRONISŁAWA WAJNGARTEN

Born in 1933

Run to the Woods!

It is with greatly mixed emotions that I approach the writing of my story, of my tragic life. Yet I have the hope that in this way perhaps someone will find me and I will not be so lonely and a total orphan for the remaining days of my life, to the very end.

I was supposedly born on September 10, 1933, in Drohobycz—that is what my baptismal certificate states (I didn't have a birth certificate)—and at present, I have an official identification document issued on the basis of this certificate. My baptism took place in Borysław in 1942 with the help of my Polish guardians, Maria and Zygmunt Gamski.

What I want to write about is hazily inscribed in my memory—a memory that has not preserved everything, no doubt due to the shock of having seen my family murdered before my eyes.

During one of the first roundups in Drohobycz—it seems it was the cold November of 1941—I was living with my aunt and her two daughters in the center of Drohobycz, probably on Borysławska Street. My mother and I had made our way there, probably with my younger sister, after we were forced to flee Młynki—a suburb of Drohobycz. Our Ukrainian neighbors there virtually forced us to leave our home, undoubtedly wanting to save us from the Germans.

My aunt's name was Frajdenhajm (I am not writing this name using German spelling, in as much as that is probably how Jewish names in Galicia were written).[1] My name is Bronia Wajngarten. Although my memory of that also is not certain, fortunately, I have an official document with it, issued by Dr. Rajnhold, the head of the *Judenrat* [Jewish council] in the Drohobycz ghetto, and that is how my name was spelled in the letter he passed on to my later guardians. The haze that surrounds my memories has nonetheless allowed me to clearly remember my name as well as the strict instructions that I was never to acknowledge it or admit to being Jewish if I wanted to stay alive. But I am getting a bit ahead with these explanations.

I remember myself as a seven-year-old, blue-eyed, blond girl, endowed with so-called "good looks." In a rather large milk can, I used to bring home remains of food that German soldiers, stationed in the barracks on Truskawiecka Street, would give me. I truly don't know how I managed to get in there, but this was the only meal for our entire family. Already at that time my father was no longer with us, having been murdered in Borysław. Perhaps I was there with my mother. I see before me a large square on which were lying naked, human bodies, massacred in a horrible manner—it looked like an animal slaughterhouse. Such an image still looms in front of my eyes.

My father had light-colored hair. He reportedly worked in the refinery called Galicja in Drohobycz.

But I must get back to the description of the death of my mother, sister, aunt, and my aunt's two daughters. It was early morning. I think we lived in the annex of a large apartment building. Trucks drove up there, and the Germans ordered us to get out of our apartments and loaded us onto the trucks like cattle, naturally, under the threat of automatic pistols pointed in our direction. We were taken to a forest not far from Drohobycz; it was probably in Dereżyce—this is a name that rattles around in my head—but it could have also been in a forest near Bronica in the direction of Sambor. At least that is what Thomas Sandkühler wrote in his doctoral thesis, *The "Final Solution" in Galicia: The Murder of the Jews in Eastern Poland and the Rescue Initiative by Berthold Beitz.*[2]

We were placed in a single long file near the forest, where

ditches had already been dug. I can't explain why I was not with my mother and my other relatives. I was the last one, and at the end of the line stood a young man in a German uniform—but not in the uniform of the SS—with a rifle ready to fire. The command was given, "Fire!" In a fraction of a second, the young man grabbed me by the hand, shielded me with his body, and yelled, "Run to the woods!" The woods were right there, and the brush was high enough that I couldn't be seen. My instinct for survival made me listen to that soldier. It seems to me that I saw my mother—her look of approval is before my eyes—and then, when I was running through the woods, all I could hear were bursts of gunfire and horrible screams.

How long I ran at this frantic pace and how I ended up in the city, in Drohobycz—I don't know. Somebody took me to Dr. Józef Rajnhold, who was probably already the chairman of the *Judenrat* by then. This man tried to save me at all costs. There is proof of this in a letter he wrote in November 1942, which was supposed to be sent to America after the war but ended up in my hands in 1953. After pulling me out of the ghetto, Dr. Rajnhold found a young, childless Jewish couple for me. Their names were Lusia and Leon Waldberg, and at that time they ran a photography studio called Artis in Drohobycz (my photographs from that period have survived). Wanting to save me, they were the first ones to insist that I learn the prayers such as "Our Father" and "Hail Mary."

However, when the sword of destruction was about to reach them as well, they turned me over to a Polish family, Mr. and Mrs. Gamski, who lived at Polmin, a well-known oil refinery in Drohobycz. They baptized me and gave me their last name, but the hunt for Jews was very intense. When it was discovered that the Gamskis were hiding a Jewish child (my adopted father was persecuted), they were forced to send me to Kraków to Lusia Waldberg's brother, Kunysz, who worked for the railroad and went by the name of Kunicki. It is difficult to describe here how I had to travel all alone from Drohobycz to Kraków, how, guided by my self-preservation instinct, I rode in a wagon marked *Nur für Deutsche* [only for Germans] and sang an old German love song, *"Drunten in der Lobau hab' ich ein Mädel geküsst"* ["Down in the Lobau[3] I Have Kissed a Maiden"]—for which I received food—not knowing what I was singing or what impression I was making on the other passengers.

Mr. Kunicki placed me with the Sisters of the Presentation in Kraków who ran an elementary school and a high school on St. John Street. Documents have been preserved there, including my certificate for completing the fourth grade in the school year 1943–44. On the certificate is written: "Religion: Roman-Catholic, Father's Name: Edmund"—although in reality, his name was Zygmunt (Gamski). Could it already have been foreseen "on high" that my husband for forty-six years would be someone named Edmund?

Life in the convent was not easy. I had to get up in the morning before six o'clock, because already at six o'clock I took part in the first holy Mass, pumping the organ bellows in the organ loft (at that time there were no electric organs as yet). In this way, with the force of my feeble arms, I helped the organist to operate the organ, and I also sang. The sisters said that God had given me a good voice and that was the way to thank him for such a gift.

Unfortunately, the subsidies paid by Mr. Kunicki for my stay in the convent came to an end, and I quickly found myself in an orphanage in Kochanów near Kraków, on the main road from Kraków to Katowice. I did not admit to being Jewish to anyone in this large orphanage. I was there with other children who had lost their parents during the war, but, as it turned out, at the end of the war many of them found their parents and families. I, however, did not.

I must absolutely mention one thing, as there is currently an ongoing discussion in Poland in the Catholic Church whether girls should be allowed to serve during Mass. In the West it is already a widely accepted practice. I performed this role already in 1944 and 1945. My duties included adorning the altar, preparing the hosts and communion wafers—which I bought twelve kilometers away in Kraków in a special store run by the Salvatorian priests—accompanying the priest behind the railing, reciting the entire liturgy in Latin, ringing the bells, and furnishing the altar with wine and water. Quite often I also played the accordion, especially on Sundays, when my male colleagues served at Mass.

Our chapel in the orphanage served as a church for the local population of Kochanów and Zabierzów. Thus I was probably one of the first girls in Poland to serve at Mass. Salvatorian priests from Kraków were in charge of our chapel. Father Wojciech Olszówka was one of them. It was he who in October 1945, when only a few children remained in the orphanage (I don't know whether he suspected my Jewish origins but probably not), decided to look after me and took me to his parents in Katowice-Ligocie, where the kindhearted Mr. and Mrs. Olszówka took me under their care. I stayed with them for five years. Then fate sent me to Wejherowo, where in 1952 I graduated from high school, simultaneously finishing a special course for the first group of teachers of the Russian language. I received the assignment to work at a police officers' school in Słupsk.

This was the end of my experiences under the occupation, but my inner hiding did not end. My later fortunes took various turns, and during the turmoil in Poland in 1968,[4] my husband and I lost our jobs, just because I was Jewish (he was not). The authorities knew this perfectly well, even though I thought they were unaware of it.

I want to note that being "thrown overboard" made me stronger. I had to search for new social circles and attempt to adjust myself to a new reality. In effect, after spending twenty years at my job and reaching the age of forty, I made a risk-taking decision—to embark on the study of German philology. After a difficult six years of study, in 1980, I received a master's diploma in German philology at Adam Mickiewicz University in Poznań. The title of my master's thesis, written in German, was *Das Bild Galiziens in den Prosawerken von Josef Roth* [*The View of Galicia in the Prose of Josef Roth*]. In this way I wanted to at least get a bit closer to my home area, of which I knew so little!

I have written down these reminiscences in the hope that through them I might still be able to find relatives. Perhaps among the readers there will be someone whom fate has brought in contact with someone from my family. I would ask that any information be sent to the Association of "Children of the Holocaust" in Warsaw at 6 Twarda Street.

I am awaiting such a moment when I will be able to forget about everyday things, and the gates of my childhood—which to this day lie hidden so deeply in the abyss of oblivion—will swing wide open in front of me.

---

1. In actuality, the German spelling of names was common in Galicia, for example, "Freidenheim" and "Weingarten."

2. *"Endlösung" in Galizien: der Judenmord in Ostpolen und die Rettungsinitiativen von Berthold Beitz 1941–1944* (Berlin: Detz Verlag, 1996).

3. Lobau is a town in Saxony with a popular summer spa.

4. See Events of 1968 in glossary.

KRYSTYNA ZIELIŃSKA, NÉE ROZENTAL

Born in 1924

I Was to Be a Boy . . .

My ten-year-old sister, Sabina, and my younger sister, Lunia, age six, were already born. My parents wanted to have a boy, so they tried once again . . . and I came into the world. Father, hearing the news, simply ran out of the clinic. He already had an army of females at home!

In the Jewish community office they didn't want to give me the name Krystyna. They said, "Perhaps Krajndla." But for a bribe of five złotys, they consented. And thus throughout my entire life, I've almost never changed my first name, but my last name—about a hundred times. I was, counting backward—Krystyna Zielińska, previously Krystyna Dąbrowa, before that my name was Aleksandra Mlonka and Krystyna Wierzbołowicz. When in the "March" years[1] we were required to fill out personal questionnaires, the item "previous name" was very important, and I had plenty to write down. Somehow, I never went back as far as Krystyna Rozental.

I was a good-looking, healthy child, but regrettably a little plump and not very well coordinated. Mama enrolled me in Tacjanna Wysocka's ballet school, but somehow I gave up on a career as a dancer. Then I began ice skating in the Rau Garden.[2] There was music, and there were eleven- or twelve-year-old boys, who, looking at my rosy cheeks and snow-white sweater, began calling me, I didn't know why, "Brightened with Radion." Radion was a laundry detergent, and an ad for it hung on the wall surrounding the rink. That white sweater and my ruddy cheeks really did make me look like a live advertisement.

My parents tried hard to turn me into a "young lady from a good home," even though, in reality, we were not that well off. And so I was not allowed to play with other children in the courtyard; that was my unfulfilled dream. I used to go out on my second-floor balcony and toss down various cutouts and toys, calling out, "Hey, kids, take these!" My contemporaries liked that a lot, but they must have thought it a bit strange, because someone wrote in chalk on my stairway, "Krysia {Krystyna} Rozental is crazy!"

A few words about our apartment building. It had three courtyards and was located right next to All Saints Church and Grzybowski Square. The front apartments were occupied by doctors and, in general, so-called better tenants. Hasidic Jews lived with their families on the left side, and on the right, all sorts of indigents. I remember a cobbler with five children. He made shoes (navy blue pumps for one złoty) but was still unable to pay the rent. Thus, without ceremony, he was thrown out into the courtyard, but, sitting at his machine, out in the open, he continued to make those shoes. Hasidic families had a lot of children. I remember a mother in a wig who had a two-year-old toddler, and her daughter had a son the same age.

At the time of the holidays, a booth was set up in the large courtyard, and the men prayed there for perhaps a week.[3] But on all other days, the courtyard belonged to the children. Its main "decorative" element was a large trash bin. The ground was paved with cobblestones. There was no question of any plants or even a bit of grass. The children of the courtyard played and danced around the trash bin. I remember one fragment from their repertoire: "Because we are young, and this is our might. Nothing can stop us, we're singing day and night. The whole world belongs to us. It's a young people's world, it's a young people's world. And he who does not believe us, let him lie like this log!!!"

Rent was very high. I remember we paid more than 128 złotys

for a three-room apartment. There were the usual tile stoves, coal was kept in the cellar, the bathtub was set up in the kitchen, and the water heater was in the lavatory. During wartime, this tub was filled with water and covered with boards. My uncle, Maks Feldberg, whose family stayed with us during bombings, fell into the water as he slept. It was not clear why he then said to my father, resentfully, "Anti-Semites."

A medical practitioner named Wiewiórka lived on the ground floor of my entry and was everything to everybody. He used to apply cupping glasses[4] (for which I despised him) and made unerring diagnoses for adults and children.

A twelve-year-old boy, Henio, with his two-year-old brother, Bobuś, was allowed to visit me for company. Bobuś's head was covered with golden curls, and he looked like an angel from one of my notebooks (because at that time we wrote with pens dipped in ink and had to use blotting paper, which was attached by a ribbon with a picture of an angel on it). Henio, when older, reasoned, "You, Krysia, are going to die first, because you are the oldest, then me, then Bobuś will be last." This prediction of the course of human destiny, though logical, did not come to pass. Both boys were gassed in Treblinka, and only I, the oldest, miraculously remained among the living.

At home, however, I was the youngest, which truly pained me. We sat in the dining room, and Mama would carve a chicken. First, she would give Father a thigh, which I really wanted, the second thigh would go to my oldest sister, Sabina, the breast to Lunia, and I, the runt—got only the wings. I was convinced that my parents did not love me, that they preferred my older sisters, and there were times when I sat in the lavatory and shed tears. Unfortunately, I was not there alone. In those days, people bought live chickens, and before they were turned into soup and meat, they were kept on a string in the lavatory. And so I daydreamed there, in the presence of this wretched bird, that I would die, have a solemn funeral, and my parents would follow the casket, crying in despair. That would be my revenge for the chicken wings, for not letting me out in the yard to play, and for my supposedly being so healthy, sturdy, and plump! I was drawn to these thoughts by a book for youngsters entitled *Jur.*[5] It was about two brothers—Tadzik, weak, sickly, and constantly looked after, and an older brother, Jur, just the opposite. He was a picture of health. And who finally died? Jur, of course!

However, Mama took care of my health very thoroughly. She gave me salt baths and took me to the vats where tar was heated, because that was good for whooping cough. And what was the worst, however, was that she constantly took me to the Saski Garden so I could breathe fresh air. I was to be at school at eleven, but my grandfather, Alfred Rozental, would come by already before eight o'clock and take me to the garden. This is where, early in the morning, all the Jewish tailors would meet. There were hundreds of them in Warsaw before the war. They held meetings in Writers' Lane (not far from the sundial), as they had plenty of common topics to discuss.

My grandfather was not just any tailor; he lectured in the vocational school for Jewish youth, which was located on Grzybowska Street, and he had his own workshop at 139 Marszałkowska Street. He mostly sewed military uniforms. In the front window of his shop there stood tiny mannequins dressed in clothes Grandpa had made. It is worth noting that in prewar Warsaw, neighborhood counted for a lot. To be a tailor on Nalewki, Franciszkańska, or on Nowolipki, that was an ordinary thing, but Marszałkowska—well, that was already French elegance.

All three of us attended the same elementary school and the same high school. Mama was active in the parents' committee, and it was probably her doing that got me accepted into first grade when I was only six years old. For breakfast[6] I would take, in a little basket, a small cake, the so-called little mushroom, because I couldn't handle sandwiches. I also had difficulty buttoning my underpants. They had little white cloth buttons that attached them to the bodice, and it wasn't at all easy, so Marysia Brodecka used to help me. Mama called her parents "Litvaks," a label I felt was pejorative.

From my youngest years I took part in school performances. My fondest dream was to play the lead parts. Once, I was supposed to be a cornflower in a group scene. Anulka Rawet was a poppy. The only thing was, she was put in front of me. There was no stopping me. Although I was pushed back to the second row again and again and even accepted it at the dress rehearsal, during the actual show, I moved out in front again!

I, as a somewhat older child of the Holocaust, recall a childhood that was, in perspective, idyllic and angelic. Since I have lived a bit longer than those unfortunate children born just before or during the war, I have retained a piece of the normal world, which I am now trying to convey in these recollections.

When "Children of the Holocaust" members who were born in 1940 or 1942 speak at psychotherapy sessions in Śródborów, the same theme comes up time and time again. They have sons and daughters, they are caring parents, but they have not been able to give their children emotional warmth because they themselves never received it. Marysia, sixty years old now, cries when she talks about this. Jurek writes poetry. His mother died when he was two, and his father raised him the best he knew how, but until his death, he never told his son that he was a Jew and that his postwar wife was not Jurek's mother. I, as a young girl older than they, stopped being a child at age fourteen, and in the ghetto, and even before it was closed off, I took care of the house. I smuggled food, sold Polonia-Luksusowe razor blades on the street and in stores, and bought a red [bicycle] rickshaw, in which my closest relatives used to cart passengers, now and then tossing me coins they had earned.

Then I became a waitress in a restaurant on Sienna Street. Dressed in a black dress with a wide black plastic belt, I sold apple charlottes and cheesecake, and I was allowed to take the leftover "corners" from the baking pan home with me. Once I was walking to work, carrying my belt in my hand, wrapped in paper. It looked like my breakfast, and a barefoot "snatcher" ran up and quickly bit the package, probably thinking he could swallow at least a bite or two before I started hitting him. My father would come home with a loaf of bread, but the food snatchers were quicker than he. His loaf had been bitten, and he was very embarrassed.

At the entrance to our apartment was a small brush with which everyone was supposed to carefully clean his clothes. Typhus, carried by lice, was spreading. My beautiful friend, Ala, lost her hair, and Celinka died, and then her older sister, Maryla, hid in the hearse, paying no heed to the danger of infection because her life was at stake! The cemetery on Okopowa Street was outside the bounds of the ghetto, so the gendarmes counted how many mourners entered, making sure the same number came back out. But even they could not imagine that someone would hide in a hearse. Anyway, they feared typhus like the plague. In fact, they put up posters saying, "Stay away from Jews. Always stay clean. Jews breed lice; lice mean typhus."

I have mentioned the "Children of the Holocaust" members and the fact that they frequently have a mother complex. I also have one, but different:

My beautiful sister, Sabina, committed suicide in the ghetto on her twenty-sixth birthday. She didn't want to wait for the German "final solution" and sought her own. First, she swallowed two vials of Luminal but was brought back to life. Then she found a simpler way—jumping out of the eighth floor of a building on Chłodna Street.

Her son, Marianek, was two years old then. Unfortunately, he was circumcised. To be sure, this fact shows a curious lack of imagination. The boy was born four weeks before the outbreak of war, just before the Nazi invasion, and was circumcised even though our family was quite strongly assimilated. My sister's suicide was probably the biggest shock I ever experienced. I decided I had to save the boy, even though I myself had nothing except a false birth certificate and a forged *Kennkarte.*

My mama had light-colored hair, a small nose, and blue eyes. She could have gotten out, she could have lived, if I had been more mature and we had been less subject to the law of the jungle, according to which it was the young and not the old that had to be saved. It's just that Mama was then forty-eight years old! This is a wound that will never heal. It is a dark spot in the story of my life.

Marianek, Lunia (my middle sister), and I went together to Kopyczyńce, near the eastern frontier. Nearby was the famous Zaleszczyki route by which our dignitaries had escaped in September 1939.[7] It was again quite a colorful scene; there were Poles, Ukrainians, and Jews who were hidden in bunkers. The front passed through several times. For a time the Germans held their ground, then the Soviet army and General Kołpak's partisans came through. Then the Germans would come back for a few days. Each army would leave behind some trucks loaded with all sorts of goods, and the local population got used to plundering them quickly, despite the bullets and shrapnel whizzing by. We called it *hapatnia* [loot], and it was very interesting—Portuguese sardines, French wines and cognacs, Italian and French women's shoes. It was all haphazardly snatched and stuffed into bags, and then swapping would follow. Whoever had one red high-heeled shoe searched for the second one from his neighbor; whoever had too many blankets (because people still had superb military blankets from September 1939) exchanged them for pillows or food.

The retreat of the Germans, who had tried hard to persuade my sister and me to run away with them before the Bolsheviks arrived, was a treat for our eyes. The main road was so crowded with tanks, trucks full of Nazi soldiers, motorcycles, and even horse-drawn carts that they all moved at a snail's pace. It took them ten hours to get from Kopyczyńce to Tarnopol, which was only twelve kilometers away.

We were liberated in the spring of 1944, a year ahead of central Poland. Our liberation came just in time, because our Marianek had gone for a swim in a clay pit with his playmates, and then we heard them calling out, "Marian, the little Jew, has his balls cut off!" The local Kripo [*Kriminal Polizei*—Criminal Police] officer, Staszek Kozioł, paid us a visit before the end of the occupation and, in jest, stuck a revolver under my nephew's pillow. However, he was in love with Janka Nowaczyk, a local beauty, and perhaps this restrained him a bit, or maybe he was just too lazy.

We were intensely affected by the "actions" against Jews, and later, the handing out of their furniture—beds, wardrobes, tables, and still-warm eiderdowns. This is when Marysia, a lovely twenty-year-old girl from Lwów, confided in us. Between sobs, she told us "Aryans" that she had gotten married before the Germans arrived. They shot her husband, and she was left alone with a baby. She somehow found out where a young, childless couple lived and deposited her baby on a straw doormat at the front of their door. After liberation she began a frantic search, but those people, anticipating that the mother might show up, had moved away in an unknown direction.

The Soviet authorities and army were generally pleasant and helpful people. Seeing two young girls raising a child on their own, they came with their horses and plowed a hectare of land that we had received from the magistrate. Questioned by the NKVD [Soviet secret police], we told them with much emotion about our experiences, that we were Jews from Warsaw and had been waiting for them to save us. They were not moved to tears. They said, "You're lying! There were too many miracles in your lives." And there were indeed quite a few miracles in our lives.

I very much wanted to study medicine, but, first of all, I had not even finished the "small" *matura*[8] (my education had stopped after three years of gymnasium). Second, I didn't have parents who could support me for seven years. Third, I had to earn a living. I started working as a nurse in a local clinic. I began by applying thousands of dressings to wounded legs. Ukrainian peasants, in order to avoid being drafted into the army, used caustic soda to create self-inflicted wounds and then said they were due to varicose veins.

Many of the Red Army's soldiers, as well as General Kołpak's heroic partisans, suffered from venereal diseases. A *Vendispenser*[9] was thus organized in the clinic, and Doctor Kolarz became its chief. The nurses from Kopyczyńce did not want to work there at any price, so they pushed me forward. I took smears on glass slides, dyed them with something very blue, and gave them to the doctor, so he could examine the gonococci under a microscope. In the meantime, I conducted so-called social interviews. I asked, "Who infected you?" Soon thereafter good-looking girls or country women would arrive who'd been assured by their partners that it would just be a visit to the dentist or gynecologist. A young Red Army soldier once asked me, "Sister, you're so young, aren't you embarrassed to be working in a venereal ward?" I replied, "You are nineteen, and this is the third time you've had the clap, so who should be embarrassed?"

Conscription for the Polish army began, and Doctor Kolarz was transferred to the *Voenkomat.*[10] I was left alone on the field of battle with the gonococci, and it turned out that I had a head for business. With help from Kazimierz Prokosz, a local pharmacist, I got addresses of his friends, pharmacists in Lwów, and repeatedly hitched rides on military trucks to buy *streptycyd*[11] and other medications. Without hesitation I would write out stamped prescriptions saying "acute gonorrhea," and everything would be in order. After all, I had previously been a forger of packages of Polonia-Luksusowe razor blades and had mass-produced Aryan documents to bring people into the Warsaw Ghetto[12]—which immediately after the Nazis entered eastern Poland seemed to Jews like the promised land. One forgery more or less didn't mean much.

I was treating people! The director of the Health Department sent me on official trips to Lwów about every couple of weeks. She was no fool, however, and would exclaim with admiration, "Miss Krysia, what a wonderful dress you are wearing!" The next day the dress would be in her closet. I also handed out money and various gifts. But like any "doctor," I also had moments of personal satisfaction. When repatriation to central Poland began, right before I was to board a cattle car (for a trip that would last three weeks), two of my patients appeared. They arrived in a sleigh decorated with beautiful rugs, wearing gray Persian lamb hats, jauntily tipped to the side, and they brought me half a pig and a ten-liter can of alcohol! With this can I arrived in Warsaw. It was my founding capital before I began a normal life, work, and study. . . .

---

1. See Events of 1968 in glossary.

2. The Rau Garden was a sports garden for children inside the Saski Garden in Warsaw.

3. The booth [*sukkah*] was for the holiday of Sukkot, the Feast of Tabernacles, which occurs in the fall right after the High Holidays of Rosh Hashanah [New Year] and Yom Kippur [Day of Atonement].

4. Cupping glasses were used to draw out what was considered "corrupt" blood from the patient as a cure.

5. *Jur* is a children's book by L. M. Montgomery (author of *Anne of Green Gables*), translated into Polish (Poznań: Wydawnictwo J. Nitecki, 1931).

6. This was probably the Polish "second breakfast," a late morning snack.

7. In September 1939 the entire Polish government evacuated through this route to Romania to escape the Germans. See Polish government-in-exile in glossary.

8. The "small" *matura* was an examination taken upon the completion of gymnasium [U.S. tenth grade].

9. *Vendispenser* was the abbreviation in Russian for venereal disease dispensary. (Author's note)

10. *Voenkomat* was a military commission set up in eastern Poland after its "liberation," which organized Polish units under the command of the Red Army.

11. Streptycyd is similar to streptomycin.

12. The razor blades were factory rejects packaged in phony wrappers. Aryan papers were needed to travel in German-occupied Poland.

WANDA ZIEMSKA

Born in 1934

In Fear Because of My Origins

I look into my childhood as into a very dark well. I recall things I had long ago erased from memory, because one cannot live with such baggage. I have decided, however, to note down what has remained and emerges from obscurity into my consciousness, because I owe it to the people who helped me stay alive. I don't know their names, not only because I don't remember them; I believe they didn't want me to know them, so I couldn't reveal them to someone I shouldn't. Besides, who would introduce themselves to a small Jewish child?

My recollections are not continuous—from the dark recesses shines through sometimes a melody, a phrase, or an image. The only constant thing is a feeling of total loneliness. To these fragments of recollection are constantly being added more pieces of the still unassembled puzzle.

I was born on May 16, 1934. We lived in Warsaw on Widok Street. Father, Edward Posner, in a haberdashery and trimmings factory at 129 Marszałkowska Street, produced items needed by the theater. Mama, Zofia, née Goldberg, played the piano. I had no siblings. I remember my mama's dresses, but I don't remember her face. I hear her playing, but I can't visualize her. Noemi, my cousin from Palestine, who visited us with her mother and two sisters before the war, managed to return home in time. The rest of the family—cousin Jurek; his mother, my Aunt Pola, who avidly collected porcelain; his father, my Uncle Herman;

my grandmother; and my other uncles—we all moved together into the ghetto in Warsaw. We stayed at first on Orla Street.

When I think "ghetto," I hear some strange, dull melody. I can't repeat it, but it's in me—monotonous, sad. In front of buildings are dead bodies covered with paper. We change apartments several times, but what I remember most clearly is that I am kept in some very strange places. From the rear wall of a wardrobe, a board is removed. I cross through the wardrobe to the other side where there is a narrow space. The board is then returned to its place. After some time I cross back through the wardrobe. I no longer have Grandma.

Bookshelves. Under the lowest shelf are heavy volumes and some mortars. A few of the books are removed, and I crawl into a dark space. I come back out—Mama, Aunt Pola, Jurek, and Uncle Herman are gone. Father comes back from the "other side," from beyond the ghetto wall, and says that they have been decimated and that Uncle Herman was allowed to stay but joined Aunt Pola and Jurek on his own. For years, I was sure that "decimate" meant to line people up in rows and take every tenth one for the transport. ("Little Wanda, and where is your family?" "One, two, three . . . ten, ten, ten—my family is the 'ten.'") Someone told me later that that railroad wagon, or that transport, was filled with lime near Małogoszcz.

I must have had something to eat in the ghetto, but I only remember two meals. The first was probably from an earlier period, because Grandma was feeding me. A horse had fallen in the street. I ate horse blood, curdled in pieces, fried in a pan. It tasted like sand and looked like a black sponge. I was the only one eating; many people all around were looking at me—no one else was eating. Mama, hunched down near the wall, was cradling her elbows in her hands. I remember her hands but not her face. The other meal I remember—in an empty office. Father got me out of my hiding place behind some wardrobes, sat me down at a tall desk, and gave me a can of thick soup. While I was eating it, I found a small strand of meat. And then my father burst into tears. That was the only time I ever saw him cry. I remember this day probably only because of the concurrence of opposites—I'd spent the whole day sitting behind a wardrobe, having to keep quiet. Now, Papa has come, I am able to talk, I am cheerful, I am eating something good—and tears are streaming down his face. . . .

For a very long time, my memories of hiding in the ghetto did not fit in with the things I knew about the war. That you have to hide on the Aryan side was clear and obvious, but hiding in the ghetto, and each time in a different place, made no sense whatsoever.[1]

I no longer had any family or friends left. Besides Papa, I saw only the brush factory workers. They sat in rows, pulling folded wires through holes in small wooden boards. They inserted precut thin bronze-colored bristles into the wire loops and pulled them in tufts into the board. They sang, "Miss Wanda, the boss's daughter—oy! What a brat, big trouble—oy!"

Now comes the time of forgetting. I get a birth certificate. All the first names are okay, but I must forget the [original] last names and dates. I follow this to the letter, as if erasing something written on a blackboard. One evening Father took me to an unfamiliar apartment. Other people were assembling there, and when night came, we went in a small group out onto the empty street. Above the entrance to the sewer, I said good-bye to Father, who stayed behind. The journey through the sewers was quite complicated. At times it looked like a dirty river, and then men in tall rubber boots put us on their backs and carried us to dry places. They carried not only me, a child, on their backs but also adults. To this day I can remember how hard it was for me to climb out of the sewer—I couldn't reach from one rung to the next.

We were taken to a narrow waiting room and told to wait in absolute silence until dawn. Some lady came for me and took me with her. The sun was shining, women were selling Easter palms and spring flowers. I don't remember during my two and a half years in the ghetto having seen even one small flower. But still, there must have been sun. Why was there no sun in the ghetto? There was very little light, sometimes none at all; I don't remember even one sunny day, while here, on the Aryan side, the sun was shining all the time.

My guardian was a set designer at one of Warsaw's theaters before the war and had worked together with my father. His wife had a dressmaking shop and employed several assistants. She did not have children; my guardian, for the Easter Holiday, brought his small son over. They took away all my things and dyed my hair blond, we got "real" *święcone*[2] to amuse us, and I was told, "Never go near the window, learn the prayers, and everything will be all right." It wasn't. One day, downstairs, in the courtyard, a woman was heard shouting, "They won't give me back my child, and they're hiding a Jewish girl!"

From that time on, I began to be moved around—a few days here and there with young women who were learning to sew, also in various places around Warsaw, in Pelcowizna,[3] with some trusted clients, one of whom had a particular impact on me, and I have remembered her all my life. She took me to the attic and showed me, through a little window, an enormous glow, saying, "Look, your father is burning there." After a few days she showed me a scrap from a postcard and, without handing it to me, said that it was a message from my papa from Treblinka, saying he was a tailor there and doing well. I did not know what the truth was, whether my papa was burning in a glow spread over the whole sky or whether there were tailors in Treblinka who were faring well. . . .

We were walking along the street. The woman looked at my birth certificate and decided it was too new. She crumpled it up. The certificate was still new, just crumpled up. She scrunched it up into a ball and dropped it through the grill into the sewer—my ticket for survival and the last thing I had from my father.

This whole period of being passed from hand to hand lasted from Easter until late autumn of 1943. I didn't know names or addresses. I don't know whom to thank for my life.

There is a book by Tim O'Brien entitled *The Things They Carried.*[4] A group of people are going through the horrors of war. They all carry something that helps them survive, to return to the normal world. Anything—a letter, a photograph, some trifle. I was alone, I was not carrying anything of my own, and I had no family name that I could associate with anything. The loneliness of a child who can't be herself and already has the awareness that people are afraid even of her looks; their negative reaction, that is something that stays with you for life.

I memorized a new life story: I escaped with my mother from Nowogródek, we stopped in a village called Brzózki, and there Mama fell ill and died. The woman with whom we were staying brought me to Warsaw, sat me down on a bench in the waiting room at the Warsaw main railroad station, told me she was going to buy a roll and hasn't returned yet. I was not supposed to remember anything else.

It must have been November 1943, it was evening, and it was sleeting. I approached a policeman standing in the square in front of the station and told him my whole story. For the next few days the railroad station became my home—the police station there. I slept there on a stretcher on the floor, I ate out of a mess kit, and during the day, I sat on a bench by a wall. The police turned me over to the RGO [Central Welfare Council].[5] An empty white hall, two attendants in white smocks on duty, lights on day and night.

I was taken back to the police station, then back to the RGO, then back again. Finally, the policeman, the same one I approached in the train station, took me to the Gestapo headquarters on Szucha Avenue. A long corridor, the right-hand wall formed by metal bars. Beyond it, the cells, two rows of benches similar to kneeling benches, people sitting with their backs to the entrance. There were no windows, lights were on all day. That was the "streetcar." The man in front of me had a bloody head. He whispered, "Ask for coffee." I was free to walk around the cell, approach the bars, while nobody else was even permitted to turn his head around. Walking up and down the corridor were armed Germans. At my request, a heavyset woman came with an aluminum pot and gave me a mug of coffee through the bars. I passed it around between the benches in my cell; the woman smiled and refilled the mug many times without a word.

For the next few days I was interrogated upstairs in room 305. The translator was a roundish man in gold-framed glasses and a light-colored suit; the others were Germans in uniform. The questions tumbled out very quickly, often the same ones many times. A big map covered the wall. An officer searched for Brzózki and found about seventeen villages with that name. Which Brzózki is it? I tried very hard, but I didn't know.

From this interrogation I have remembered: Translator: "Why did you run away from Nowogródek?" Me: "From the army." The translator repeated, after the interrogator, who was in a gray uniform, "Were the soldiers in uniforms like mine?" I was not prepared to answer this question. I did not know in what uniforms were the soldiers in Nowogródek in November 1943. I had to think. If they wore the same kind, he would not have asked. "No, different ones," I replied. "Did they talk like me?" "No, differently." There were enough questions for several days, but these are the ones I remember.

From the "streetcar," we were taken to a transport. People were called out from the cells behind the bars and lined up facing the wall. The Germans shouted horribly. I knew they were going to Palmiry, but I didn't know what that meant.[6] Upstairs, I was ordered to kneel down by the desk and say my prayers loudly. I recited "Our Father," "Hail Mary," "I Believe In God." They interrupted me at "Under Thy Protection." I was lucky they didn't tell me to sing—Christmas carols, for instance! A man in a navy blue uniform, I don't know whether he was a railroad worker or an official, swore that he was a neighbor of my parents in Nowogródek, that he knew them and knew that they had a daughter. . . .

I returned to the "streetcar," but then I was led into an office or a large guardroom. On one side sat a heavily made-up girl chattering away, and on the other, by the door, stood a woman with a child in her arms. A German, from behind a desk, asked me which one of them I wanted to go with. He gestured with his hands so that I would understand what he was asking me about. Everyone, except for the woman with the child, was laughing loudly. I cautiously took a step toward the woman who was not laughing. We left.

The woman was shaking all over, burst out crying, and couldn't calm down. From the subsequent oft-repeated accounts given to neighbors and acquaintances, I understood what had happened. "My" policeman found out that the Gestapo would release me provided somebody registered me. He dropped in on his friends who worked for Schiele (the firm Haberbush and Schiele) and asked whether anyone would be willing to register a little girl for a few days. Some man said that he could do it, but before he managed to return home to alert his wife, the Gestapo had already been at his house and taken his wife with them. She brought with her only the younger daughter, thinking it would be safer that way. When she understood that nothing had happened, that it was all about picking up a girl, she cried with joy, having previously been in shock. I slept in the kitchen on a reclining beach chair. Then there was Christmas, with a tree, and I got a pink sweater.

At the beginning of the new year, 1944, I sat in the corridor of the emergency shelter on Sienna Street. I held a shoe box containing sandwiches and holiday cake on my lap. I was led into a room full of children. They sat on tables, benches, on the floor, and several older ones watched the door. The teacher was reading aloud *Pan Tadeusz.*[7] I stayed almost until the end of July, mostly in isolation. I was told I had typhus. Father Stefański was taking care of me.

A woman psychologist conducted psychological tests on me. At the end of July, a nun in lay clothing took me and several other girls away. We entered an overcrowded train through the window. This was supposedly the last train departing from the

Warsaw East Station, perhaps due to the approaching Soviet army from the east, or maybe due to the outbreak of the Warsaw Uprising. We arrived at St. Joseph's Institution in Otwock. I entered the recreation room upstairs. At long tables sat about fifteen girls who, in the margins and between the lines of old filled-up notebooks, were writing as punishment, "I am a thief because I stole tomatoes." Five hundred times. This was my home for the next five years.

My guardians clearly did not want me to remember my origins, and they succeeded in that. I do not think my further fate differed much from that of any other orphaned child. I did not associate the unpleasantness or adversity I encountered with my origins, but rather with being an orphan, with my loneliness, and my own faults. As a rule, some people come from the country, others from cities, but I came from nowhere. I did not know any of my family's surnames, so I wrote to the Social and Cultural Association of Jews in Poland,[8] asking whether anyone had inquired about me. I was told I should turn to the Polish Red Cross, but from them also came a negative reply.

I changed schools, jobs, places of residence; for a long time, I could not find my place in life.

Eventually, I arrived at a stopping point. I met my husband and took up a normal, stable life and work. The martyrology of Jews became the subject of a series of paintings by my husband, which have been exhibited both in Poland and abroad. They have received positive reviews, and most of them have been sold.

In March 1968 something started happening in Poland, but I didn't feel it related to me in any way. At the beginning of April, a coworker came to my office, where the phone had not rung for several days, and whispered, "You're going to have problems." "For what?" "For Zionism." "And what is Zionism?" "Well, I don't really know, but it has something to do with your origins."

Then there was a general meeting, accusations from the podium; I see in the hall my coworkers crying. I have nightmares about this meeting to this day. Reading aloud an anonymous letter, which the authorities received, "She hates Poland. She says that she will shoot at workers."

"This is obviously a mistake." "They will apologize in a few days. This can't be about me, it's out of the question."

I take my accumulated vacation, and we go to my husband's parents. My father-in-law takes me aside for a "private" conversation. He has friends who are foresters and can place me "for safekeeping" in some well-hidden place until everything clears up. My husband makes the final decision—he will not let me go into hiding anywhere, and we will not leave the country of our own free will. We expect that he will now face a lot of unpleasantness, but he does not. He continues to teach art in a lyceum, only that previously commissioned paintings of the martyrological series are returned to him, and he is not invited to participate in an exhibition. My husband's friends find me a job, but the Municipal Committee of the PZPR[9] does not consent to my being hired. When I step out into the street, it seems to me as if someone had pinned a label on my back, and every few minutes I check that nothing is hanging there. When I hear steps on the stairs when I am alone at home, I hide behind the curtain or the sofa.

I begin suffering from joint problems and am granted a third-degree disability pension, having been diagnosed with rheumatic joint inflammation. The director who signed my dismissal from work brings to my house a huge bouquet of roses. He is very sorry, he says, and ashamed that it had fallen to him to do it.

My husband buys me a typewriter. I accept work to be done at home from the Translation Cooperative as long as my fingers can still type. My husband teaches me the Bible on the basis of reproductions of paintings by old masters. I also read books by Singer[10] and learn from them about the customs and what it means to be a Jew. As if I didn't know . . .

It is exactly thirty years and five months since I learned that I am not a full-fledged citizen of my homeland. My illness has progressed very far; I can move only with the greatest difficulty, my eyesight is weak, and I rarely go out of the house.

When Solidarity[11] first started, I was working just part-time. The leader of our union came to me and invited me to join this great, wonderful movement. I replied that I would very gladly do so, but I feared that my very presence would only do them harm. He understood but contradicted me, saying that it was certainly not so, that I did not realize how noble Solidarity was and how far above any divisions, and that this was its very idea.

Shortly after that, I had to quit and stopped working professionally. Today, it has become evident that my fears were justified. At this very moment, as I am writing this, crosses are being assembled along the fence of the largest Jewish cemetery in the world, in Auschwitz—against Jews. Someone is playing his own game, for reasons I cannot understand, drawing into it the dead and the living. Those who should be silent are screaming, and those who should be screaming are silent. I am beginning to be afraid. For the third time in my life, I am in fear because of my origins.

---

1. In order not to be deported, a person had to have a *Kennkarte,* an identity card showing that he/she was employed and "useful." A child who had no *Kennkarte* was subject to deportation and thus had to be hidden.

2. Author refers to small figurines sometimes included with delicacies blessed by the priest on Holy Saturday before Easter.

3. Pelcowizna is an area of Warsaw on the eastern side of the Vistula.

4. *The Things They Carried* (New York: Broadway Books, April 1999) is a book about Vietnam.

5. RGO is the acronym for *Rada Główna Opiekuńcza.*

6. Palmiry is a village in the Kampinos National Park northwest of Warsaw, where mass murders of Poles and Jews took place.

7. *Pan Tadeusz* [*Mr. Tadeusz*] is a very famous Polish epic poem by Adam Mickiewicz.

8. TSKŻ, *Towarzystwo Społeczno-Kulturalne Żydów w Polsce.*

9. The PZPR, *Polska Zjednoczona Partia Robotnicza* [Polish United Workers' Party] was a Communist party formed in December 1948 in Warsaw. It performed administrative functions on behalf of the state and had full control of many work assignments.

10. Nobel laureate Isaac Bashevis Singer (1904–91) was a Polish-born American author whose works about Jewish life in the shtetl have been translated into Polish and are very popular in Poland.

11. Solidarity [*Solidarność*], headed by Lech Wałęsa, began in 1980 as a democratic workers' movement. It was later outlawed but returned in 1989 to be a part of the government, eventually leading to the downfall of Communism. See "Historical Notes."

Glossary

Action/*Aktion:* Forced roundup for deportation to concentration or death camps.

Anders Army: An army of Poles under the command of General Władysław Anders, also known as the Polish Second Corps. When Germany attacked the Soviet Union in 1941, Stalin, in order to get the cooperation of the Allies, agreed to release Poles who had been exiled to Siberia during the Soviet occupation of eastern Poland (1939–41) and allowed them to form this army. The Anders Army left the Soviet Union and went to Iran and then to Palestine, where it became part of the British Eighth Army. It took part in the Italian campaign, including the famous Battle of Monte Cassino.

AK/*Armia Krajowa:* Organized underground army in Poland that reported to the Polish government-in-exile in London; known in English as the Home Army.

Aryan papers: Documents attesting that the person named in them was Aryan, not Jewish. Jews who were able to obtain falsified Aryan papers were able to live on the Aryan side, though always in danger of being uncovered and denounced.

Aryan side: Outside the ghetto, where only non-Jews were permitted to live.

Auschwitz: Largest German concentration and death camp in Poland, located thirty-seven miles west of Kraków in the town of Oświęcim. Beginning as a concentration camp for Polish political prisoners, it was greatly expanded into a death camp by the addition of Auschwitz II-Birkenau. More than one million people were killed there, ninety percent of them Jews.

Banderowcy: Guerrilla bands of Ukrainian nationalists, named after their leader, Stepan Bandera. They were anti-Polish as well as anti-Jewish.

Blue-uniformed policemen: Polish policemen (in contrast to Jewish or German policemen).

Disability pension: Beneficiaries of disability pensions are classified into three groups and receive pensions according to the level of severity of their disability and suffering.

Events of 1968: In 1968, there were student demonstrations in Poland against government censorship. They were crushed by the Communist regime and blamed on "Zionists" (*some* of the students and professors who backed them were Jewish). A wave of anti-Zionism and anti-Semitism followed. Jews were accused of not being loyal to Poland and were often demoted or summarily dismissed from their jobs. Many Jews who had survived in Poland or returned to Poland after the war then emigrated (about 30,000).

First Polish Army: Soviet-controlled Polish army formed in the Soviet Union in 1944 under the command of Polish General Zygmunt Berling.

General Government: Polish territory occupied and governed by the Germans but not formally annexed to the German Reich (as were territories closer to Germany). Divided into four districts—Warsaw, Kraków, Radom, and Lublin.

Gestapo/*Geheime Staatspolizei:* German secret police, known for their brutality.

"Good looks": Not having a Semitic appearance.

Green border: Border out in the countryside where it was easier to cross illegally into another country.

Gymnasium/*gimnazjum:* Secondary school, corresponding at that time to U.S. grades seven through ten.

Home Army: English name for *Armia Krajowa* (AK), the organized underground army in Poland that reported to the Polish government-in-exile in London.

Judenfrei: Free of Jews.

Judenrat: Jewish council, appointed by the Germans to interface with the Jewish population and carry out German orders.

Kapo: Prisoner who received special privileges for supervising (often cruelly) other prisoners.

Kennkarte: Identification document issued by the Germans to those authorized to work and receive ration cards.

Lager: German forced labor or concentration camp.

Łagier: Forced labor camp in the Soviet Union, usually in a remote region.

Lyceum/*liceum:* Corresponds to the last two years of U.S. high school.

Matriculation/*matura:* Final examination of the secondary school years, a prerequisite for admission to a university.

NKVD: Soviet secret police, forerunner of KGB.

Polish government-in-exile: Polish government evacuated from Poland in September 1939 and reestablished first in Paris, then in London; it continued to direct the Polish underground and Polish troops in Allied armies.

Polish People's Army [*Ludowe Wojsko Polskie*–LWP]: Formed in 1944 when the Soviets re-entered Poland. Was a combination of the First Polish Army, formed in the Soviet Union, and the People's Army [*Armia Ludowa*], a leftist resistance movement operating inside Poland.

Reich: German state.

Repatriation: After the war ended, eastern territories, formerly in Poland, became part of the Soviet Union (Ukraine, Belarus, Lithuania). Poles were given the opportunity to remain and become Soviet citizens or relocate to Poland and be "repatriated."

Righteous Among the Nations of the World: A title of honor bestowed by Yad Vashem in Israel upon non-Jews who risked their lives to save Jews in occupied countries during World War II.

SA/*Sturmabteilungen:* Nazi storm troopers; also called "Brown Shirts."

Schupo/*Schutzpolizei:* German security police.

Selection: Separation of those fit to work from those to be killed.

"Shop": Workshop of Jewish slave labor, organized to produce goods for the German war effort.

SS/*Schutzstaffel:* Elite military unit of Nazi party that served as a special police force; also called "Black Shirts."

Szmalcownik (pl. *Szmalcownicy*): Blackmailer(s), those wanting their palms greased (*schmaltz* = rendered fat).

Treblinka: Death camp fifty miles northeast of Warsaw where most of the Jews of Warsaw were deported. More than 800,000 Jews were killed there.

Umschlagplatz: Transfer place. Large square on the edge of the Warsaw Ghetto that served as the transfer point for Jews (approximately 400,000) rounded up to be shipped to labor or extermination camps.

Volksdeutscher/Volksdeutsche: Polish man/woman of German origin who received extra privileges by declaring self loyal to Germany.

Volksliste: List of Poles of German descent who had declared loyalty to Germany.

Warsaw Ghetto Uprising: Uprising in the Warsaw Ghetto by the small population remaining after the deportation of some 400,000 Jews to the Treblinka extermination camp. Organized by the Jewish Fighting Organization (ŻOB), it began on April 19, 1943, and continued until the burning of the ghetto in mid-May.

Warsaw Uprising: Not to be confused with the Warsaw Ghetto Uprising. Uprising by the general population of Warsaw against the Germans, beginning August 1, 1944, just as the Red Army was approaching Warsaw. The Red Army, however, delayed its arrival in Warsaw, and the Germans were able to suppress the uprising and destroy the city. The Germans then dispersed masses of people from Warsaw to the countryside, many to camps in the nearby town of Pruszków.

Wehrmacht: Regular German army, thought to be less brutal than other units.

Żegota: Branch of Polish underground organized to give assistance to Jews.

Złoty: Unit of Polish currency (consisting of 100 groszy).

Historical Notes

1772, 1793, 1795: Poland is partitioned three times, progressively causing it to vanish from the map of Europe. After the third partition, the division is as follows:

1. Russian Poland, consisting of two parts:
   a. Territory governed directly by Russia, including Białystok and Wilno.
   b. Congress Kingdom of Poland, a separate province covering central Poland, including Warsaw and Łódź. The czar of Russia is "king" of Poland.
2. Austrian Poland (province of Galicia), an area governed by Austria-Hungary, consisting of southeastern Poland from Kraków to beyond Lwów (Austrian name for Lwów—Lemberg; present-day Ukrainian name—Lviv).
3. Prussian Poland, an area governed by Prussia/Germany, consisting of western Poland, including Poznań (Posen) and Gdańsk (Danzig).

January 1863: January Insurrection, ill-fated uprising in Kingdom of Poland against Russia; program of Russification follows. After 1868 all official documents in Kingdom of Poland are in Russian. School instruction is also in Russian.

July 28, 1914: Austria-Hungary declares war on Serbia; World War I begins.

February–March 1917: Russian Revolution begins.

November 7, 1917: Bolshevik (Communist) coup d'état occurs in Russia.

November 11, 1918: World War I ends. Independent Poland reestablished.

1919–21: Polish-Soviet War. Poland's borders expand.

September 1, 1939: German troops attack Poland from the west; World War II begins.

September 3, 1939: Britain and France declare war on Germany.

September 17, 1939: Soviet Army invades eastern Poland under secret agreement between Germany and Soviet Union, the so-called Ribbentrop-Molotov Agreement. Polish government evacuates through Romania, first to Paris, then to London.

September 28, 1939: Germany and Russia divide Poland between them. Many Jews flee to Russian-occupied areas to escape Nazis.

October 1939: Northern and western Poland are annexed to Germany proper. Five hundred thousand Poles living there are relocated to the General Government (see glossary) to make room for Germans moving into these territories. Many Poles are executed. Jews among them are shipped to newly established ghettos.

February 1940: Beginning of mass deportations (between 1.5 and 2 million) of Poles living under Soviet occupation to Siberia and Soviet Far East. People are forced into slave labor. Between one-third and one-half die by June 1941, when Germany invades eastern Poland.

June 22, 1941: Germany attacks Soviet troops without warning. War between Germany and Soviet Union erupts.

June 30, 1941: Germans enter Lwów, soon chase out Russians and occupy all of Poland.

July 30, 1941: Agreement is signed in London between Poland and Soviet Union to give amnesty to Polish "political" prisoners and allow the formation of the Polish Second Corps under Polish General Władysław Anders (Anders Army). Between 120,000 and 150,000 former prisoners, including women and children (4,000–5,000 Jews among them), leave the USSR to go to Iran, Iraq, and then to Palestine. Anders Army goes on to fight in Italian Campaign as part of British Eighth Army.

December 7, 1941: Japanese attack Pearl Harbor; United States enters war a couple of days later.

July 1942: Beginning of deportation of Jews from Warsaw Ghetto to Treblinka death camp.

April 13, 1943: Germans report finding mass grave of Polish officers killed in Katyń Forest by Russians.

April 19, 1943: Warsaw Ghetto Uprising begins (see glossary). Ghetto destroyed by May 16, 1943.

May 1943: Kościuszko Division is formed in the Soviet Union under Polish Colonel (later General) Zygmunt Berling from Poles still in Russia. Later expanded to become First Polish Army. Remains under Soviet command.

January 1944: Soviet troops push back Germans and recross eastern line of old Polish frontier.

July 1944: Polish (Communist-dominated) Committee of National Liberation (PKWN/*Polski Komitet Wyzwolenia Narodowego*) is installed in Lublin.

August 1, 1944: Warsaw Uprising begins (see glossary). Soviets cease their offensive to liberate Warsaw.

September 10, 1944: Soviets to east of Vistula River finally mount attack. A few units from the Berling Army manage to cross Vistula to establish bridgeheads in the main part of Warsaw.

October 2, 1944: Warsaw Uprising suppressed by Germans. More than 200,000 lives lost, city in ruins. Polish population expelled from city.

December 1944: PKWN proclaims itself provisional government of Poland and is recognized by Soviet Union a few days later. Prime minister: Osóbka-Morawski; head of state: Bolesław Bierut; deputy prime minister and head of Communist Party: Władysław Gomułka.

January 17, 1945: Warsaw finally liberated by army led by General Berling.

February 1945: Secret agreement confirmed in Yalta by British Prime Minister Winston Churchill, U.S. President Franklin Roosevelt, and Soviet Premier Joseph Stalin to cede Eastern Poland to the Soviet Union and to allow installation of Communist government in Poland.

May 8, 1945: V-E Day, war in Europe ends.

July 5, 1945: Britain and United States recognize new provisional Communist government of Poland. Polish boundaries shift west. Ukraine, Belarus, and Lithuania take parts of Poland east of the River Bug; Poland takes East Prussia and lands beyond its prewar western border formerly belonging to Germany.

July 4, 1946: Pogrom in Kielce, Poland. A building sheltering Jews who had returned from the USSR en route to Palestine is attacked. Someone had spread rumor of "blood libel," that is, that Jews had killed a Polish boy to use his blood in the making of matzo. Forty-two Jews are killed. Smaller pogroms occur elsewhere in Poland.

July 22, 1952: A new Polish constitution is adopted, formalizing the establishment of a Soviet-type Communist state. The Republic of Poland is renamed the Polish People's Republic.

March 1953: Stalin dies; Khrushchev comes to power.

November 4, 1956: Soviet tanks invade Hungary.

August 1961: Berlin Wall is erected.

June 1967: Six-day Arab-Israeli conflict. Used by General Moczar, head of Polish Secret Police, as opportunity for nationwide anti-Zionist and anti-Semitic purge.

March 1968: Students demonstrate in Warsaw against censorship. Some students and professors involved are Jewish. General Moczar again attacks Jews as cause (see Events of 1968 in glossary). Party head Gomułka condemns liberals and revisionists. Most Jews lose jobs or are demoted. Thirty thousand Jews leave Poland.

August 1968: Warsaw Pact armies (including Poles) invade Czechoslovakia.

Late 1970s, early 1980s: Rise of labor movement in Poland.

October 16, 1978: Polish Cardinal Karol Wojtyła elected pope of Roman Catholic Church, takes name John Paul II.

August 30, 1980: People's Republic of Poland (Communist government) agrees to allow independent trade unions to form.

September 17, 1980: *Solidarność* [Solidarity] is created as a nationwide trade union, integrating recently formed regional unions. Lech Wałęsa, leader of the July 1980 strike at the Gdańsk shipyards, becomes its head.

December 13, 1981: Martial law declared; Solidarity leaders imprisoned.

July 1983: Martial law ends.

Fall 1989: Solidarity wins elections. Communist rule in Poland comes to an end peaceably.

May 23, 1997: New Polish constitution approved by referendum of population.

March 12, 1999: Poland joins North Atlantic Treaty Organization [NATO].

May 1, 2004: Poland enters European Union.

Index of Persons

Certain conventions have been used in compiling this index to facilitate the identification of persons who may have been known by more than one name. Married women are listed under both their maiden name, e.g., Obremska, Stella m. [married name] Kolin, and their married name, e.g., Kolin, Stella b. [born] Obremska. Those with aliases are listed under both names, e.g., Rudziński, Ryszard/Ryś (*alias of* Arnold, Henryk) and Arnold, Henryk (*alias* Rudziński, Ryszard/Ryś). If a person has an alternate surname or first name, it is listed in parentheses.

Polish letters with diacritical marks are alphabetized after those without diacritics. Names ending in "*cka/ska*" are the feminine forms of Polish names ending in "*cki/ski.*" For a couple, the "*cki/ski*" form is used.

Names of those who contributed accounts to this volume are listed in bold.

Index of Places

Jewish Lives

For a complete list of titles, see the Northwestern University Press Web site at www.nupress.northwestern.edu

THOMAS TOIVI BLATT
From the Ashes of Sobibor: A Story of Survival

IDA FINK
A Scrap of Time and Other Stories

LALA FISHMAN AND STEVEN WEINGARTNER
Lala's Story: A Memoir of the Holocaust

LISA FITTKO
Escape through the Pyrenees
Solidarity and Treason: Resistance and Exile, 1933–1940

HANS FRANKENTHAL
The Unwelcome One: Returning Home from Auschwitz

RICHARD GLAZAR
Trap with a Green Fence: Survival in Treblinka

MICHAŁ GŁOWIŃSKI
The Black Seasons

HENRYK GRYNBERG
Children of Zion
The Jewish War *and* The Victory

JAKUB GUTENBAUM AND AGNIESZKA LATAŁA, EDS.
The Last Eyewitnesses: Children of the Holocaust Speak, Volume 2

INGEBORG HECHT
Invisible Walls *and* To Remember Is to Heal

JOST HERMAND
A Hitler Youth in Poland: The Nazis' Program for Evacuating Children during World War II

Gertrud Kolmar
My Gaze Is Turned Inward: Letters, 1934–1943

Arnošt Lustig
The Bitter Smell of Almonds
Children of the Holocaust
The House of Returned Echoes
The Unloved (From the Diary of Perla S.)

Liana Millu
Smoke over Birkenau

Thomas Nolden and Frances Malino, Eds.
Voices of the Diaspora: Jewish Women Writing in Contemporary Europe

Bernhard Press
The Murder of the Jews in Latvia, 1941–1945

Wiktoria Śliwowska, Ed.
The Last Eyewitnesses: Children of the Holocaust Speak, Volume 1

Isaiah Spiegel
Ghetto Kingdom: Tales of the Łódź Ghetto

Jiří Weil
Life with a Star
Mendelssohn Is on the Roof

Joanna Wiszniewicz
And Yet I Still Have Dreams: A Story of a Certain Loneliness